IMAGES
of America

AMHERST

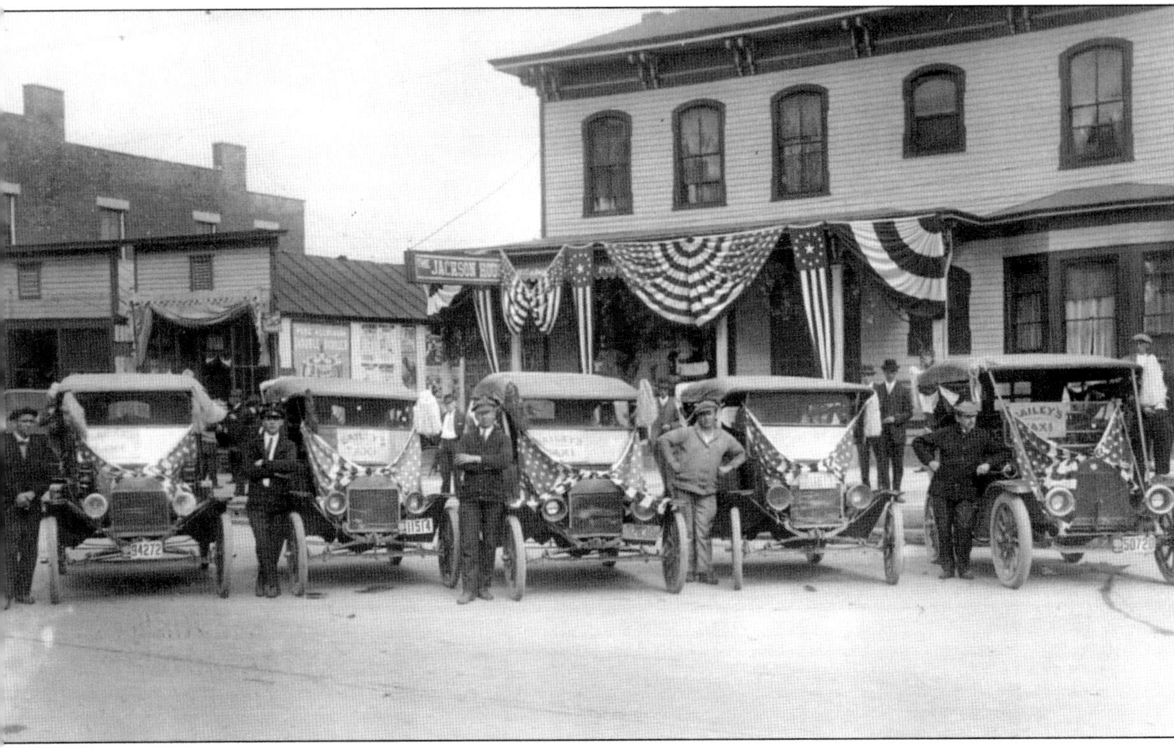

Taxi Cabs, 1914. Drivers for the Bailey Taxi Company prepared for Old Home week in 1914 by decking out their cabs with patriotic bunting. They appear here lined up in front of their dispatch office located next to the Jackson Hotel on South Main Street. (Courtesy of the Amherst Historical Society.)

On the Cover: Amherst Post Office, c. 1900. Located at 256 Church Street, the Amherst Post Office also provided rural free delivery. Here wagons loaded with mailbags are ready to set out on their routes. (Courtesy of the Amherst Historical Society.)

IMAGES
of America

AMHERST

Donna M. DeBlasio and
Martha I. Pallante on behalf of
the Amherst Historical Society

ARCADIA
PUBLISHING

ISBN 978-0-7385-7733-3

Published by Arcadia Publishing
Charleston, South Carolina

Printed in the United States of America

Library of Congress Control Number: 2009929849

For all general information, please contact Arcadia Publishing:
Telephone 843-853-2070
Fax 843-853-0044
E-mail sales@arcadiapublishing.com
For customer service and orders:
Toll-Free 1-888-313-2665

Visit us on the Internet at www.arcadiapublishing.com

Dedicated to the members of the Amherst Historical Society and the citizens of Amherst

Contents

Acknowledgments

Producing this book for the Amherst Historical Society has been a real joy for the authors. It would not have been possible without the cooperation of a myriad of people who gave freely of their time, talents, and gifts. All of the images used in this project are from the collections of the Amherst Historical Society, which has been blessed with an embarrassment of riches. Special thanks go to those individuals who have devoted their energies to the care and cultivation of the collections.

Members of the Amherst Historical Society have been extraordinarily generous with their time, providing the necessary background information to compile this work. Marilyn Jenne, Dale and Judy Rosenkranz, Orville Manes, Mary Powers Miller, Dick Rice, John Dietrich, Ruth Haff, Judy Ryan, Lilly Krebs, Robert Bechtel, and Mary Roberts provided additional clarification and specific details. Valerie Jenkins Gerstenberger graciously reviewed each chapter as it was completed and made helpful suggestions and provided useful guidance. Three individuals, Roy Jenkins, David Bauman, and Robert Pallante, shot many of the contemporary images on behalf of the Amherst Historical Society. Pallante also did yeoman's work scanning and organizing the images. Amy Pallante, Section 106 compliance coordinator of the Colorado Historical Society State Historic Preservation Office, wrote the descriptions for chapter 6, for which we are grateful. Finally, special thanks go to Laurie Pallante Lynch, for her intrepid investigator skills, and also to Martha A. Pallante and Donna Rumpler, who put in as many hours on the project as we did. Not only did they organize all the materials for us, making our job much easier, but they also made sure that we were cared for. Besides making this project enjoyable, they also gave us one of our best lines ever: four women, two first names.

—Donna M. DeBlasio and Martha I. Pallante

Introduction

Amherst, since its establishment as one of the westernmost communities in the Connecticut Western Reserve in 1811, has kept pace with the larger world around it. Developed originally as Amherstville, a small, agricultural community, it had little that distinguished it from its contemporaries to the east and south. Only gradually did the residents of the area find a way to set themselves apart from their neighbors. The discovery and early use of its sandstone resources began in the 1840s. From their humble beginnings, the small and independent enterprises emerged as a world famous industrial center. Henry Warner is generally credited with opening the first commercial quarry in the area in 1847, known as the Brownhelm Quarry. A year later, Sylvester Silsby began the extraction of grindstones from the John Elliott quarry, shaping the stones manually with chisels. George E. Hall built the first mechanical stone mill in 1868. From these early operations, the Cleveland Quarries eventually developed. The catalyst of Amherstville's initial success in the sandstone industry resulted from another city's misfortune. The catastrophic Chicago fire of 1871 created a vast market for the high-quality Amherst Blue sandstone. As a consequence, the Amherstville quarries reached an unprecedented level of production that lasted through the beginning of the 20th century.

In July 1886, a number of the smaller quarries in the Amherst area incorporated into the Cleveland Stone Company. Their enterprise encompasses operation not only in Amherst but also in nearby Berea, Kipton, Elyria, and Euclid, making it into the largest sandstone conglomerate in the world. The successes of the Cleveland Stone Company drew competitions, most specifically the Ohio Quarries Company, organized by Chicago banker John R. Walsh in 1903. This company created a small vertical monopoly centered out of its Buckeye Quarry. In addition to operating a milling operation and one of the deepest quarries in the world, the company constructed a railroad spur line that connected it to the Lake Shore and Michigan Southern Railway. Smaller enterprises, the Blum and Delbridge Cut Stone Company (1911) and the Amherst Cut Stone Company (1914), provided additional competition.

The merger of these four enterprises occurred during the period between the end of World War I and the beginning of the Great Depression. The Cleveland Stone Company gradually acquired the smaller operations and renamed it Cleveland Quarries Company, headquartered in South Amherst, in 1929. Through the remainder the 20th century, Amherst Blue became the material of choice for construction companies throughout the United States. The product graced structures throughout the nation and the world. These were as diverse as the Cleveland Hope (Lorain-Carnegie) Memorial Bridge, the city hall of Philadelphia, and the Hancock building in Boston. Builders found uses for Amherst Blue in governmental, memorial, and private construction projects.

The peopling of Amherst mirrored its industrial growth and development. Its initial population originated primarily from regions along the East Coast, stretching from New England to Virginia. As the quarries developed, so did the need for labor, and similar to many other American boomtowns, the local population was supplemented by immigration from southern and eastern Europe. By the beginning of the 20th century, the population was smaller, but it was as heterogeneous as its much larger neighbor to the east, Cleveland. The churches and social organizations reflected the changing nature of the population, becoming more diverse. Ethnic parishes joined older Protestant congregations that migrated with early settlers from the East Coast.

The citizens of Amherst have long had a commitment to the basics of good citizenship and solid education. The dedication of the community to creating strong institutions, such as schools, infrastructure, civic services, and commercial enterprises, were as durable as the sandstone they quarried. Private citizens, as well as elected officials, continue to give freely of their time and talents. Perhaps the most visible efforts resulting from this community spirit are the establishment and maintenance of the Amherst Sandstone Village and the preservation efforts of Main Street Amherst.

As Amherst and its citizens begin the 21st century, they work hard at simultaneously retaining the important portions of their past while preparing for a new post-industrial future. The community, while erecting new structures, has also adapted its older built environment in other ways. While the quarries themselves cannot be replaced, they have diversified and are seeking other sources of employment and revenue.

One

The Early Years

Located on the southern rim of Lake Erie, Amherst was established in 1811 as part of the Connecticut Western Reserve. Originally known as "the Corners" and briefly recognized by the state government as Plato, by 1830, local inhabitants referred to their village as Amherst. Legend has it that the township was named in honor of early resident Jonas Stratton's hometown in New Hampshire. Officers of the first local government were elected in the same year at a private home on Middle Ridge Road. In April 1836, those officers officially registered a town plat under the name Amherstville. During the 1830s and 1840s, the population rapidly expanded and the area acquired many of the institutions characteristic of an established community, including churches, schools, a post office, and government buildings. By 1850, the population reached 1,400 and swelled to nearly 1,600 by 1880. In 1873, village officials prepared to incorporate the community under a new name, North Amherst. By 1909, the community officially became Amherst.

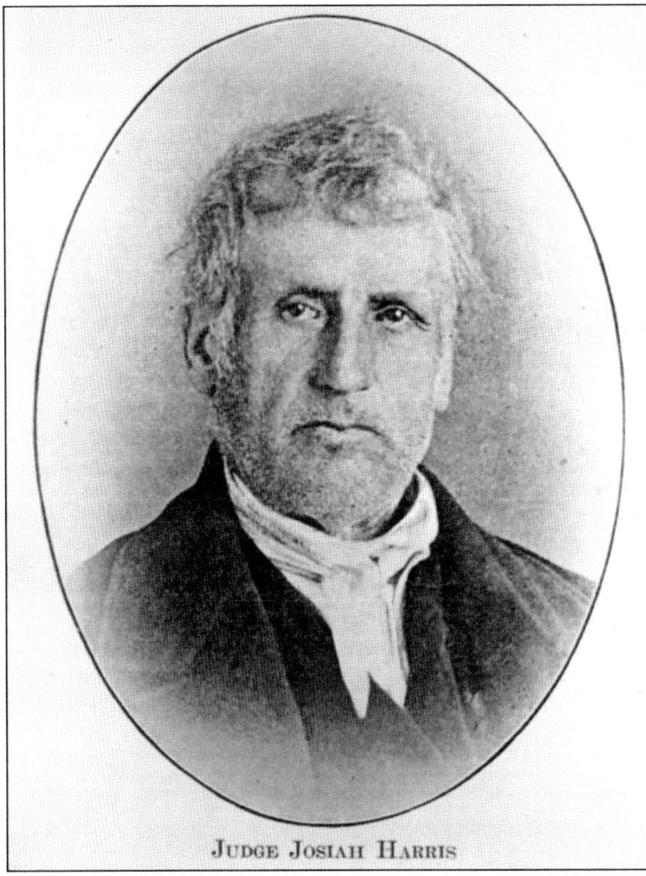

JUDGE JOSIAH HARRIS

JOSIAH HARRIS AND HIS COMMISSION AS JUSTICE OF THE PEACE. Josiah Harris (left), born in Massachusetts in 1783, ventured into Amherst Township as part of a surveying team in 1815. He returned in 1818 to take up permanent residence. His house served alternately as a post office, office of the justice of the peace, and a tavern. Harris was appointed justice of the peace (below) for the township on November 1, 1830. He subsequently continued his service to the community as associate Lorain County judge, postmaster, and state senator. He died at the age of 84 in 1868.

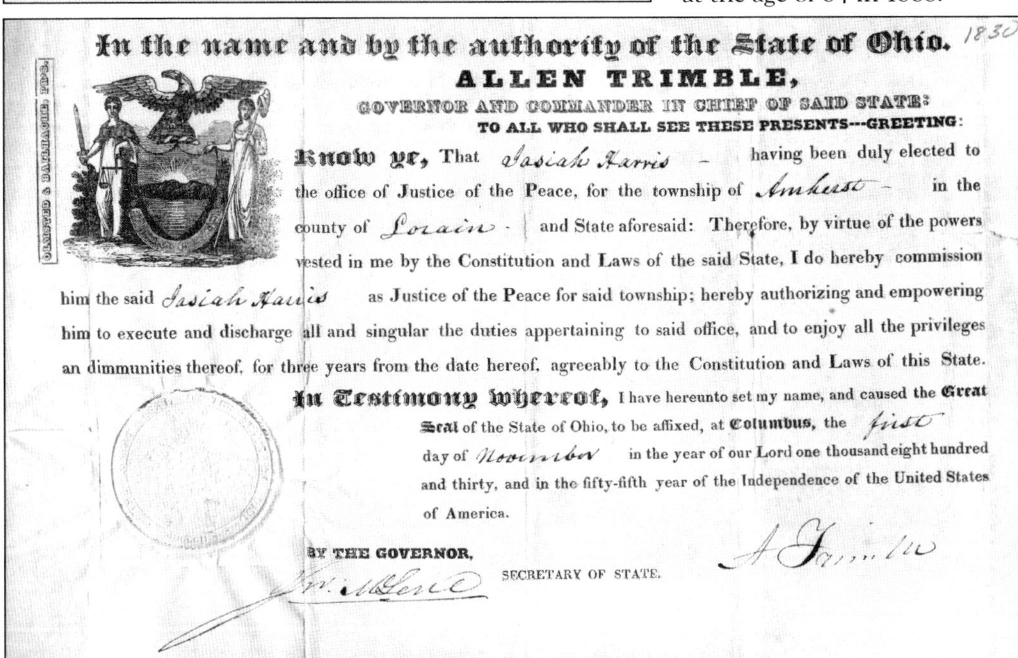

In the name and by the authority of the State of Ohio. 1830

ALLEN TRIMBLE,

GOVERNOR AND COMMANDER IN CHIEF OF SAID STATE:

TO ALL WHO SHALL SEE THESE PRESENTS---GREETING:

Know ye, That Josiah Harris - having been duly elected to the office of Justice of the Peace, for the township of Amherst - in the county of Lorain - and State aforesaid: Therefore, by virtue of the powers vested in me by the Constitution and Laws of the said State, I do hereby commission him the said Josiah Harris as Justice of the Peace for said township; hereby authorizing and empowering him to execute and discharge all and singular the duties appertaining to said office, and to enjoy all the privileges an dimmunities thereof, for three years from the date hereof, agreeably to the Constitution and Laws of this State.

In Testimony whereof, I have hereunto set my name, and caused the Great Seal of the State of Ohio, to be affixed, at Columbus, the first day of November in the year of our Lord one thousand eight hundred and thirty, and in the fifty-fifth year of the Independence of the United States of America.

BY THE GOVERNOR,

Jn. McLene SECRETARY OF STATE. A Trimble

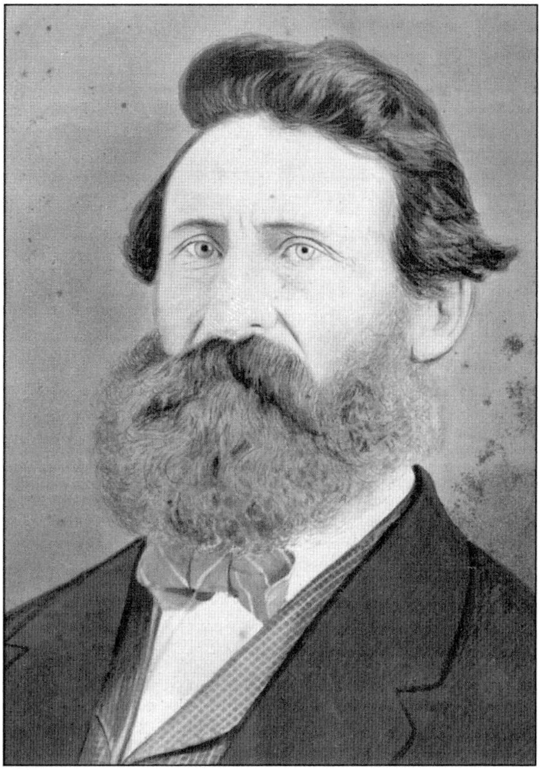

Isaac and Minerva Richmond Shupe. Isaac Shupe (right), was born in 1825 as the youngest son of Jacob Shupe, who migrated from Pennsylvania to Amherst Township by 1811. Locating on Beaver Creek, family enterprises are credited with the first sawmill, gristmill, and whiskey distillery in the township. Isaac and his wife, Minerva Richmond, matured along with their community and became respected citizens and leaders until their deaths in 1896 and 1913, respectively.

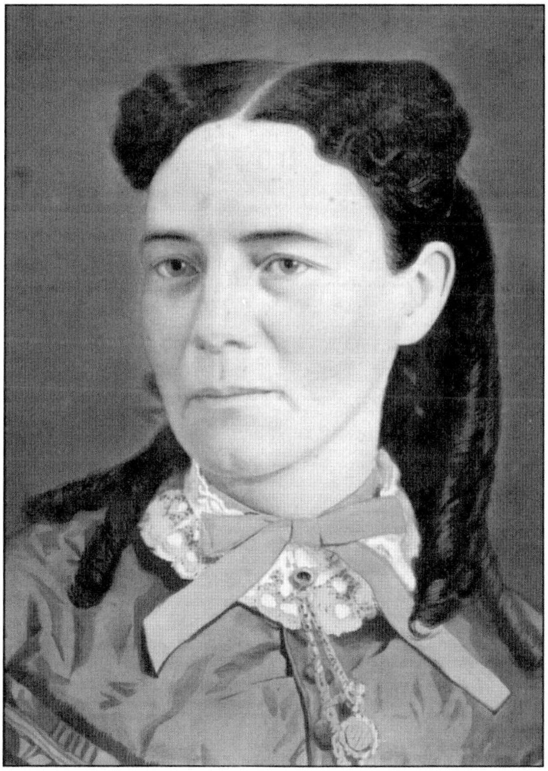

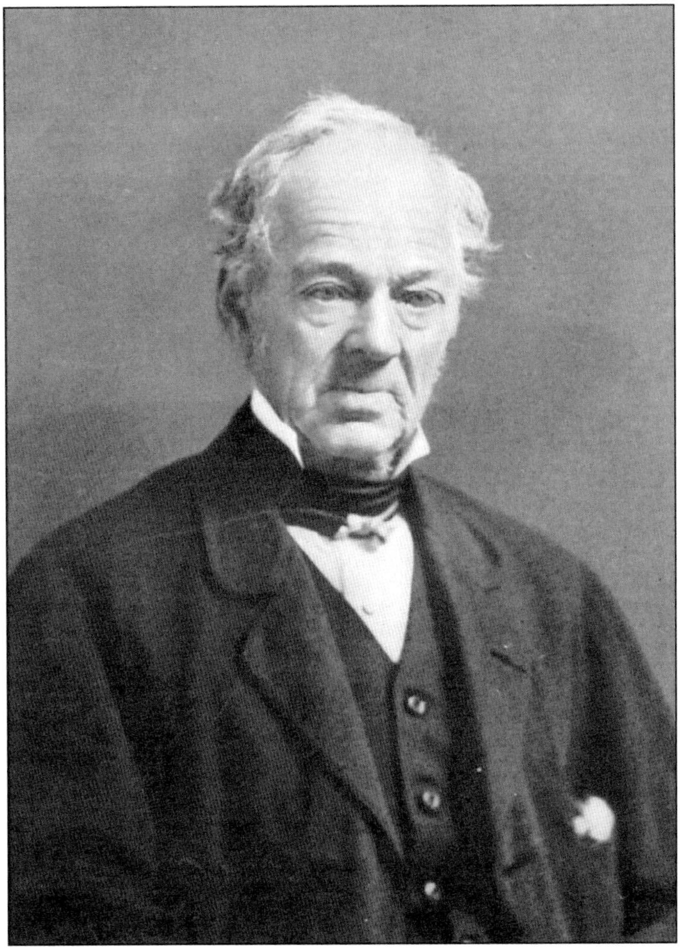

HIRAM BELDEN AND HIS MASSACHUSETTS HOUSE. Hiram Belden (left) came west from Massachusetts in 1830 and served as one of the early schoolmasters for Amherst Township. An educated man, he also functioned as a surveyor and in 1836 received a commission from Josiah Harris to lay out plots for the township. His linked chains measured 7.92 inches, reaching a total length of 66 feet. Ten chains equaled a furlong, and there were eight furlongs to a mile. A square 10 chains on a side equaled an acre. Belden's earlier house in Sandisfield, Massachusetts (below), hints at the origins of many similar dwellings constructed in the Western Reserve. Known as a New England central chimney plan, this five-bay structure had a central hall with two rooms on either side. This substantial house type provided a model for aspiring citizens of the Western Reserve.

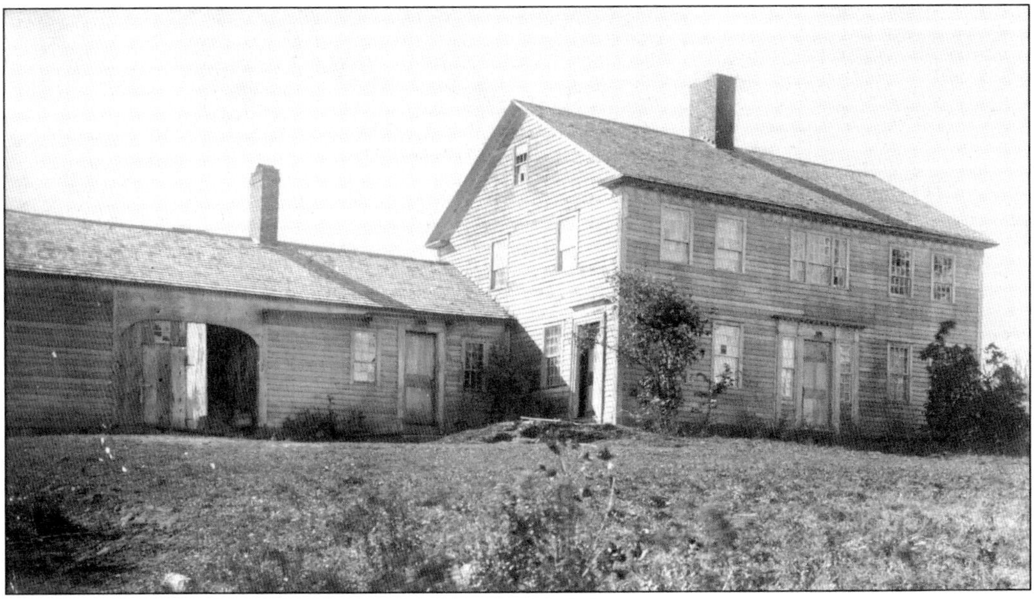

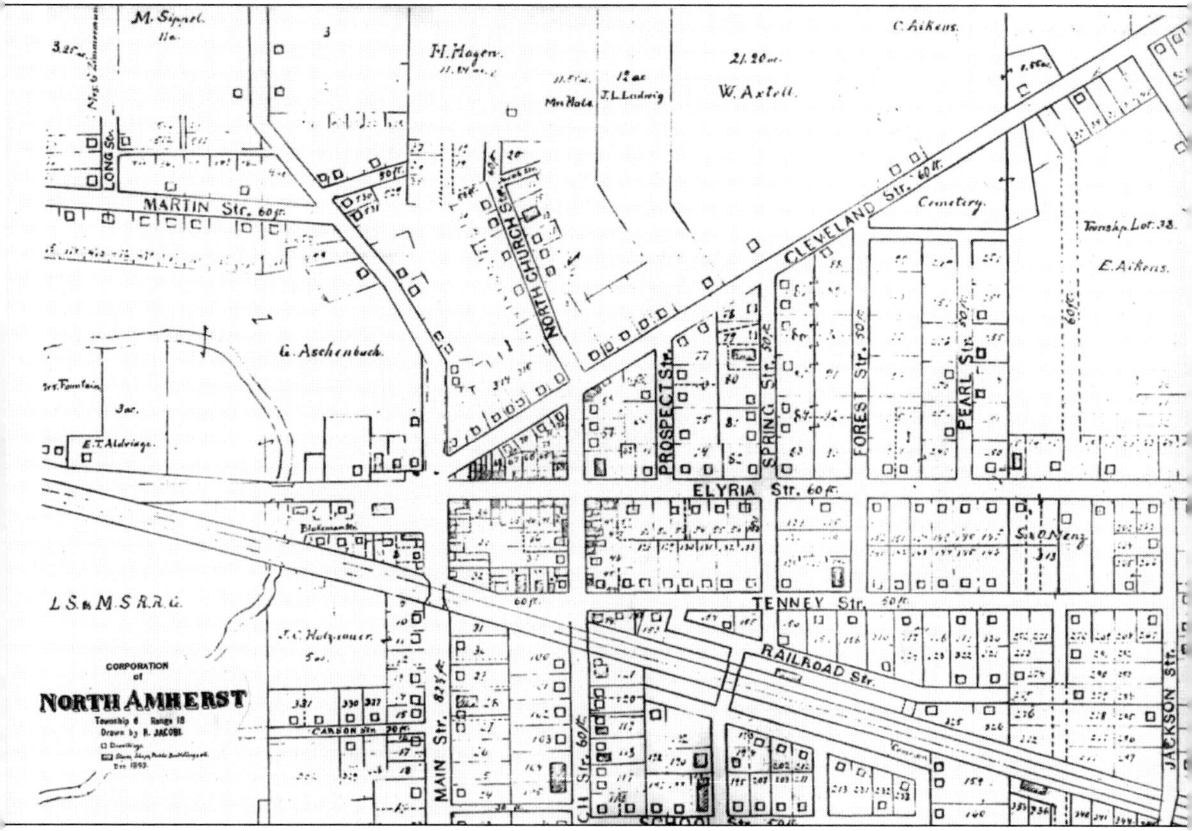

Corporation of North Amherst Plat, 1836. This town plat map, produced in 1836, illustrates the kind of work done by Belden and his fellow surveyors. Present-day Amherst is recognized on the map as Amherstville, with its boundaries defined by Cleveland Avenue to the north, Elyria Avenue (not in the image at bottom) to the south, the Beaver Creek to the west, and Prospect Street to the east. The community was not known as Amherst until 1909.

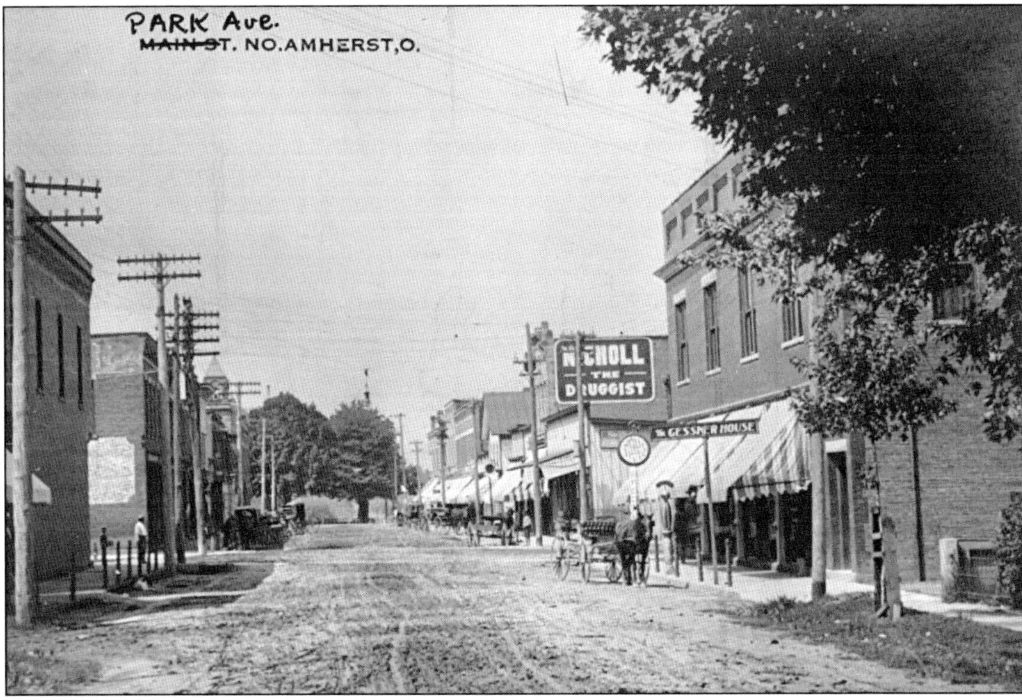

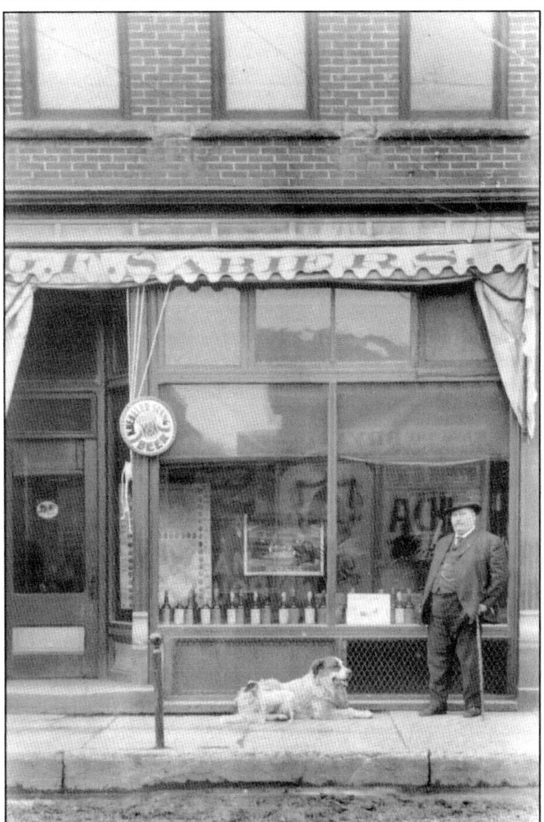

Park Avenue Looking West, c. 1905. Originally named Elyria Street, Park Avenue hosted a thriving commercial district by the beginning of the 20th century. Note the various establishments, such as the Manhattan Hotel and the Nicholl Drugstore, as well as the tower of the town hall at the end of the street. Newly electrified, the tracks for the trolley can be seen in the distance, and the presence of the unpaved road and horse-drawn carriages typifies the state of transportation.

Sabiers's Saloon, c. 1900. Sabiers's Saloon, owned by August F. Sabiers and located at 135 Park Avenue, provided entertainment for the local population. Primarily a male domain, the sign posted on the exterior of the building advertised Kuebeler Stang Beer for 5¢ a mug.

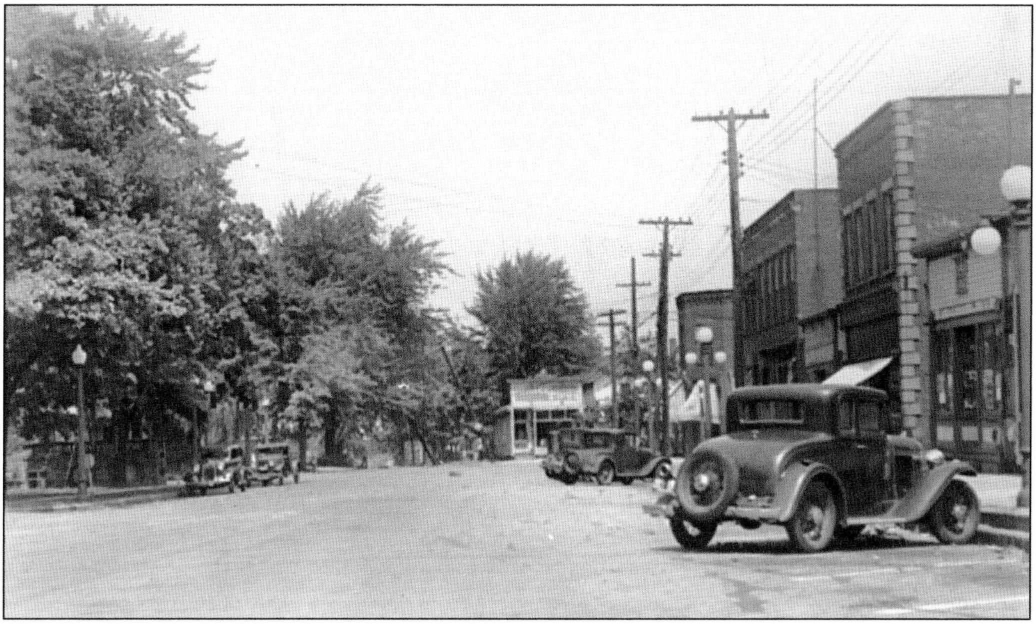

SOUTH MAIN STREET LOOKING NORTH. By 1920, visible changes had occurred in the community. Automobiles had appeared, the streets were paved, and streetlights lined the thoroughfares. Early streetlights were arc lights that operated on a moonlight schedule. In other words, the city turned the electricity on at dusk and off at midnight, and streetlights operated only when moonlight was insufficient.

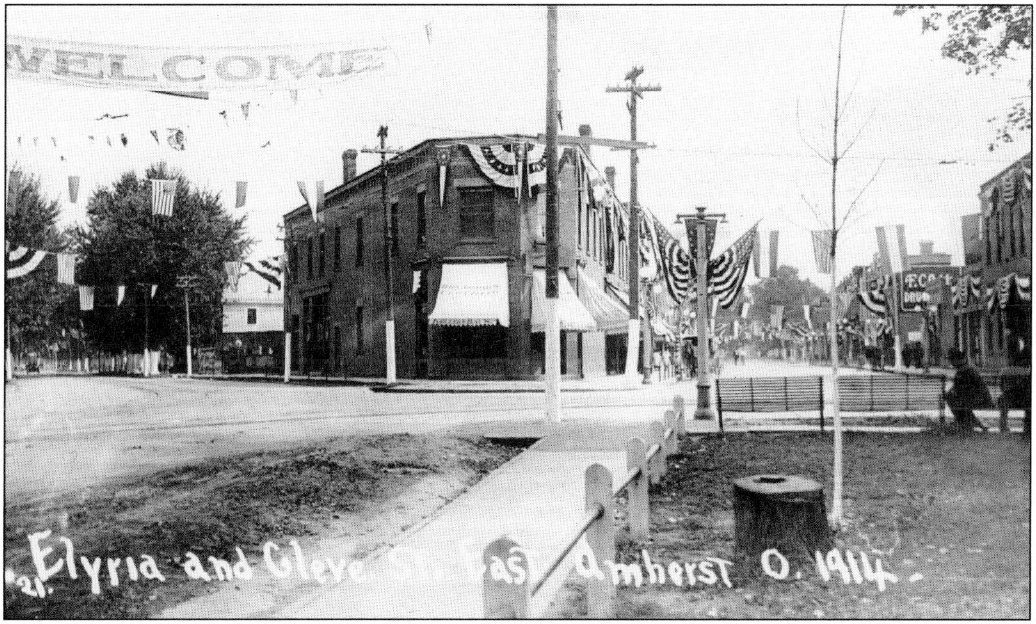

FLAT IRON BUILDING, 1914. Located at the corner of Cleveland and Park Avenues, the Flat Iron building, constructed in 1894 by John Holzhauer, remains one of the city's most recognized structures. Sitting at the juncture of five roads and across the street from the town hall, the building was at the center of community life. In this image, the building is decked out in patriotic bunting for the Old Home week celebration.

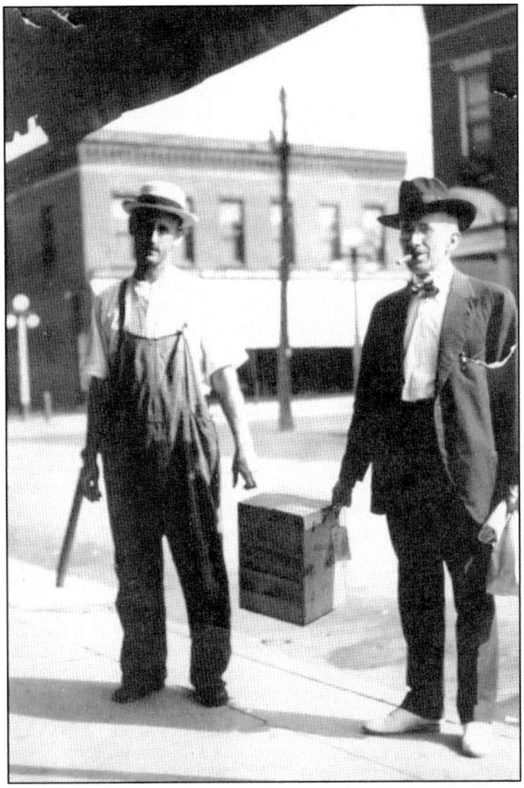

STREET SCENE C. 1910. Two Amherst businessmen transport a strong box, crossing the street in front of Bodman's Dry Goods Store. The delivery of goods and services often required cooperation and a hands-on approach.

COBBLER JOHN ULRICH SR., DECEMBER 1910. John Ulrich Sr. takes a break from his work in his cobbler's shop, located on Church Street. He is surrounded by the tools of his trade in an open space that he shared with his customers. Note the presence of electrical light and the cast-iron stove.

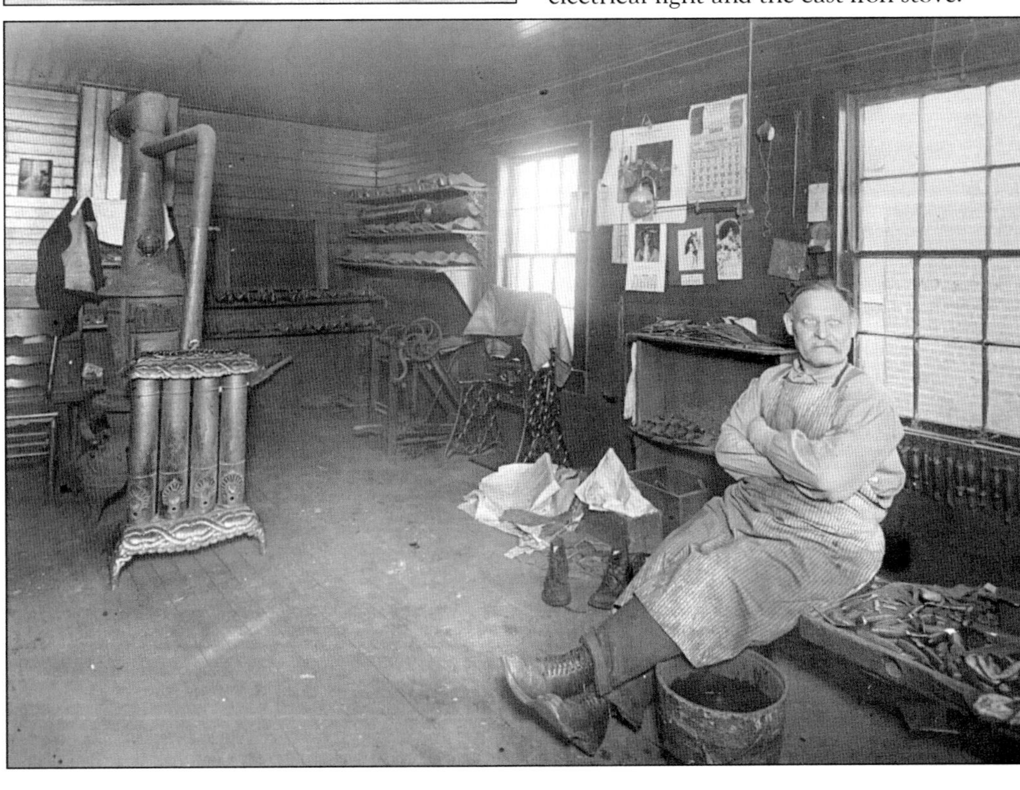

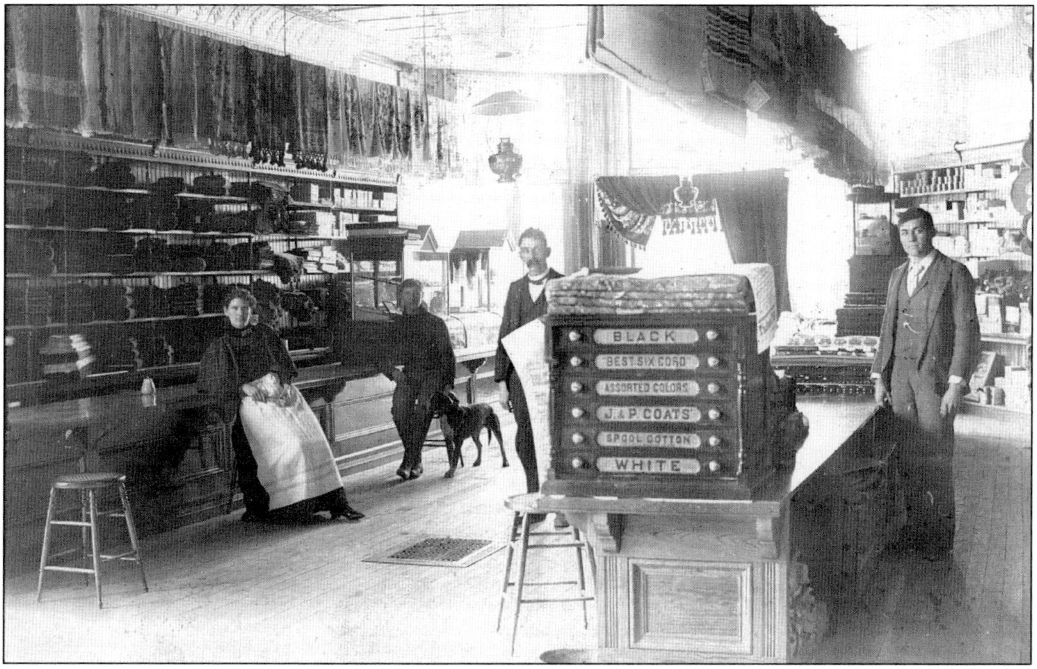

John Holzhauer's General Store, c. 1884. John Holzhauer's General Store, located at 110 Park (Elyria) Avenue, provided the community with most of what they needed to furnish their homes and clothe their families. Pictured here from left to right are Lena Beller Lersch, Charles Merthe, Holzhauer, and Conrad Aschenbach. Keeping watch over the proceedings is the pet dog.

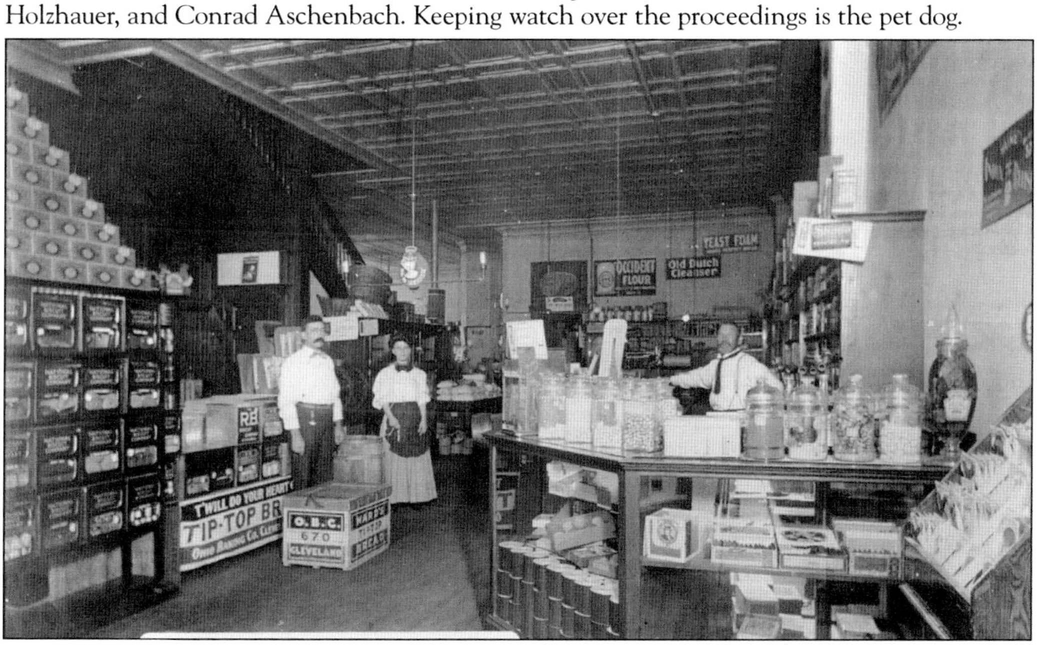

Bodman's Grocery and Dry Goods Store, c. 1905. Bodman's Grocery and Dry Goods, at the corner of Church Street and Park Avenue, provided Amherst residents with those foodstuffs and household items they could not produce themselves. The store carried both national and local brands and featured the R. B. Biscuit Company, the National Biscuit Company (Nabisco), Tip Top Bread (Ward's Ohio Baking Company), Occident Flour, and Old Dutch Cleanser.

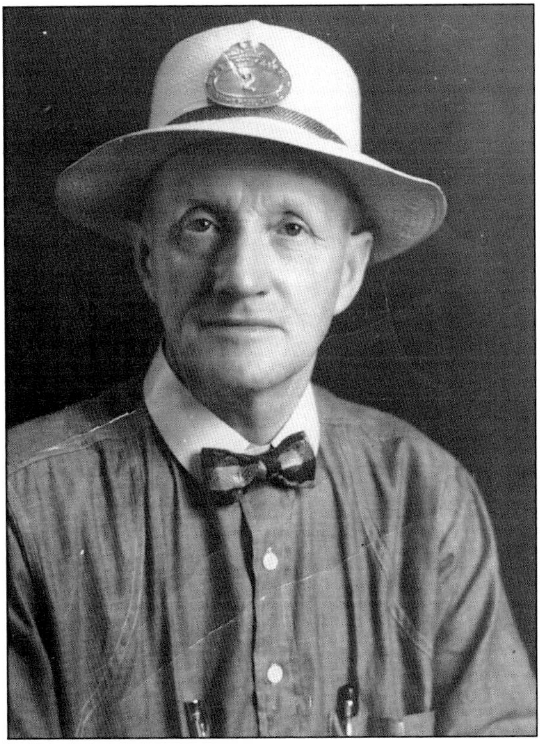

HERMAN BEESING AND HIS PAY BOOK. Herman Beesing (left), born in 1872, was the first rural free delivery mailman for Amherst in 1916. The last in a family of eight children, he lived across from the Old Spring. Prior to his work as a postman, Beesing labored in the local stone quarries, as his pay book (below), dated November and December 1889, illustrates. Later in life, Beesing also served as treasurer for three terms and a single term as councilman.

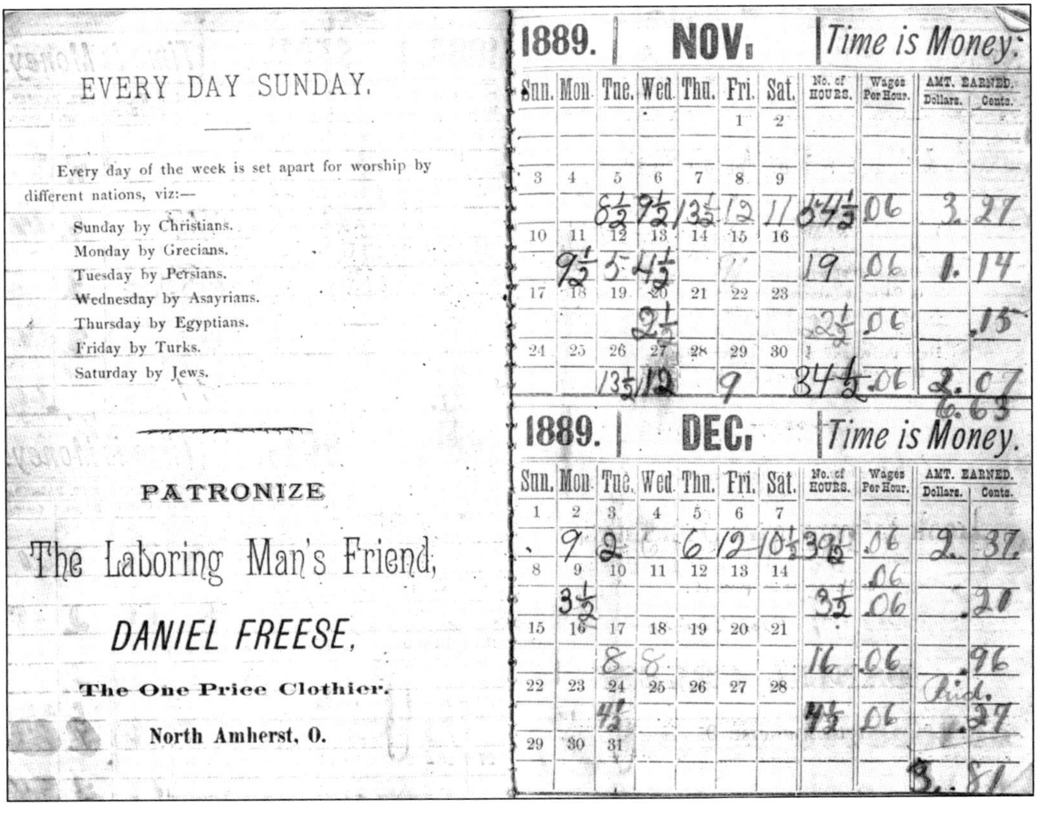

EVERY DAY SUNDAY.

Every day of the week is set apart for worship by different nations, viz:—

Sunday by Christians.
Monday by Grecians.
Tuesday by Persians.
Wednesday by Asayrians.
Thursday by Egyptians.
Friday by Turks.
Saturday by Jews.

PATRONIZE

The Laboring Man's Friend,

DANIEL FREESE,

The One Price Clothier.

North Amherst, O.

1889. NOV. Time is Money.

Sun.	Mon.	Tue.	Wed.	Thu.	Fri.	Sat.	No. of HOURS.	Wages Per Hour.	AMT. EARNED. Dollars.	Cents.
					1	2				
3	4	5	6	7	8	9				
		8½	9½	13½	12	11	54½	.06	3.	27
10	11	12	13	14	15	16				
	9½	5	4½				19	.06	1.	14
17	18	19	20	21	22	23				
			2½				2½	.06		.15
24	25	26	27	28	29	30				
		13½	12		9		34½	.06	2.	07
									6.	63

1889. DEC. Time is Money.

Sun.	Mon.	Tue.	Wed.	Thu.	Fri.	Sat.	No. of HOURS.	Wages Per Hour.	AMT. EARNED. Dollars.	Cents.
1	2	3	4	5	6	7				
	9	2		6	12	10½	39½	.06	2.	37
8	9	10	11	12	13	14		.06		
	3½						3½	.06		21
15	16	17	18	19	20	21				
		8	8				16	.06		96
22	23	24	25	26	27	28			Paid.	
		4½					4½	.06		27
29	30	31								
									3.	81

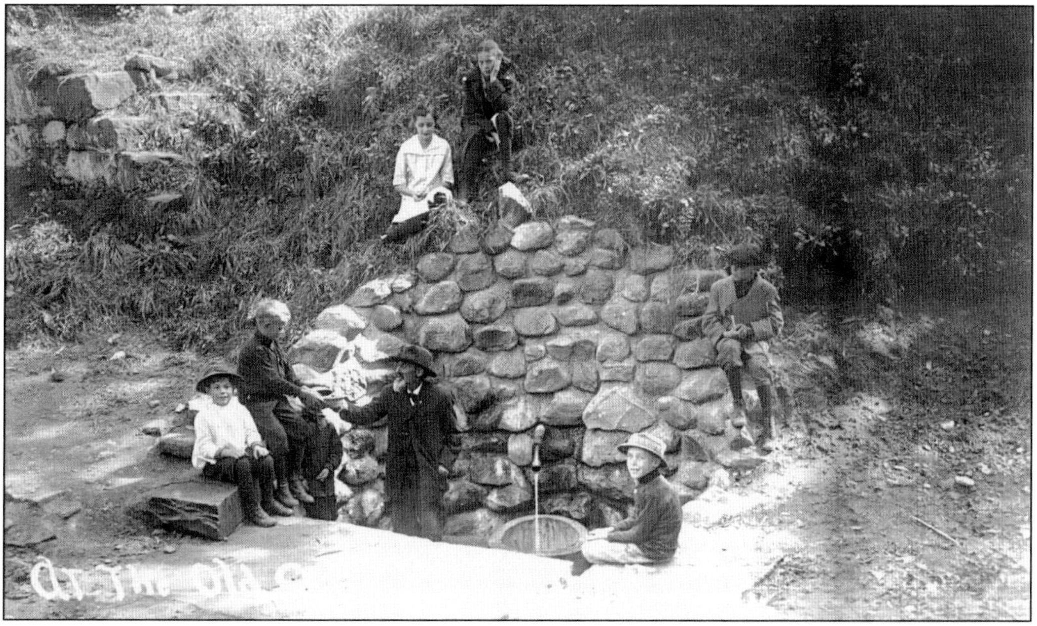

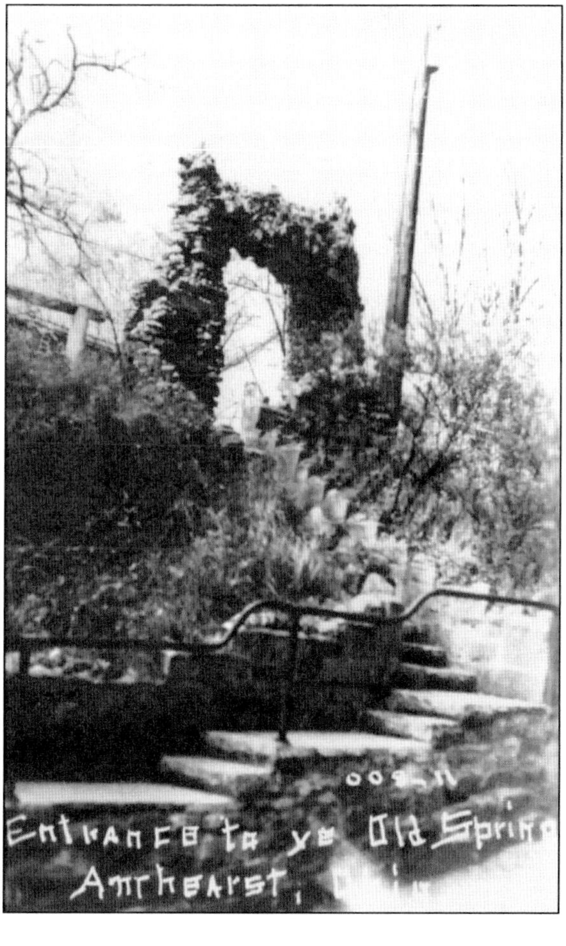

The Old Spring. One of Amherst's most recognizable landmarks, the Old Spring is located on Milan Avenue just west of town hall. In its early days, the spring provided residents of Amherst with a guaranteed source of clear, cool water. As the community matured, improvements in the sanitary system spelled the end of the spring's usefulness as the sole source of water but turned it into an important marker in the town's history. In 1955, bacteria found in the water rendered it unpotable. The initial improvements to the spring, seen above in 1914, reinforced the side of the hill from which it emerged and provided a free-running pipe. In 1930, August Nabakowski created an arch and signage to commemorate the site. Further improvements by the Works Progress Administration (WPA) around 1936 (seen at right around 1949) included an upper retaining wall and stairs to provide access, as well as tables and a fireplace for picnics.

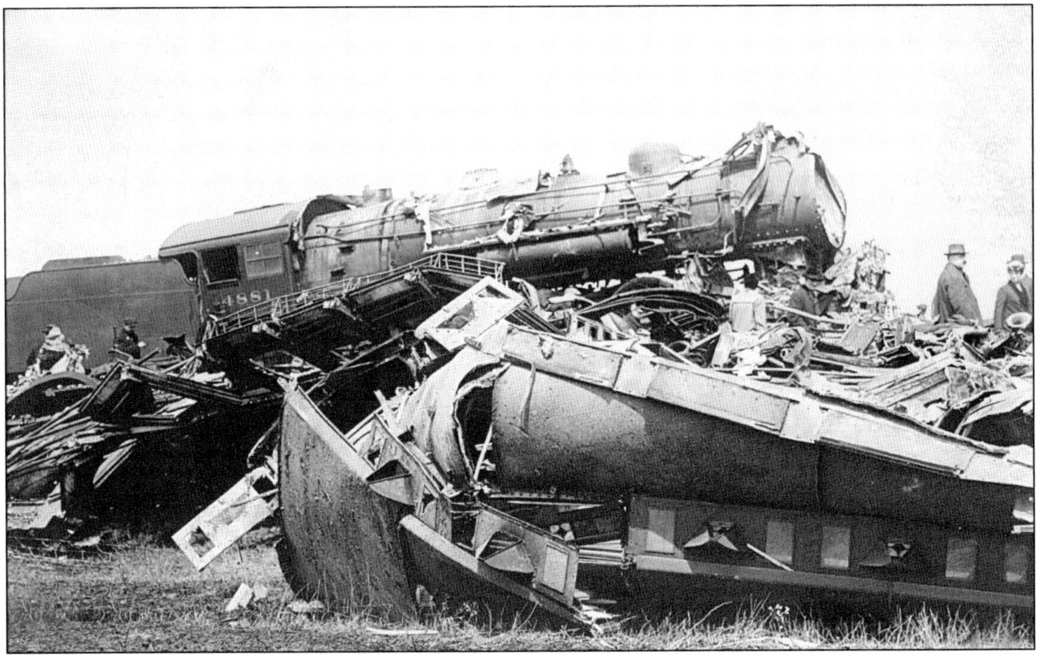

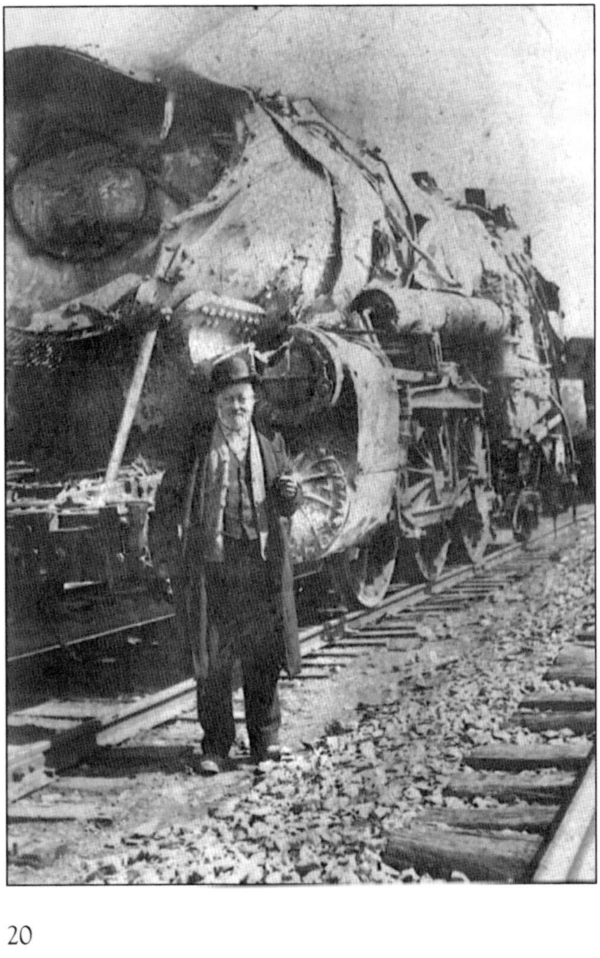

The Train Wreck, 1916. One of the signal events in the history of Amherst was the train wreck of March 29, 1916 (above). The collision, which involved three New York Central Railroad trains, occurred on a very foggy morning at 4:20 a.m. and resulted in 28 fatalities and serious injuries to at least 50 others. The destruction engendered by the collision is clearly evident above. At left, Joseph Richardson Miller stands beside the engine of the *20th Century Limited*. Miller's farm abutted the railroad tracks and the accident occurred a quarter of a mile from his farm.

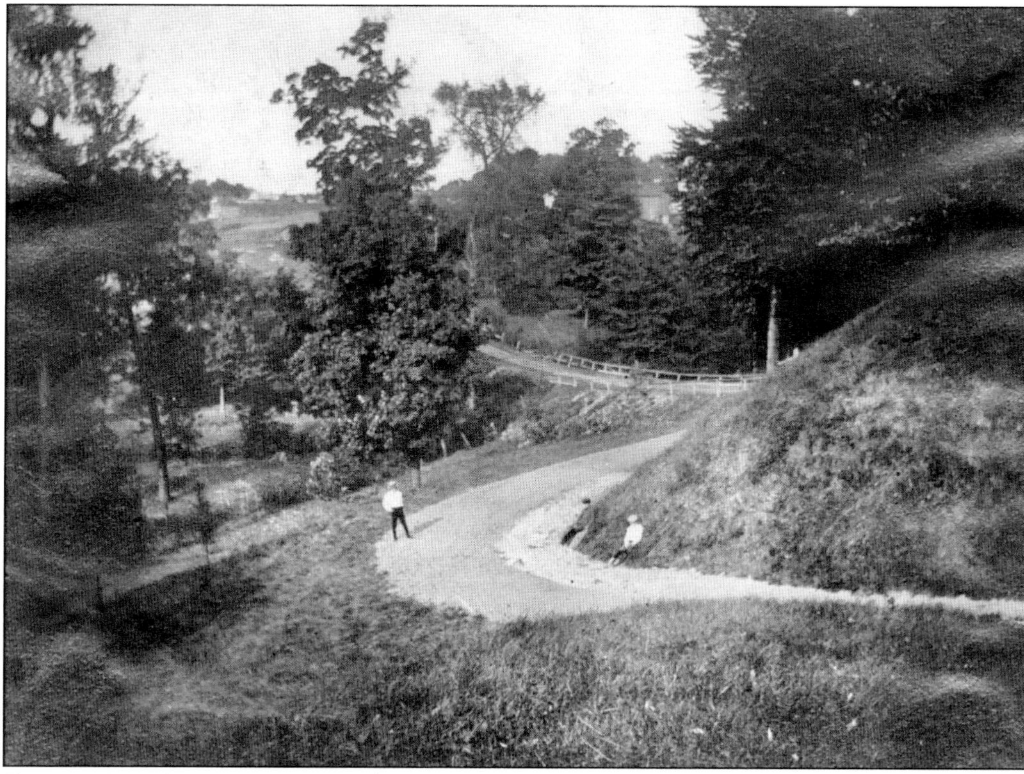

CROWN HILL CEMETERY, 1904. The grounds for Crown Hill Cemetery were purchased by the village in 1894 from H. G. Remington for $1,100. The earliest gravestone, a simple boulder, marks the final resting place of Charles and Jenny Schubert. Interned with the Schuberts were Bet and Belle, the family's horses.

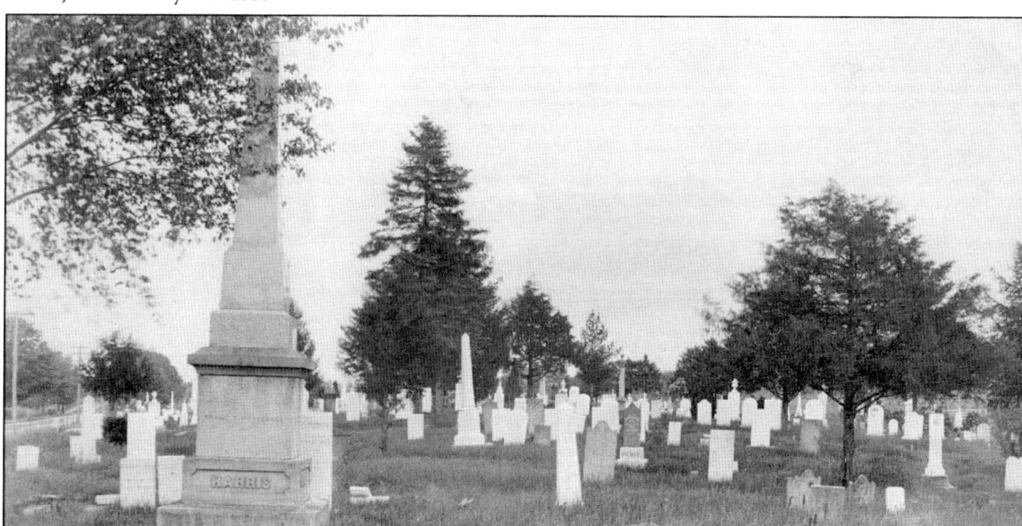

CLEVELAND STREET CEMETERY, c. 1900. The Cleveland Street Cemetery, also known as "God's Little Acre," became the final resting place of some of Amherst's earliest residents. The earliest known internment occurred in 1819. Among the notables were members of the Josiah Harris family, as indicated on the stone at far left.

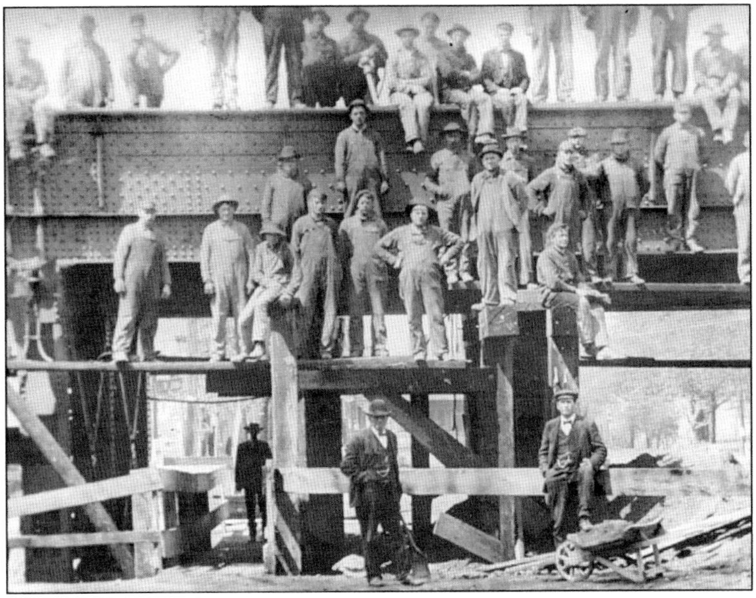

Raising the Rail Lines, 1892. As Amherst grew so did its access to the outside world. The railroad came to the town in 1852, and as the commercial district expanded, the presence of rail lines impeded traffic. In 1892, to remedy the situation, the Amherst town fathers built a trestle to raise the tracks over Main Street. Citizens boasted, "No school bus has to wait for trains in our town."

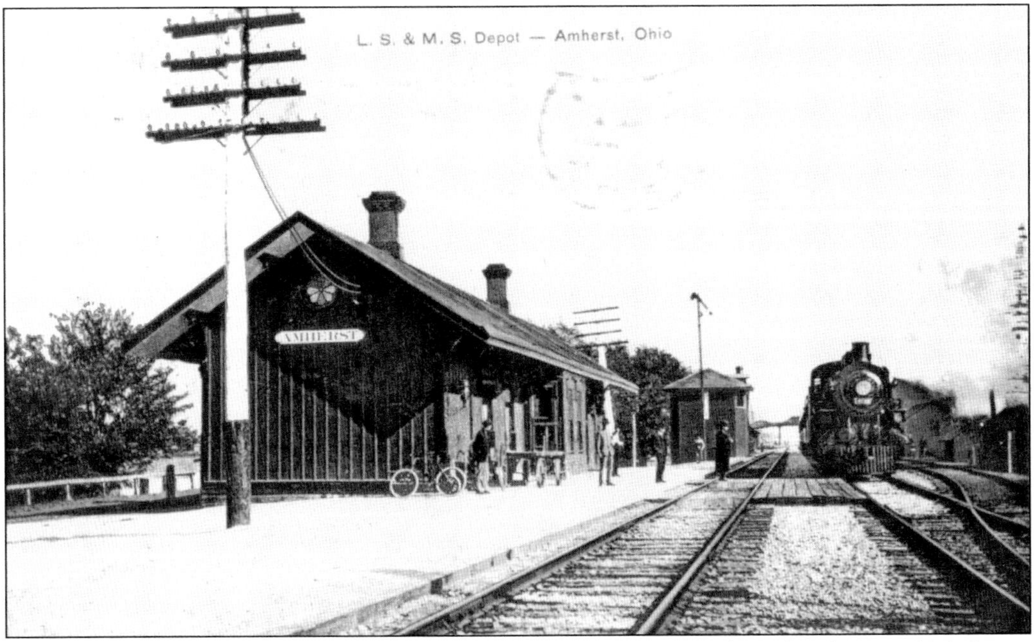

Lake Shore and Michigan Southern Railway Depot, c. 1907. The Lake Shore and Michigan Southern Railway built a passenger depot, located on the north side of the tracks near Mill and Spring Streets, in the 1890s, after the raising of the trestle. The company provided passenger service for the town along the Lake Erie shoreline. The depot operated until 1947, when service was discontinued. It was torn down in 1951.

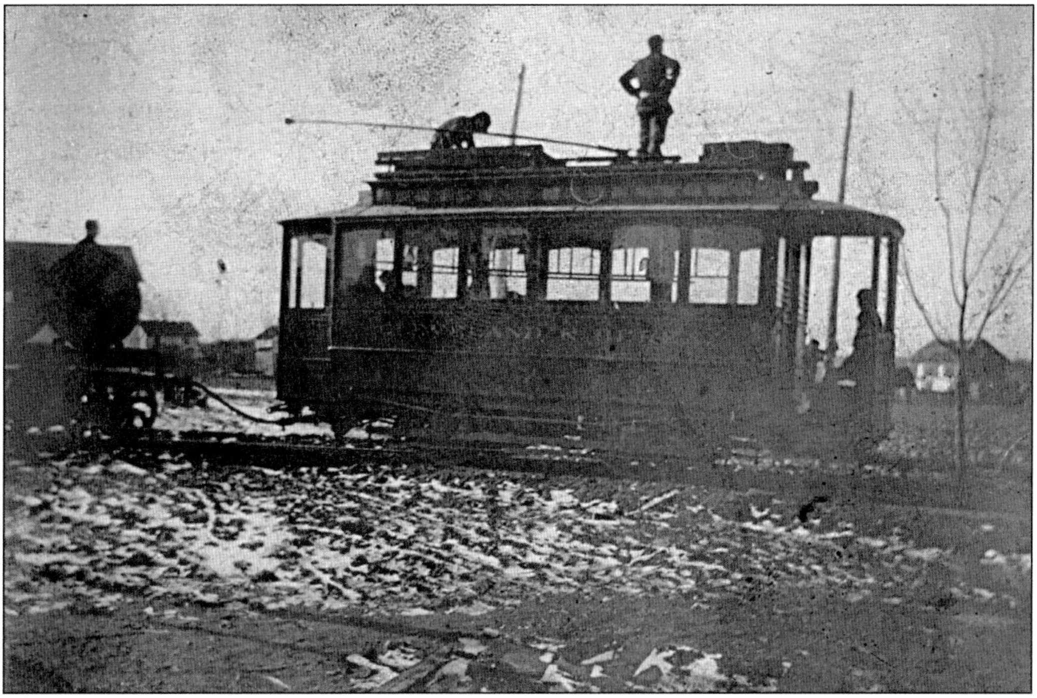

The Green Line Streetcar, c. 1900. Electric trolley service began in Amherst on February 8, 1900. Sam Delafield, a local meat dealer, paid 25¢ for the first ride. The streetcar route ran from Amherst to Lorain and functioned as part of the interurban line. The streetcars prospered for approximately 25 years, when they were replaced by bus lines.

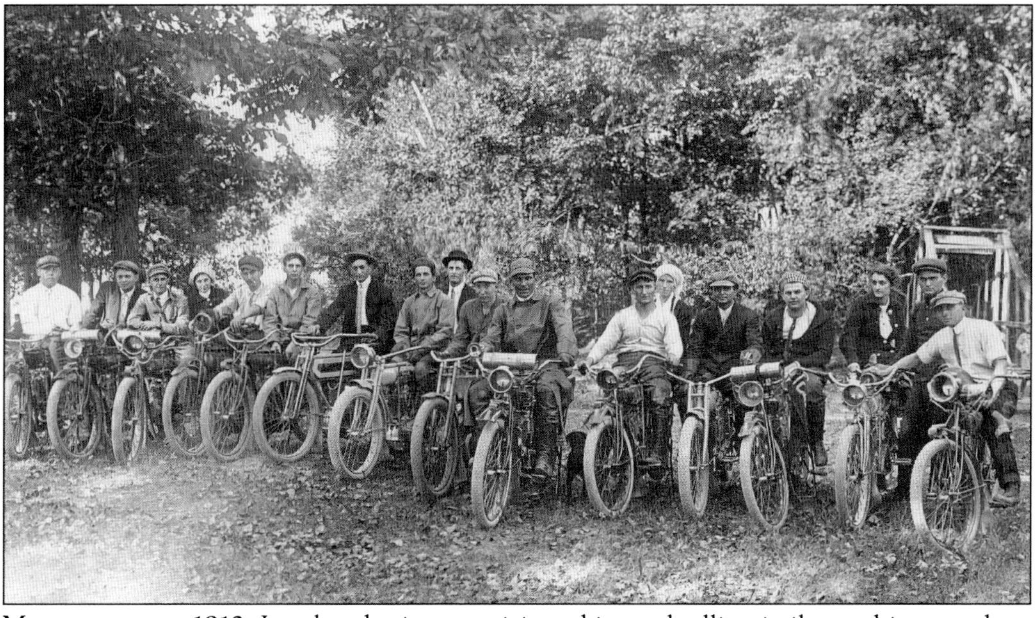

Motorcyclists, 1913. Local enthusiasts participated in road rallies similar to this one, where riders gathered at Slater's Grove in Lorain. All of the motorcycles, mainly Harleys and Indians, were manufactured in the United States. At least half sported gas-powered headlights. Note that the women in the background were motorcyclists themselves.

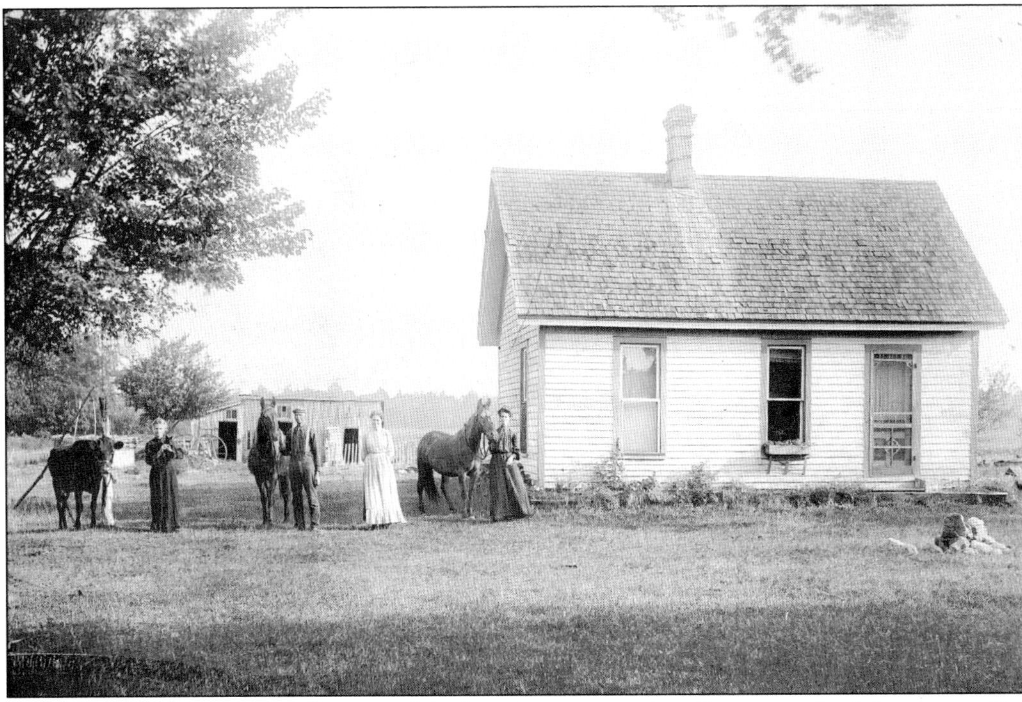

Eugene Linn House, 1907. In spite of Amherst's growing urban flavor, much of the surrounding area remained rural. The Linn homestead on North Ridge Road characterized the outskirts of the community in the opening decades of the 20th century. Among those pictured are Eugene and Mary Linn, at left in the photograph.

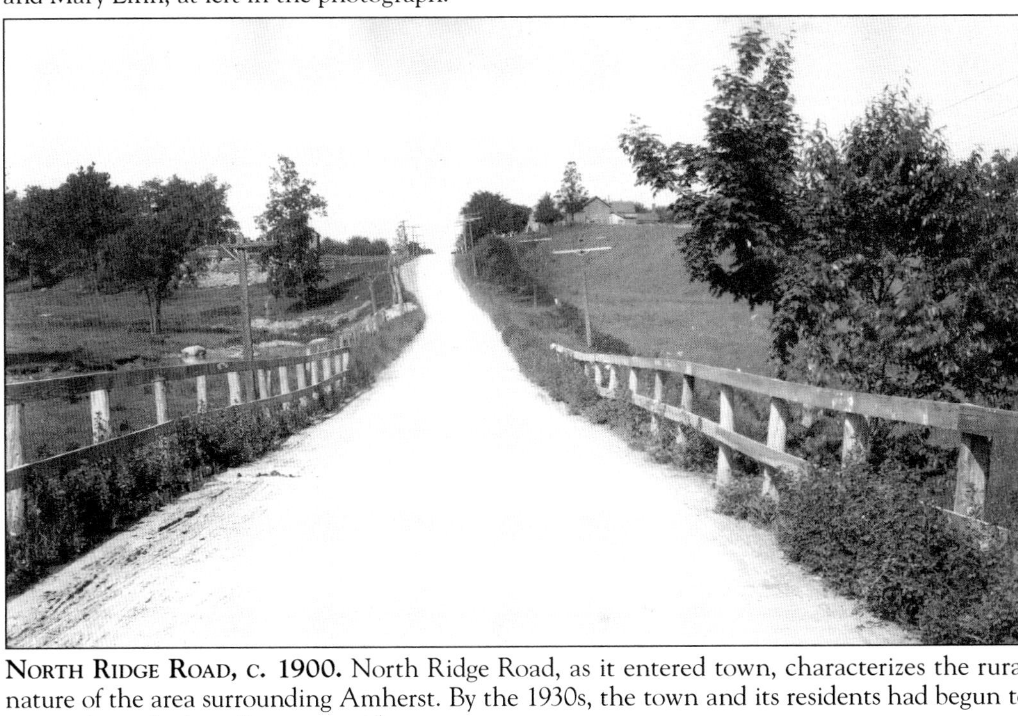

North Ridge Road, c. 1900. North Ridge Road, as it entered town, characterizes the rural nature of the area surrounding Amherst. By the 1930s, the town and its residents had begun to encroach on the bucolic countryside.

Two

The Quarry Story

While Amherst initially developed as an agricultural settlement, its residents soon came to rely on the rich deposits of sandstone that abounded in the area. Early residents saw the shallow, rocky soil as the bane of their existence but gradually realized its true value. By the mid-19th century, the community boasted several small, independent quarries. In 1847, an entrepreneur from Toronto, Ontario, Canada, moved to the area and purchased a tract of land to develop the first quarry in Amherst Township. John Worthington founded a prosperous enterprise based on the extraction and rough finishing of Amherst Buff sandstone. In the years that followed, a number of others, including George E. Hall and R. P. Wilson, followed his lead. Hall, in 1868, opened the first stone sawmill, and Wilson, a year later, began operations at the Gray Canyon No. 6 quarry, later to become the largest single sandstone quarry in the world. Capitalizing on their growing market, John Worthington and Sons constructed a railroad spur from Brownhelm station to the Vermilion docks on Lake Erie in 1871. Two years later, the Lake Shore and Michigan Southern Railway constructed a spur to the No. 6 quarry. Worthington was joined in 1886 by the Cleveland Stone Company and in 1903 by the Ohio Quarries Company, organized by Chicagoan John R. Walsh. Their Buckeye Quarry is reputed to be one of the deepest in the world, mined to a depth of 240 feet. In the second decade of the 20th century, taking advantage of locally quarried product, two concerns—Blum and Delbridge Cut Stone Company and the Amherst Cut Stone Company—prospered in Amherst. The two merged in 1919 into the Ohio Stone Company after being purchased by the Ohio Quarries Company. In 1929, the Ohio Quarries Company and the Cleveland Stone Company merged into the Cleveland Quarries Company. This entity maintained its operations until the latter part of the 20th century. The quarries provided the foundation for the community's prosperity and the magnet for attracting its growing population.

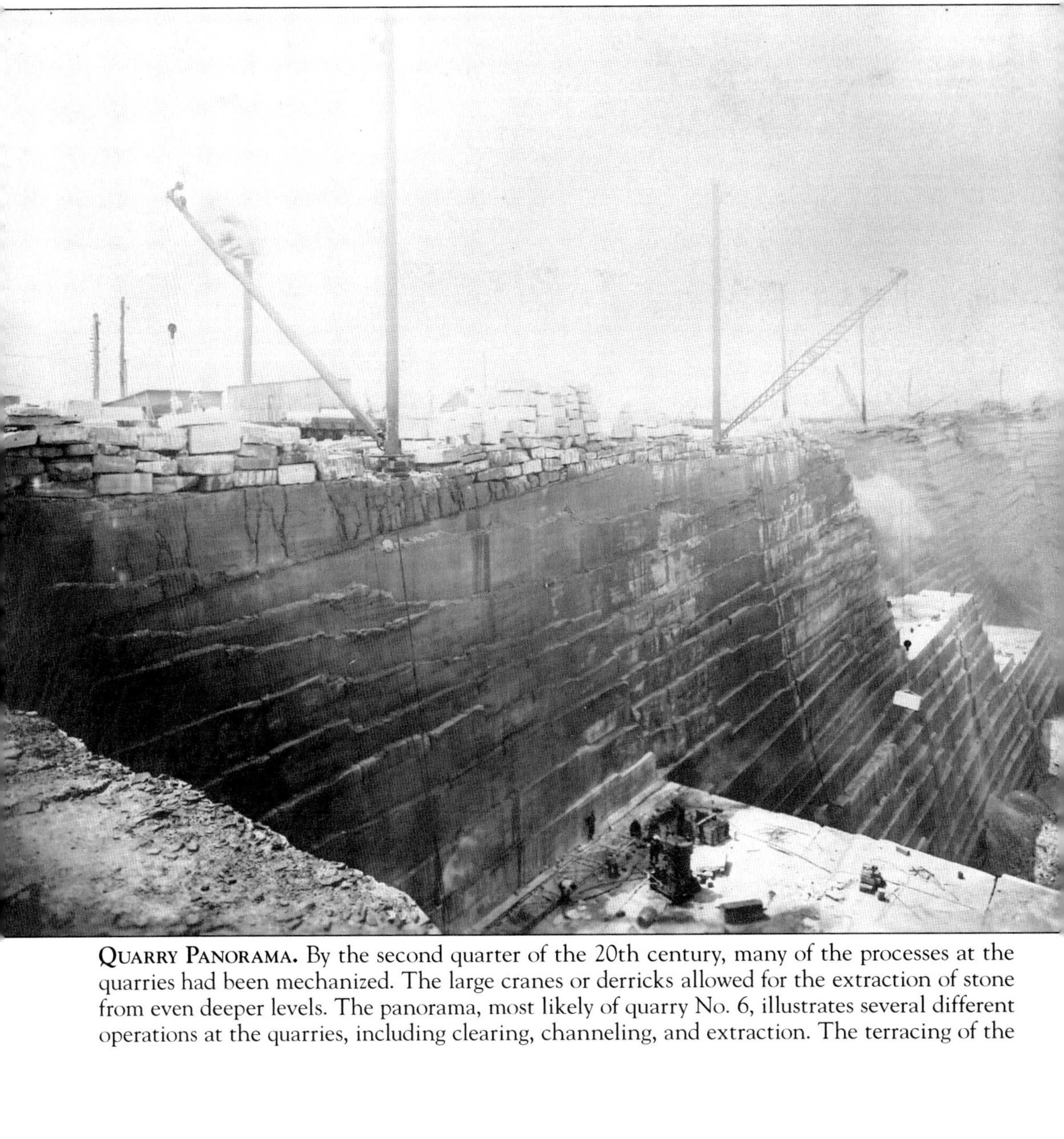

Quarry Panorama. By the second quarter of the 20th century, many of the processes at the quarries had been mechanized. The large cranes or derricks allowed for the extraction of stone from even deeper levels. The panorama, most likely of quarry No. 6, illustrates several different operations at the quarries, including clearing, channeling, and extraction. The terracing of the

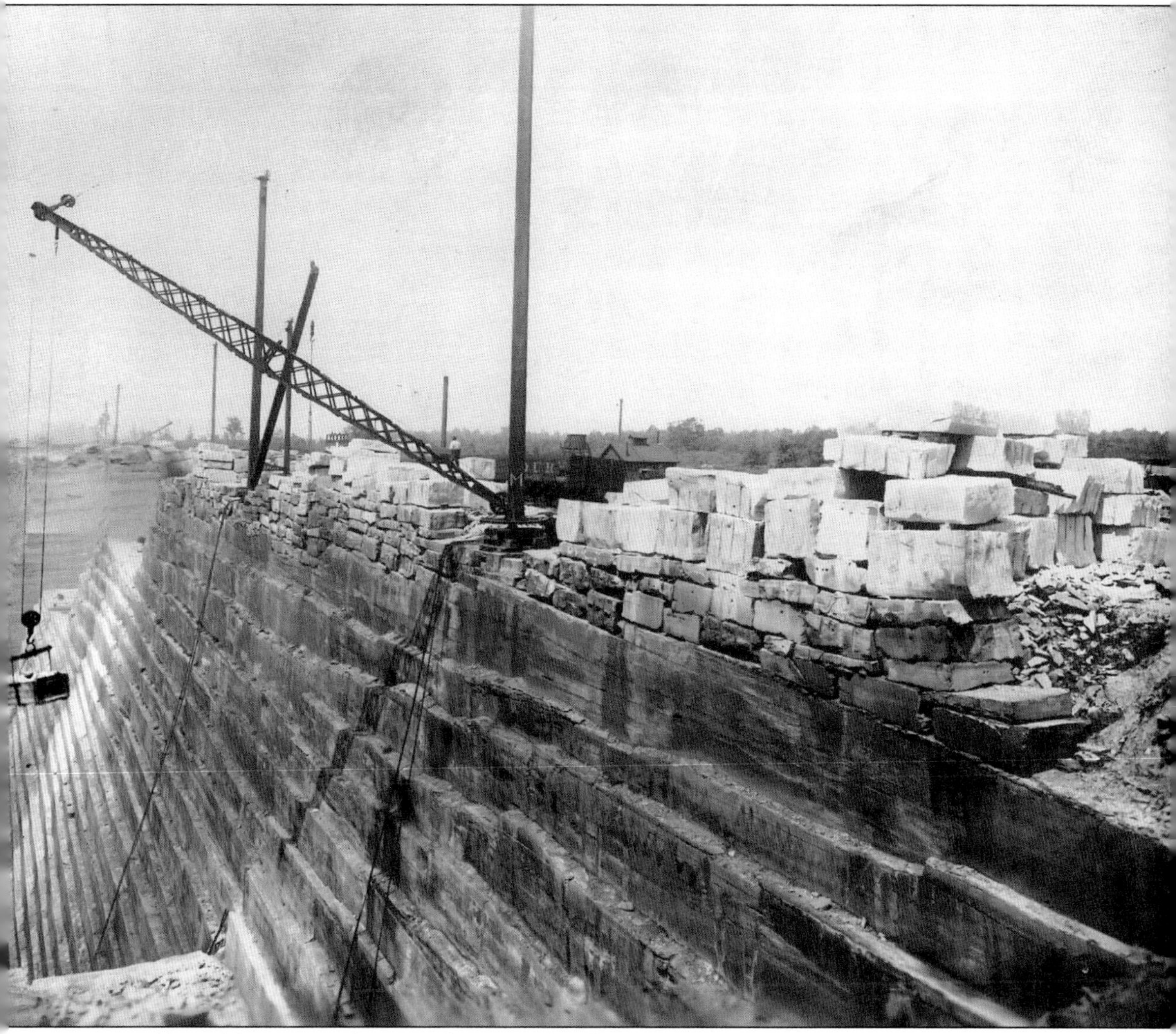

quarries allowed for stone to be mined at several different levels simultaneously. The large blocks, weighing 12 to 40 tons, were placed on waiting railroad cars and taken to the mills for further processing. The panorama also clearly illustrates the breadth and depth of the operations.

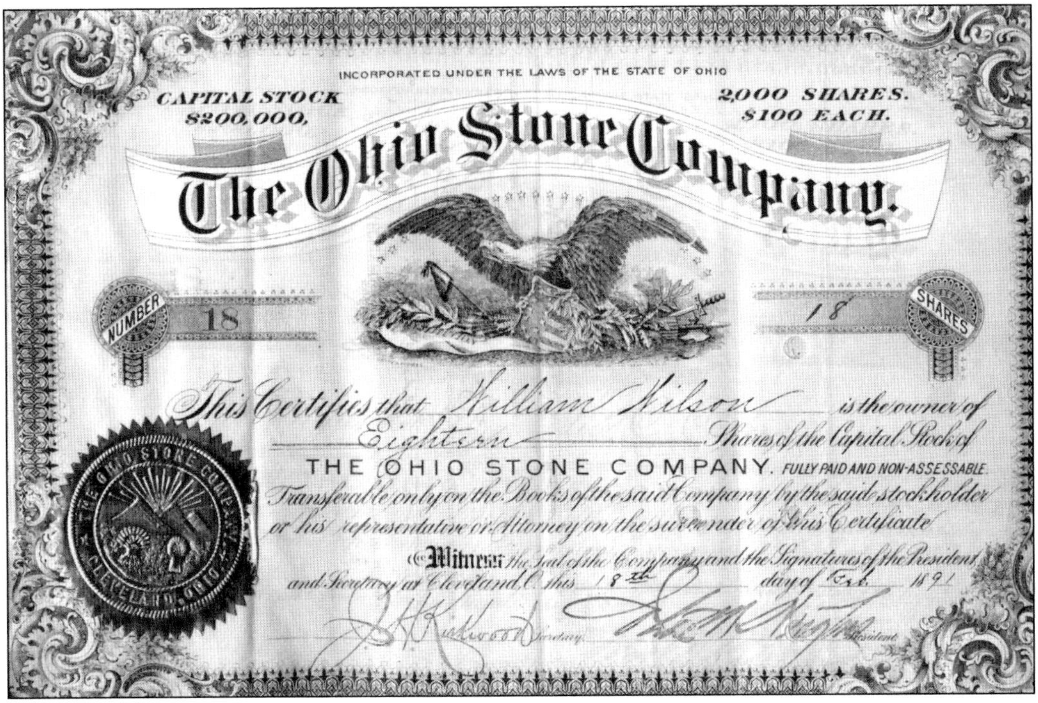
INCORPORATED UNDER THE LAWS OF THE STATE OF OHIO

CAPITAL STOCK $200,000.

2,000 SHARES. $100 EACH.

The Ohio Stone Company.

NUMBER 18

18 SHARES

This Certifies that William Wilson is the owner of Eighteen Shares of the Capital Stock of THE OHIO STONE COMPANY. FULLY PAID AND NON-ASSESSABLE. Transferable only on the Books of the said Company by the said stockholder or his representative or Attorney on the surrender of this Certificate.

Witness the Seal of the Company and the Signatures of the President and Secretary at Cleveland, O. this 18th day of Feb 1891

J. H. Kirkwood Secretary

President

THE OHIO STONE COMPANY CLEVELAND, OHIO

OHIO STONE COMPANY STOCK CERTIFICATE. This document certified that John M. Hughes and Alex C. Caskey, trustee for the Hughes estate owned 50 shares of the capital stock of the Ohio Stone Company. The certificate, numbered "one," was dated February 3, 1891, and signed by J. H. Kirkwood and Hughes. Hughes and Caskey purchased 196 shares that day.

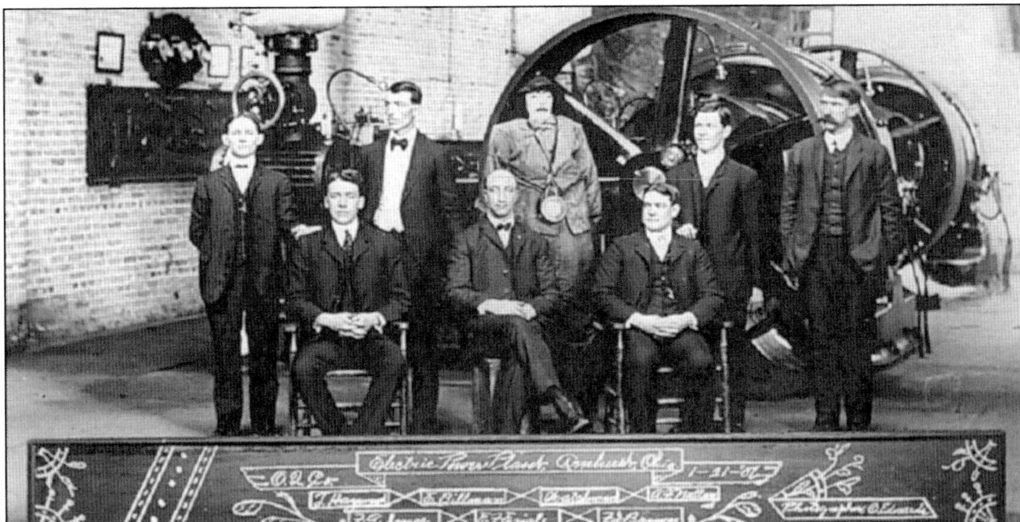

OHIO QUARRY COMPANY POWER PLANT. The electric power plant at the Ohio quarries site illustrates growing mechanization of the stone quarrying industry. Representatives of the company management are seated in front of the generator. From left to right (seated) are F. A. Jones, E. F. Engle, and F. J. Brown; (second row) T. Haywood, E. Billman, "Watchman," A. F. Nalley, and an unidentified man. Note Watchman, the stuffed figure in the center of the second row, complete with a large lock around his neck. The photograph was taken about 1901.

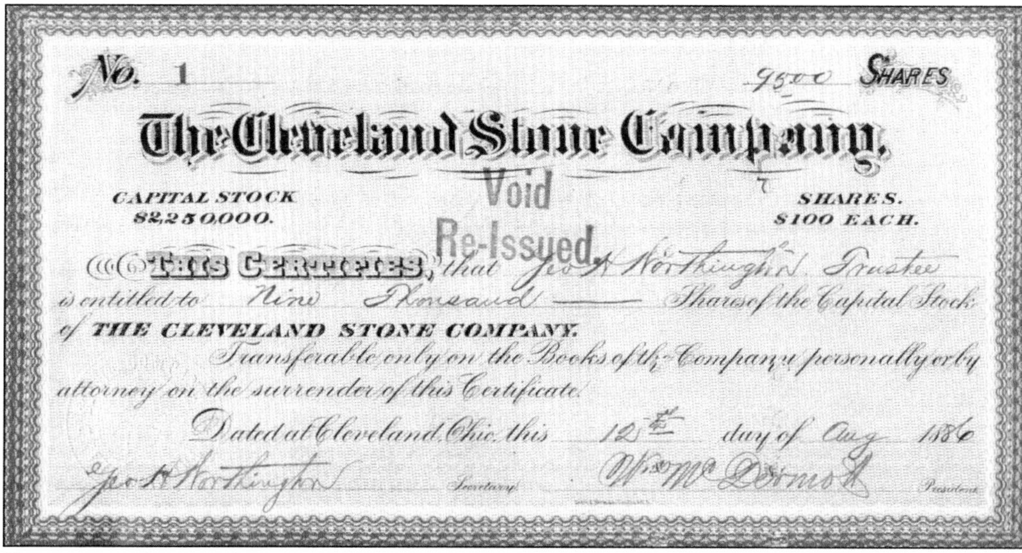
No. 1 9500 SHARES

The Cleveland Stone Company.

CAPITAL STOCK $2,250,000. Void SHARES. $100 EACH.

Re-Issued

THIS CERTIFIES, that Geo H Worthington Trustee is entitled to Nine Thousand —— Shares of the Capital Stock of THE CLEVELAND STONE COMPANY. Transferable only on the Books of the Company personally or by attorney on the surrender of this Certificate.

Dated at Cleveland, Ohio, this 12th day of Aug 1886

Geo H Worthington Secretary. Wm McDermott President.

CLEVELAND STONE COMPANY STOCK CERTIFICATE. This document certified that George H. Worthington, trustee, owned the majority shares—9,000 of them—of the Cleveland Stone Company. Issued on August 12, 1886, it verifies Worthington's importance in the quarries and the community.

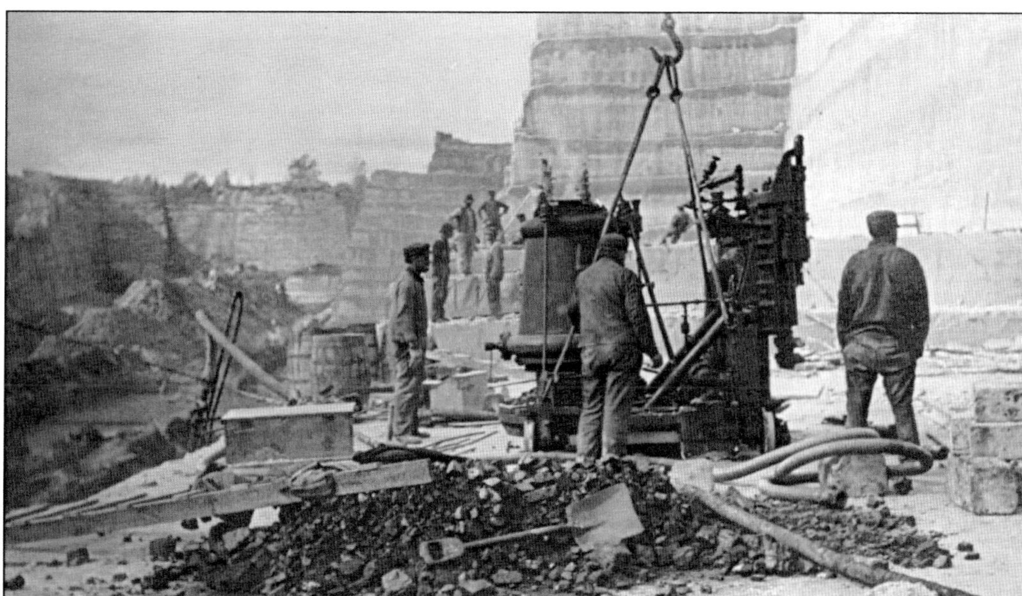

CHANNELING MACHINE, C. 1919. A channeling machine, driven by compressed air, made the extraction of stone more efficient. It drove steel rams up to 15 feet deep into the rock, allowing quarries to eliminate blasting, which caused fissures and cracks in the stone. For the machines to work, the air had to be heated with the coal piled directly behind the operators. They were portable enough to be moved with the aid of derricks.

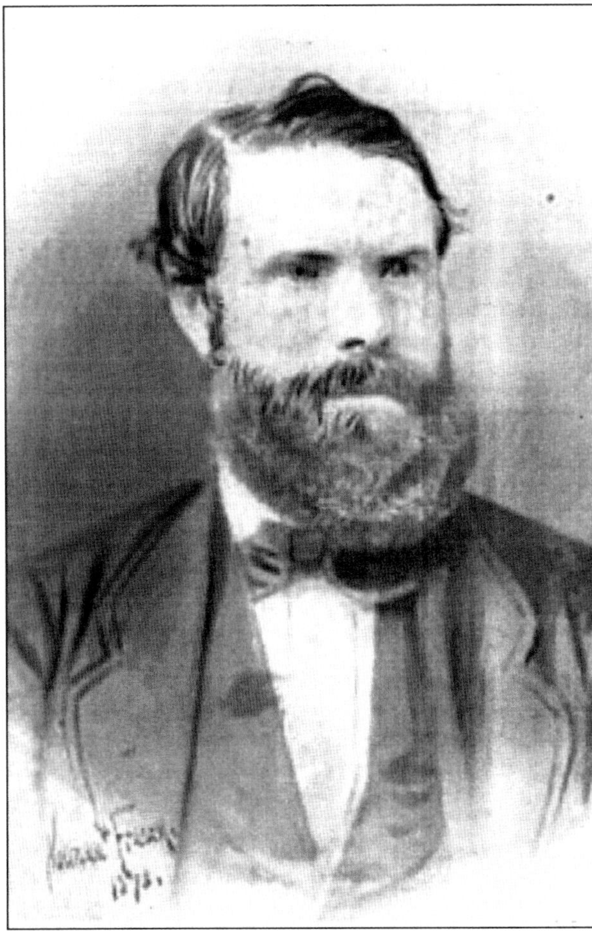

George Worthington and the Berea and Huron Stone Company. George Worthington (left), a native of Toronto, Ontario, Canada, was responsible for introducing Amherst to large-scale quarrying operations. By the 1880s, he was the major shareholder in the Cleveland Stone Company, as well as a variety of other ventures. On January 20, 1880, he and four others subscribed to capital stock (below) of the Berea and Huron Stone Company. The agreement also made provision for them to assume positions on the board of directors. The cost of subscription was $100 per share. It is signed, "George H. Worthington, Frank M. Steams, William McDermott, and Frank B. Wallace."

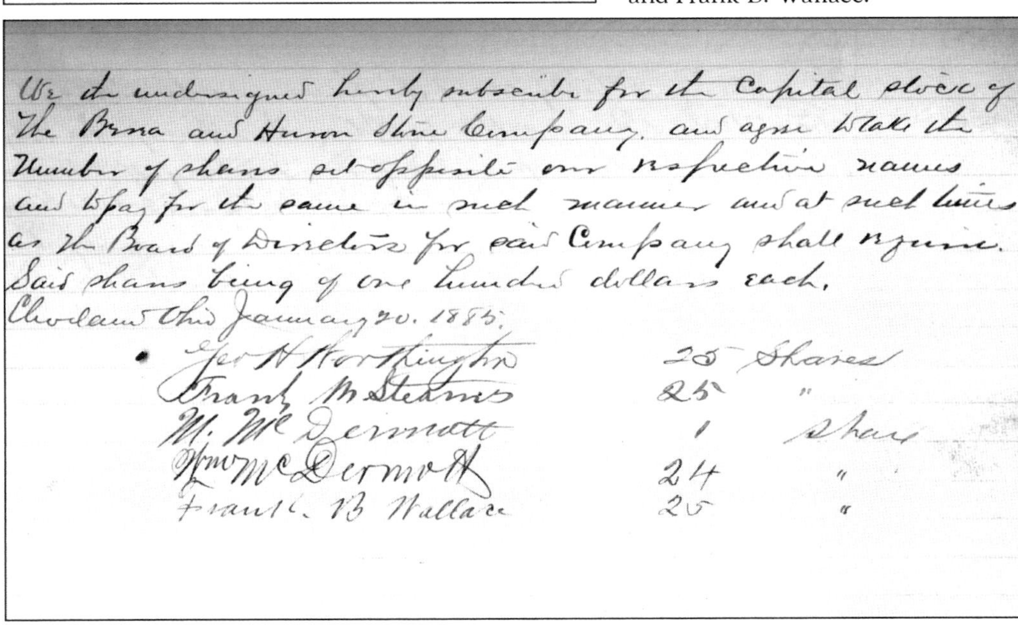

We the undersigned hereby subscribe for the Capital stock of The Berea and Huron Stone Company and agree to take the Number of shares set opposite our respective names and to pay for the same in such manner and at such times as the Board of Directors for said Company shall require. Said shares being of one hundred dollars each.
Cleveland Ohio January 20. 1880.

Geo H Worthington	25 Shares
Frank M Stearns	25 "
W. McDermott	1 Share
Wm McDermott	24 "
Frank B Wallace	25 "

WORKERS AT THE NICHOL QUARRY. This photograph from about 1900, probably taken at the Nichol Quarry on North Ridge Road East, clearly illustrates the diversity of the quarry's workforce. Middle-aged craftsmen, young laborers, and boys populated the workforce. Take particular note of the two youngsters with their water pails and shoulder yokes in the bottom left corner. Also of interest is the cornfield that abuts the quarry in the background.

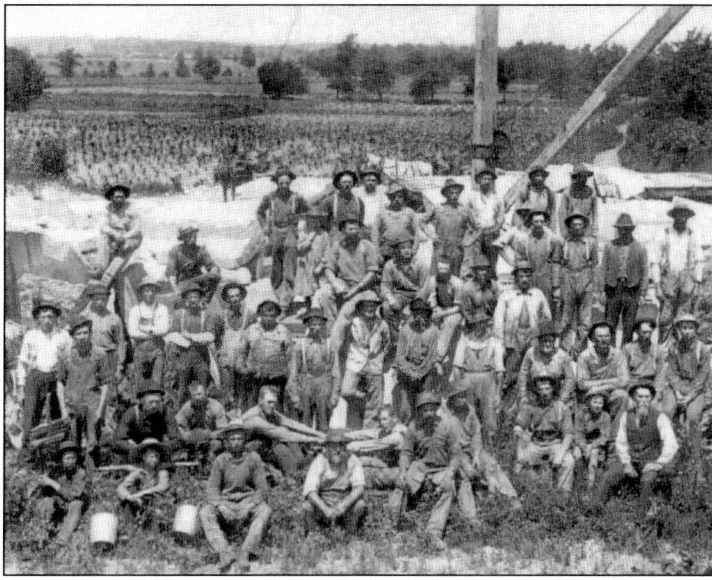

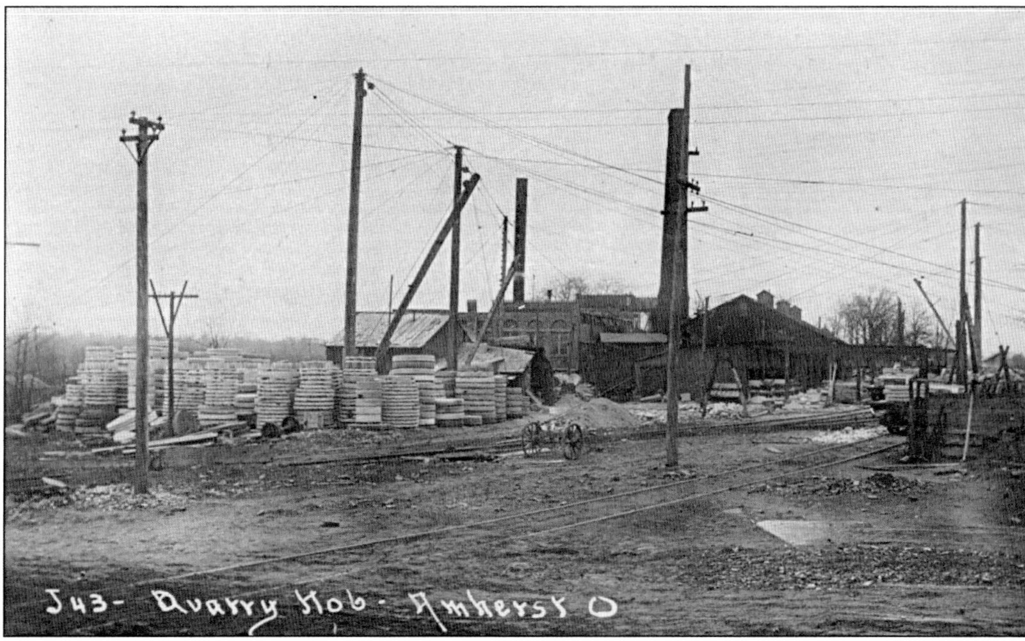

RAIL SIDING AT THE NO. 6 QUARRY. Grindstones, finished in the building at the rear, are stacked by the rail siding of the Lake Shore and Michigan Southern Railway for shipment to their final destinations. These grindstones, highly prized for their resistance to wear, were cut from firm stone, which consisted of grains tightly cemented by silica or quartz. The grindstones were used for sharpening and in various grain milling operations.

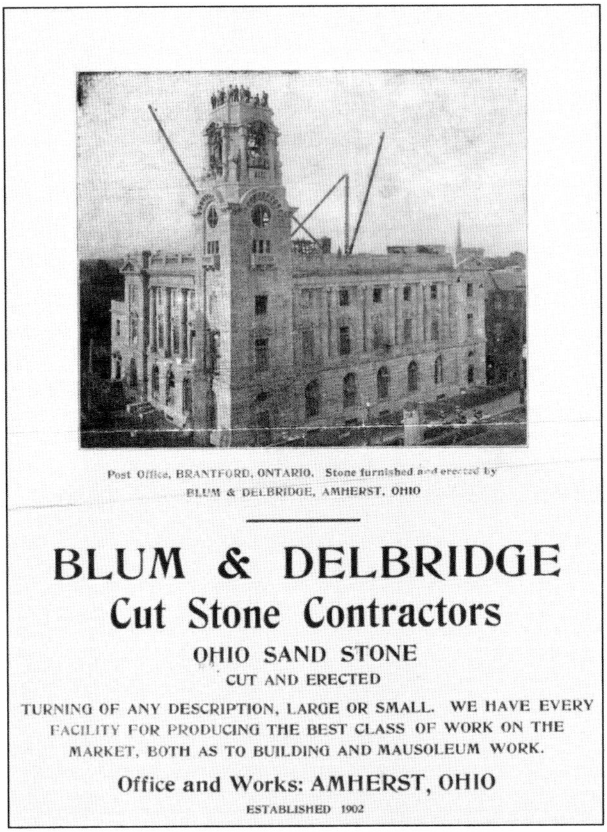

BLUM AND DELBRIDGE ADVERTISEMENT. The Blum and Delbridge Cut Stone Company specialized in the finishing of sandstone for major construction projects throughout the United States and Canada. This advertisement proclaimed the company's willingness to work on projects from large to small and promised the "best class of work on the market." It featured the post office in Brantford, Ontario, Canada, a project for which Blum and Delbridge not only provided the stone but also did the construction of the building.

BLUM AND DELBRIDGE WORKERS. Workers gathered outside the Blum and Delbridge Cut Stone Company just prior to World War I were probably stonecutters, finishers, and masons. The presence of the quarries allowed for the growth of subsidiary industries to dress and finish quarry products. Note the presence of boys in a time before child labor laws.

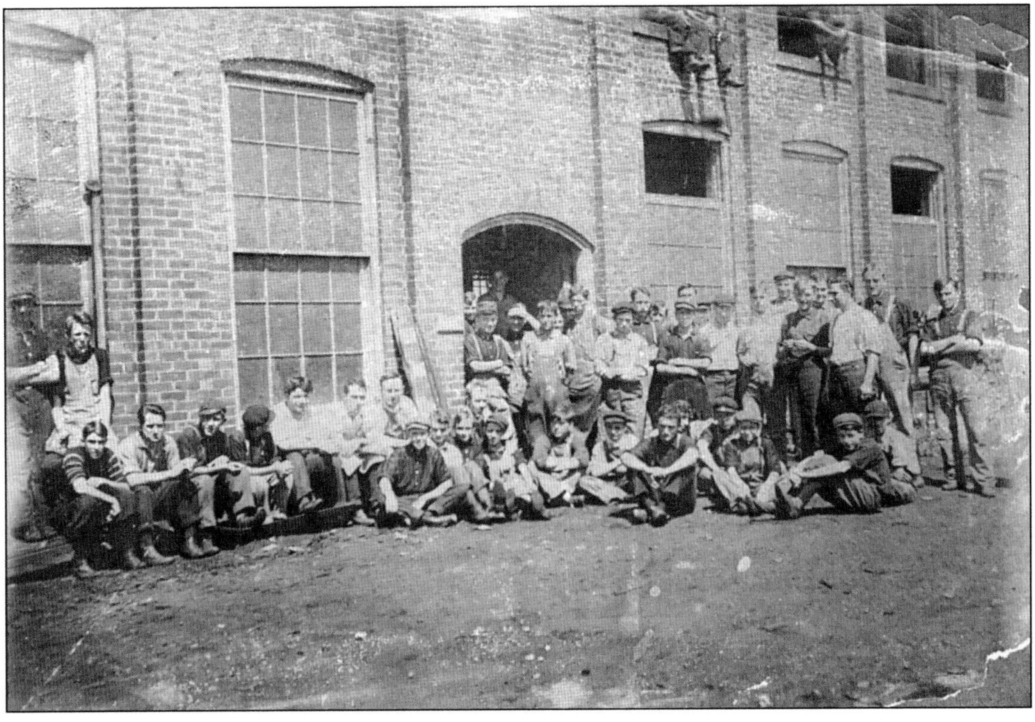

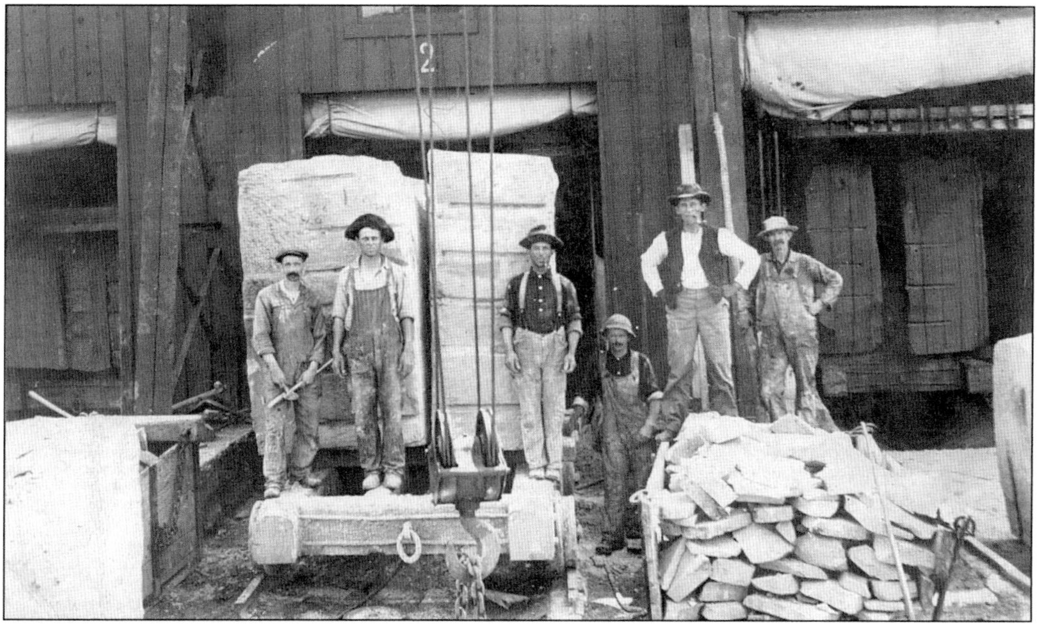

WORKERS AT THE OHIO CUT STONE COMPANY. These workers negotiate the process of prefinishing the stone before moving farther into the plant to complete the process. Working outside dock No. 2, these men are part of Martin Dock's crew.

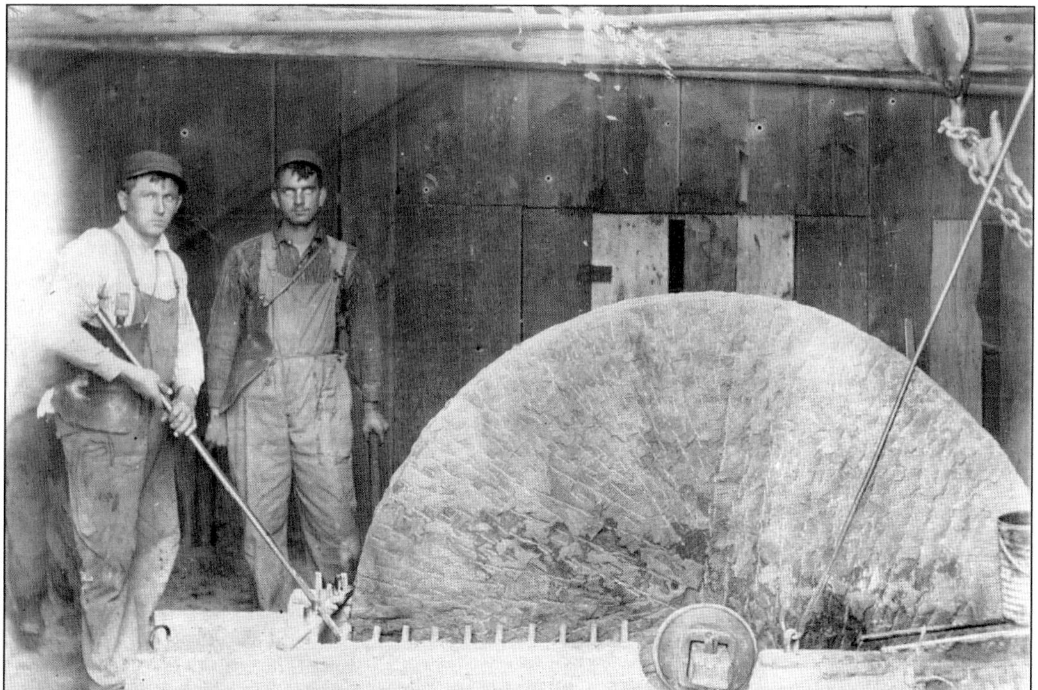

CUT STONE WORKERS. Martin Dock and Frank Hutton are working at the factory. They appear to be finishing a grindstone.

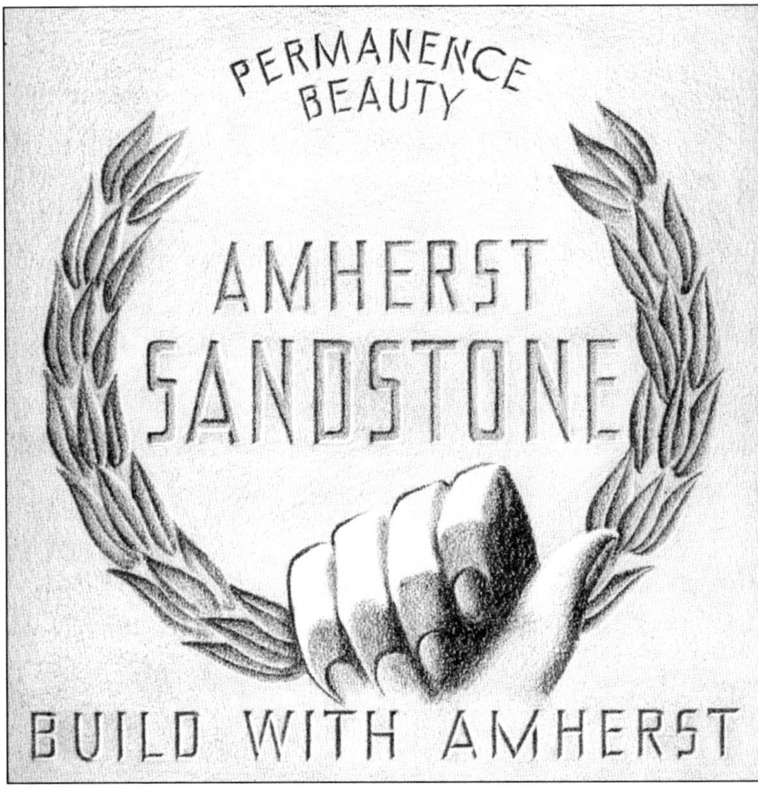

ADVERTISEMENT FEATURING AMHERST STONE. By the end of World War II, the Cleveland Quarries Company had become the preeminent source of fine quality sandstone from the Berea drift. In 1955, they copyrighted this trademark image and used it to advertise the products of their various quarries; in this case, those located in Amherst.

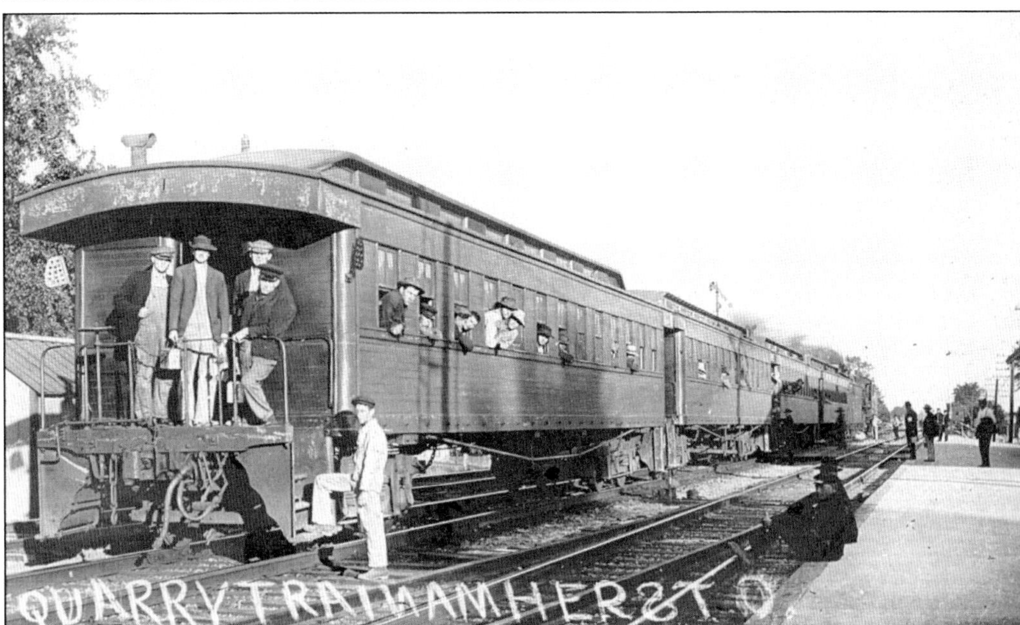

THE QUARRY TRAIN. The quarry train transported workers from Amherst to the various quarry locations. The train provided convenient transportation for workers who lived in town to the more remote quarry locations. Those unfortunate enough to miss the train walked to work. Once a year, the train carried workers and their families to Cedar Point for the annual company picnic.

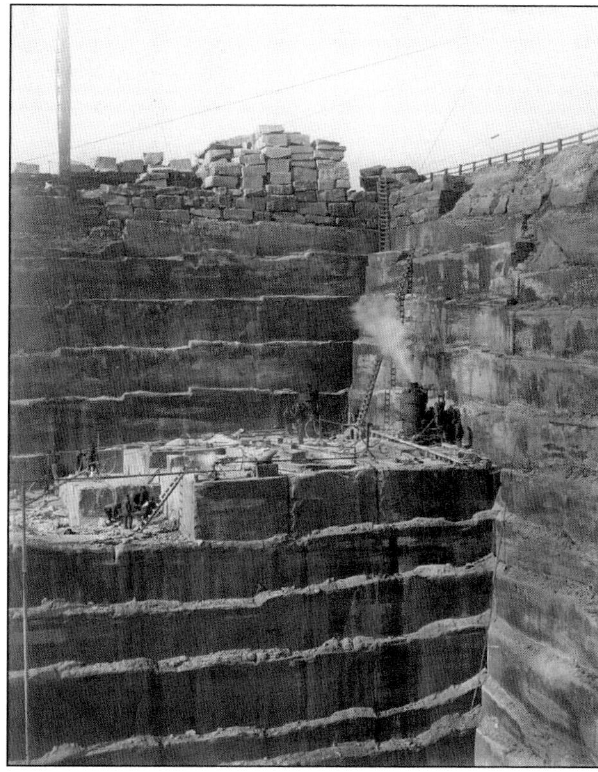

QUARRY NO. 7, MAY 1921. This image clearly depicts the scale of operations at the various quarries. At the center of the photograph, a channeling machine creates fissures in the rock to depths greater than 10 feet. A notion of scale is provided by the workers and the ladders they used to descend and ascend from the quarry's various levels. The derrick at the top left corner stacks irregular blocks of stone channeled from the levels below.

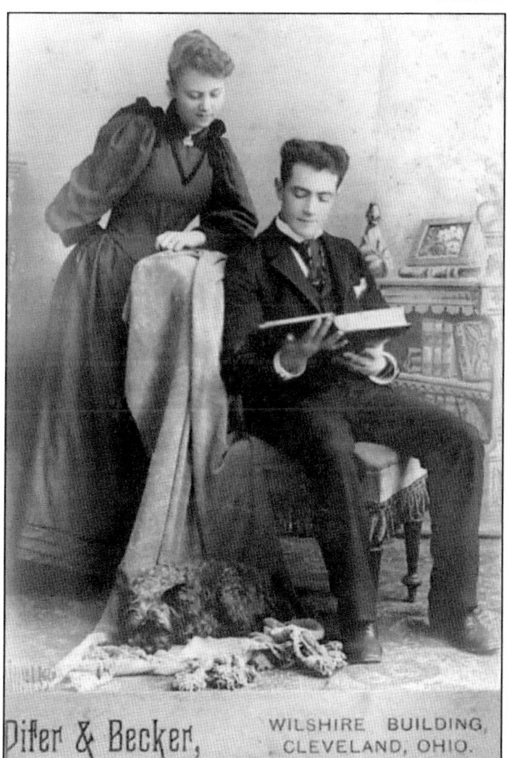

ALLIE AND CLAYTON ENGLE, c. 1894. The story of Allie and Clate Engle demonstrates the hazards and dangers of quarry work at the dawn of the 20th century. When 19-year-old Allie packed her husband's lunch and sent him off to work, she had little notion that he would never return. Later that day, a quarry supervisor came to inform her that her husband had died when he was knocked into the quarry by a swinging crane. This left young Allie with an infant daughter to rear by herself.

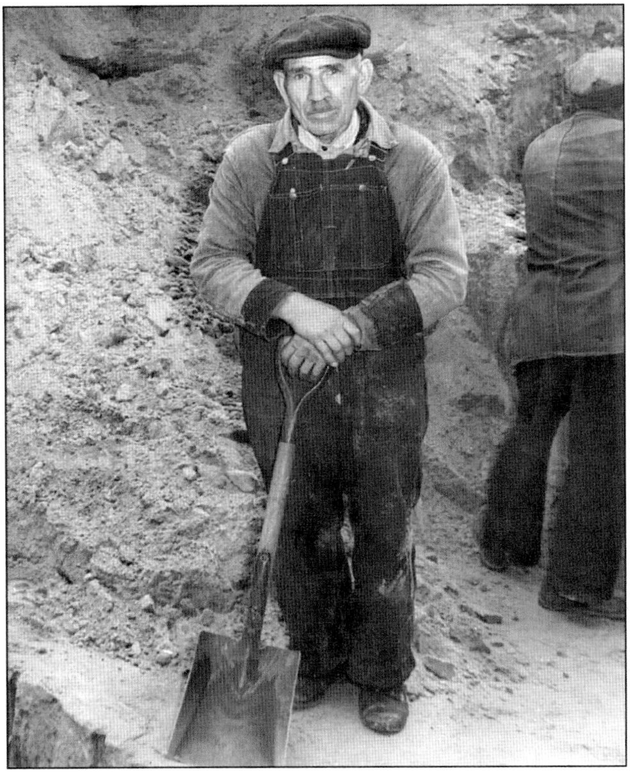

JOHN CHIHAY AND HIS MEDICAL FILE. John Chihay, a Polish immigrant (seen at left around 1925), came to the United States in 1913 from Poland. Upon arrival, he began working for the Cleveland Quarries Company and advanced to channel machine helper by the mid-1920s. As his medical reports reveal (below), silicosis was a frequent hazard by the time rock workers reached middle age.

DUPLICATE

DATE 6-9-26

REPORT OF X-RAY EXAMINATION

—OF—

FILM NO. 417

Name John Chichay

Address Henry St., City or Village Amherst, Ohio.

PERSONAL	
Sex M / Age 48 / Color W / M.S.W.D. W / Racial Stock Polish	
Present Trade or Work	Rockman
Particular Kind of Work	Rock Worker in Quarry
Date Hired by Present Co.	Sept. 1913
*Have You Been Transferred?	Yes — If so, When? 1920
From What Dept. Transferred?	Channel machine helper

Previous Occupations	Year Entered	Year Left
Came to U.S.	1913	

Lost Time Due to Previous Disablement	Year
Head bruised 10 days	1915
Toe Smashed 2 weeks	1925

*Use Reverse Side for Additional Data.

MEDICAL	
Pain: No	Hemoptysis: No
Cough: No	Expectoration: No
Loss W't.: No	Shortness of Breath: No
Malaise: OK / Nutrition: OK	Musculature: OK
Rate of Resp.	Chest Expansion Measurement Insp'n Exp'n
Sputum Exam.	

X-RAY FINDING

Early far advanced silicosis.

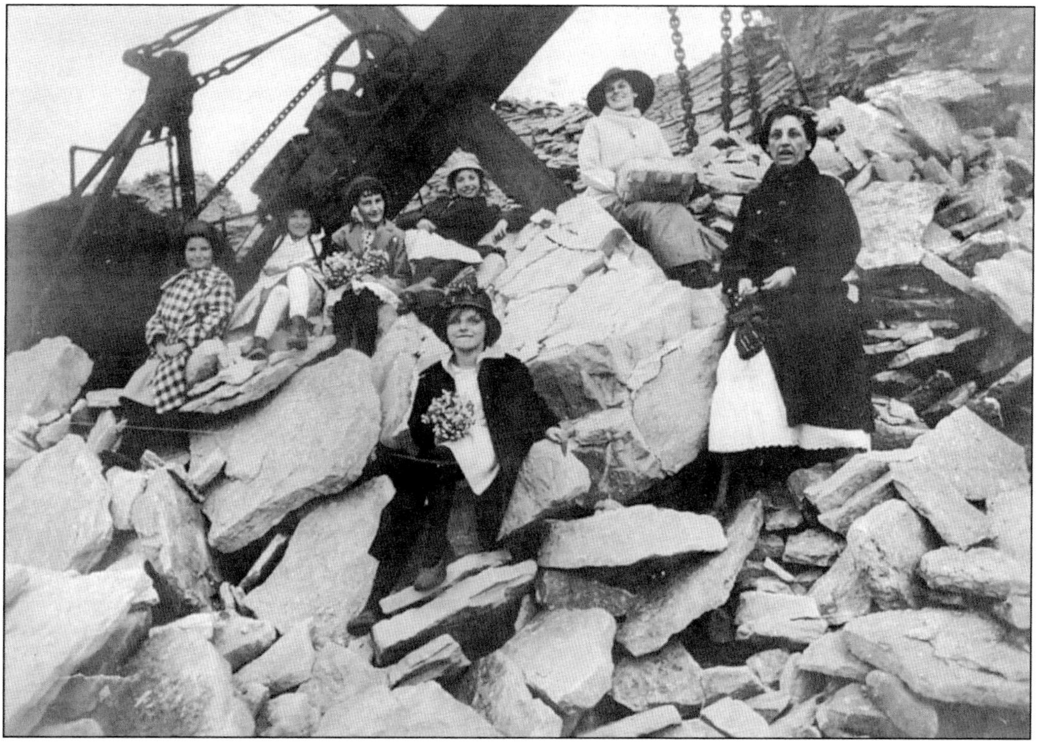

Visitors to the Quarries, c. 1917. The quarries' management frequently hosted tours of their facilities for the families of their workers, local school groups, and other interested parties. Such tours were limited to the buildings where stone was processed rather than the actual quarry sites, which were deemed too dangerous. In the above photograph, a group of children and their chaperones perch on partially crushed stone. The large machine in the rear was used to pulverize lesser-grade sandstone for use as ganister or aggregate. In the photograph below, a group of young boys participating in a school field trip pose amid the quarry stone. They carry with them tools of the rock man's trade.

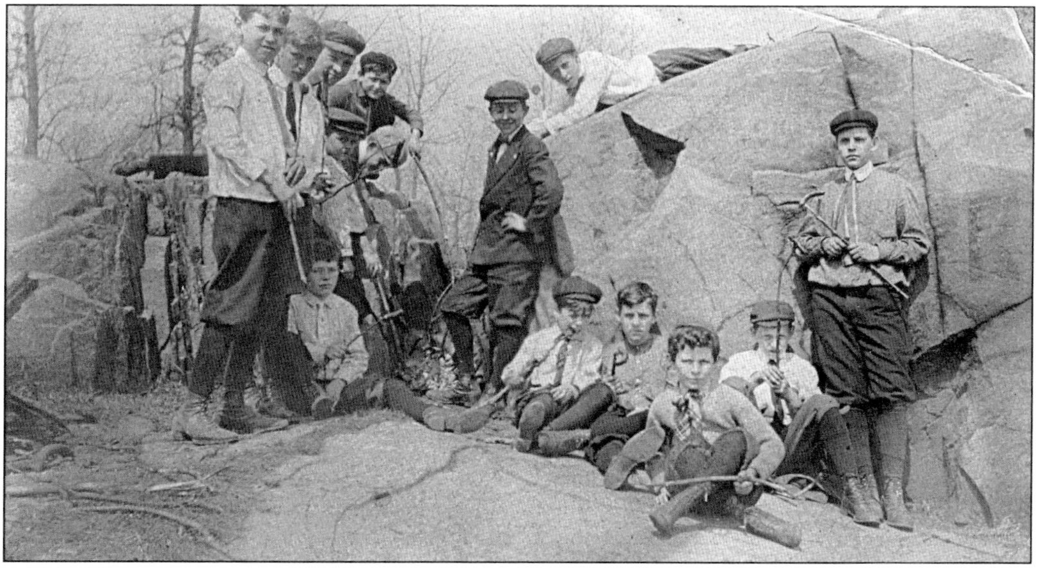

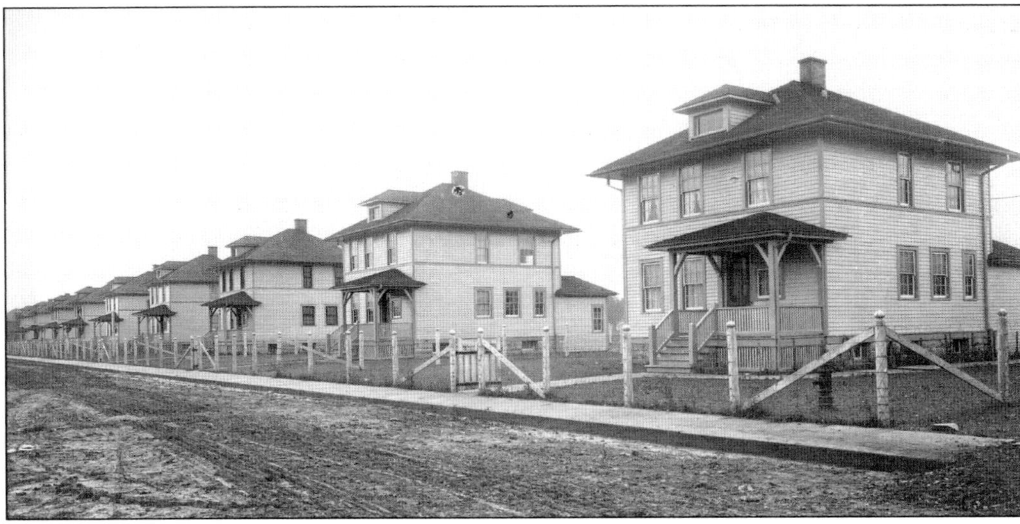

QUARRY HOUSING AND THE QUARRY MASTER'S HOUSE. Located on Buckeye Street, these houses (seen above about 1905) were built by the Cleveland Quarries Company to house its workers. American Four Squares, buildings of fairly substantial construction, were typical of domestic architecture in the early 20th century. At the far end of the street sat the Buckeye Hotel, the first home to many southern and eastern European immigrants drawn to the area in search of employment. At the corner of Quarry Road and Milan Avenue is the quarry master's residence (below). Probably constructed around the time of the Civil War, this house exhibits elements of both the Greek and Gothic Revivals. The house type is referred to as a "hen and chick" because of the one-story ell attached to the main block. Note that this house was much larger and better appointed than those of the ordinary workers.

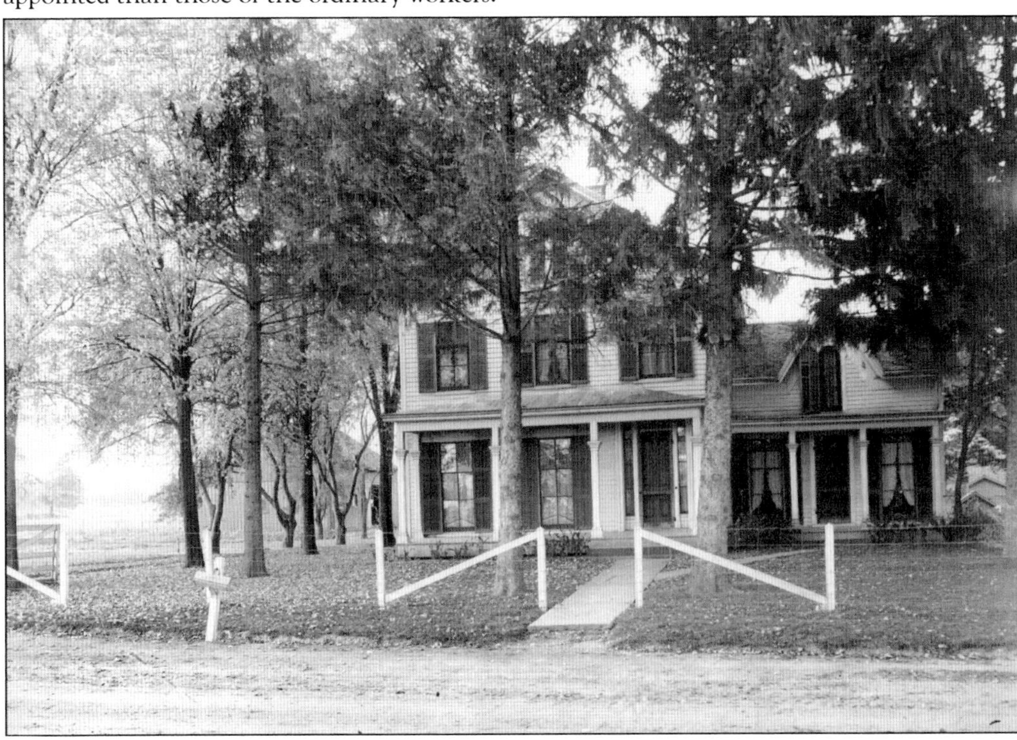

Three

Celebrations and Commemorations

Among the rituals of community life are celebrations or commemorations marking significant milestones in its history. During the first decades of Amherst's existence, the people were more concerned with the building of their community and marked important occasions informally. As it entered its second century, Amherst town leaders looked for ways to mark important events. At the advent of World War I, Old Home week made its debut. The event, the first held in 1914, celebrated Amherst's over 100 years of existence. As the name suggests, Old Home week was also a time for current and former residents to get together and reminisce. By the 1930s, the event had evolved into an annual homecoming, complete with community gatherings and a parade. In the post–World War II period, community gatherings became more frequent and focused on holidays and events connected to local culture. National holidays, such as Memorial Day, along with more esoteric events, such as the Potato Festival, became focal points for community activity. Parades, fairs, competitions, and other such festivities bring together all of the citizenry, including the young and old, longtime residents, and newcomers.

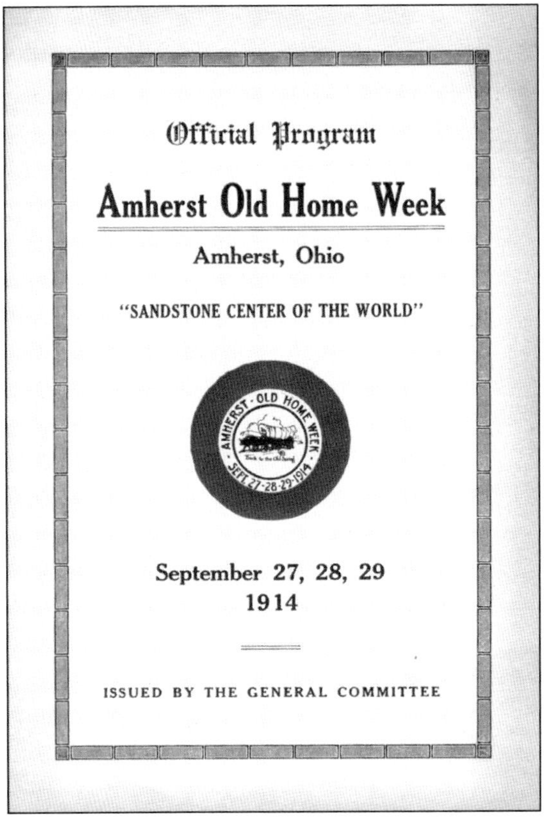
Official Program

Amherst Old Home Week

Amherst, Ohio

"SANDSTONE CENTER OF THE WORLD"

AMHERST · OLD HOME WEEK · SEPT 27-28-29-1914

September 27, 28, 29
1914

ISSUED BY THE GENERAL COMMITTEE

OLD HOME WEEK, 1914. The Amherst Old Home Week program (left) boasted as its slogan "Back to the Old Spring." Organized by a group of community leaders, the event welcomed residents and visitors to "a town of rapid advance, progressive policies of hardy fellowship." The schedule of events included Sunday church services, a concert, field events, and a ball game, all culminating in a parade (below) on Tuesday morning. Note the placard for the Stone Cutters' Union, a fraternal organization serving social and labor needs. Its membership, largely Scottish, hosted an annual Burns Night, celebrating poet Robert Burns's birthday.

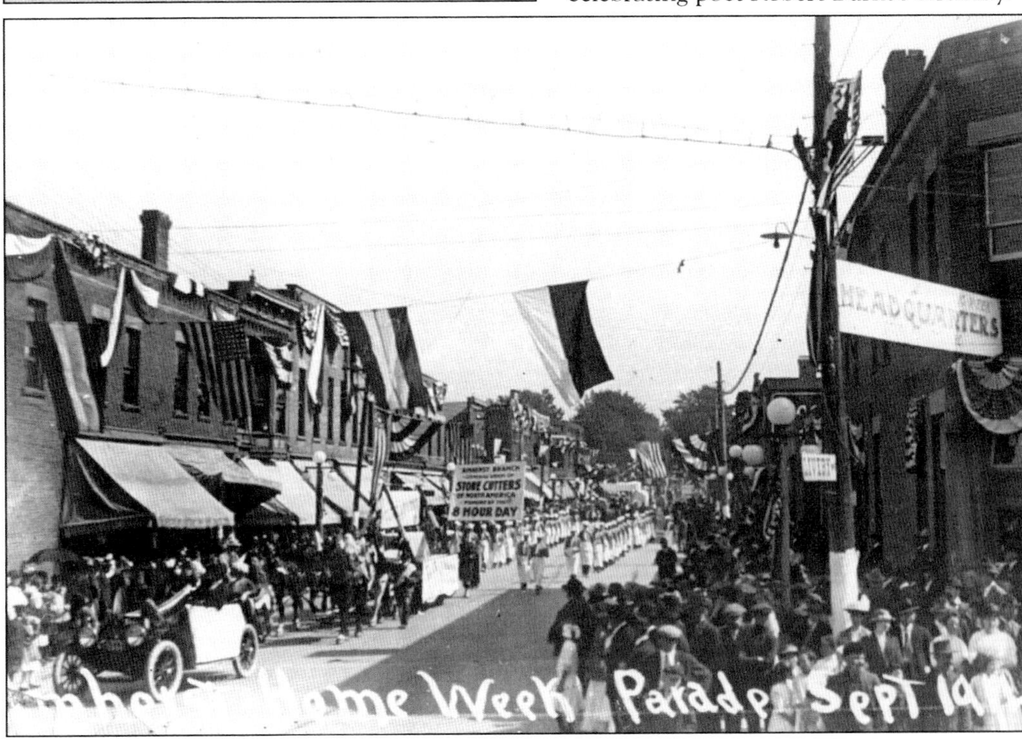

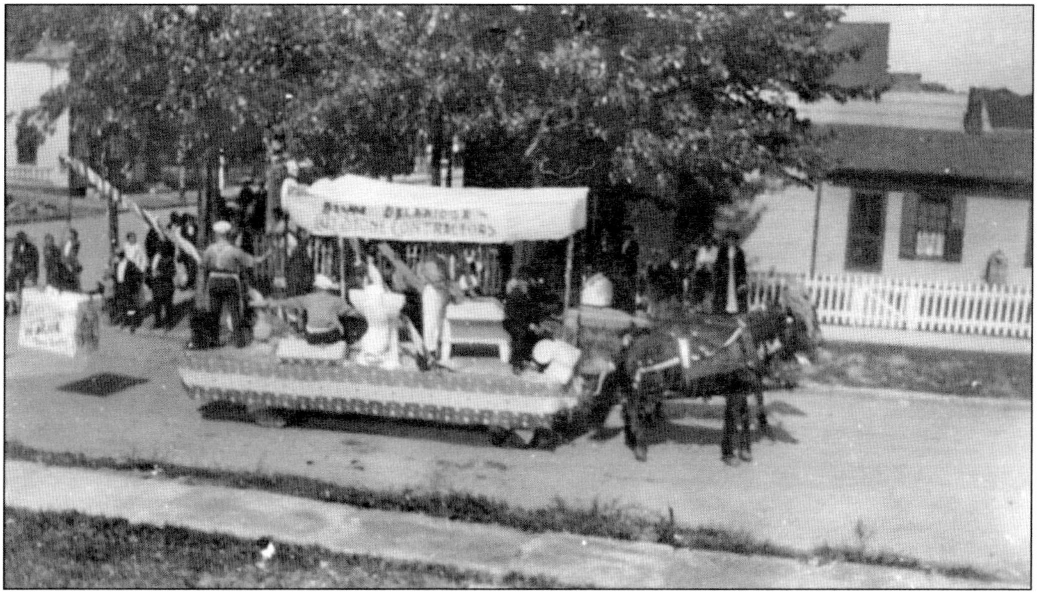

Old Home Week Parade Floats, 1914. The parade featured a number of floats sponsored by local businessmen. The Blum and Delbridge Cut Stone Company contractors' entry (above) featured a horse-drawn platform upon which stonecutters demonstrated on models of their workshop. Below, William Guild, grocer, transformed one of his delivery carts into a parade float with patriotic bunting. Even the horse sports American flags as part of its gear.

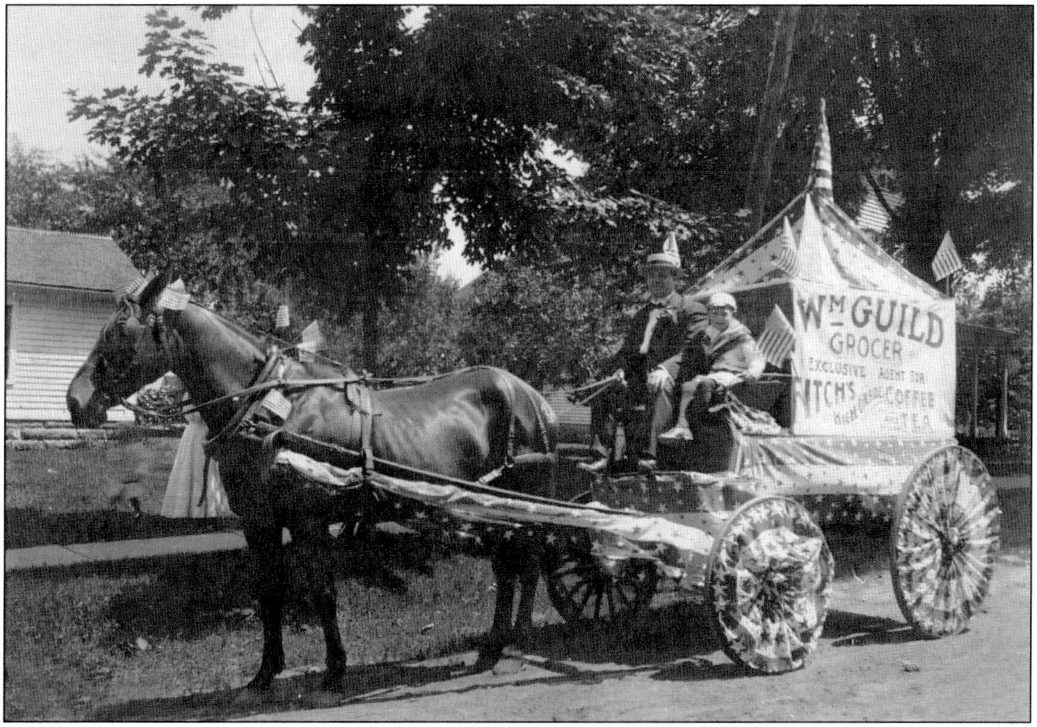

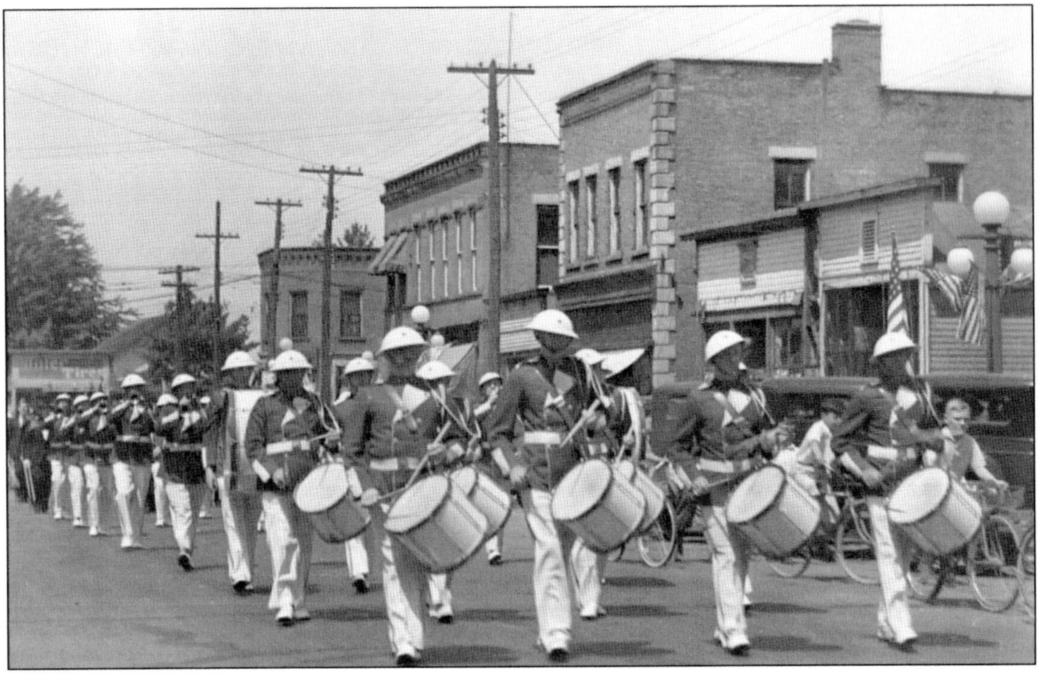

Memorial Day Parade, c. 1930. A drum and bugle corps parades down South Main Street as part of Amherst's annual Memorial Day commemorations. This holiday is a time to remember those who died in wartime service to the nation.

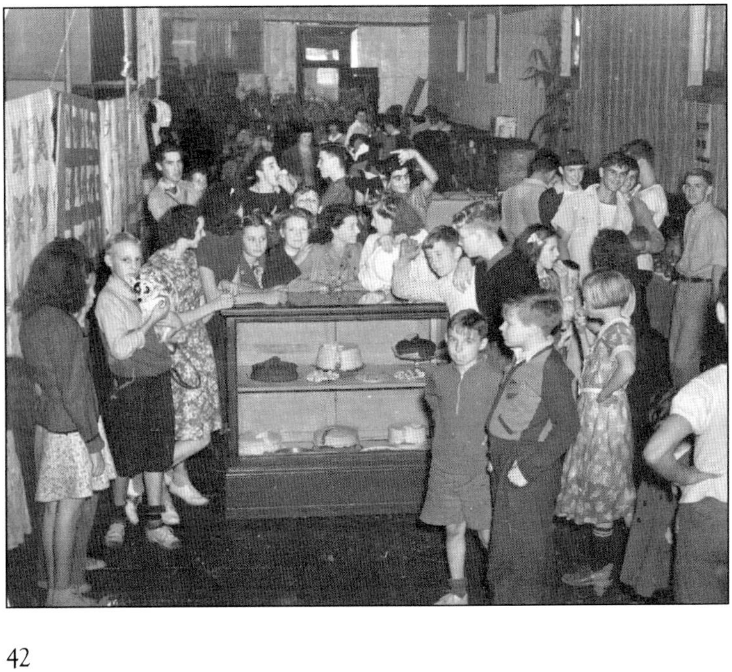

Amherst Day Street Fair, c. 1940. Amherst Day, celebrated in mid-summer, created an occasion for its residents to socialize and celebrate. Merchants planned races, rides, games, and fireworks as a thank you to local residents for their patronage and support. The event also permitted Amherst schoolchildren to utilize an empty downtown building for a craft and bake sale. The street fair allowed participants to sample local goods and crafts.

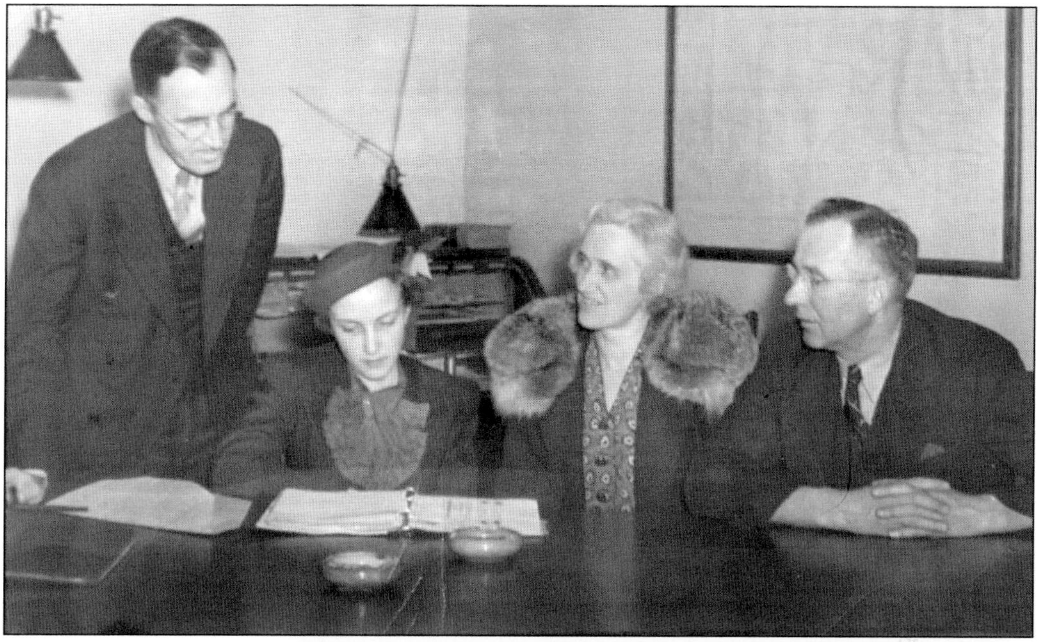

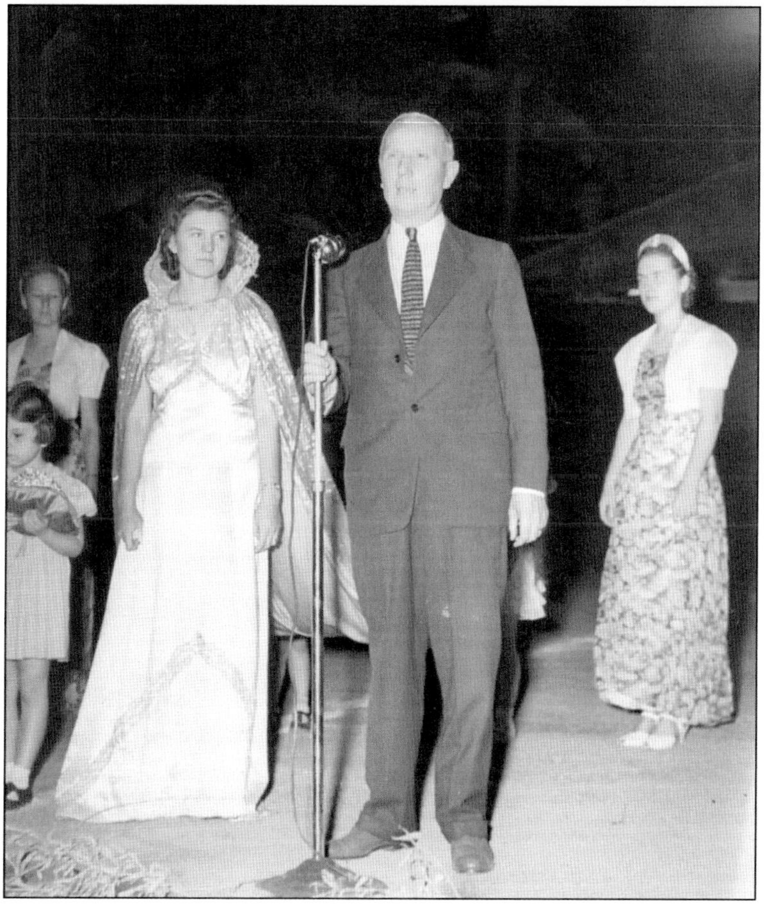

OLD HOME WEEK, 1939. In 1939, community organizers used the occasion of Old Home week to celebrate the town's 125th anniversary. The committee (above) for the 125th homecoming planned the four-day event for September 24–27. From left to right are John Smythe, Norma Beesing Streiker, Marion Steele, and August Nabakowski. An integral part of the celebration was the crowning of the homecoming queen Beverly Bruce King (with cape), crowned by Judge D. A. Cook of Elyria. Also pictured are Judy Brown (left front), Rhoda Schwitzke (left back), and Bev Sprague (right).

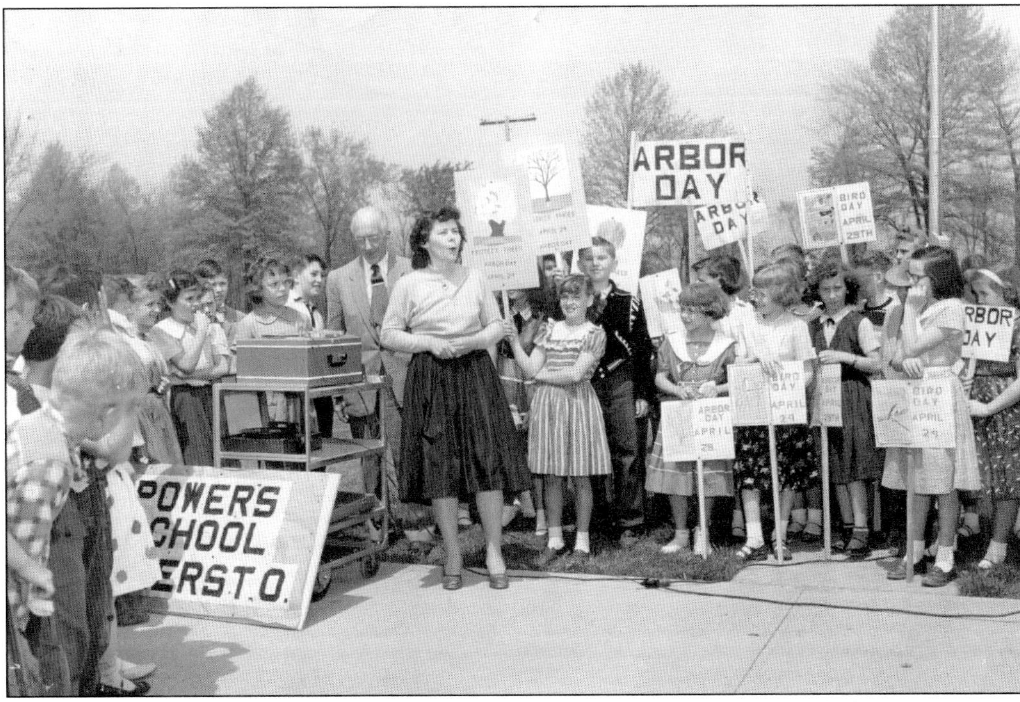

CELEBRATING YOUTH. At the end of World War II, in keeping with the national shift in temperament focusing on youth and the future, celebrations in Amherst frequently centered on activities aimed at the city's children. Above, the 1955 Powers School Arbor Day program, an annual event hosted by the Amherst Garden Club, advocated conservation long before it was fashionable. The garden club provided a tree or shrub to be planted on school grounds. Pictured at center, principal Fred Powers listens to garden club member Alice Penton whistling. Part of another annual celebration was a parade and horse show sponsored by the Amherst Lions Club. The picture below features the 1956 show winners, with club president Clem Rice (center, in plaid shirt), presenting the awards.

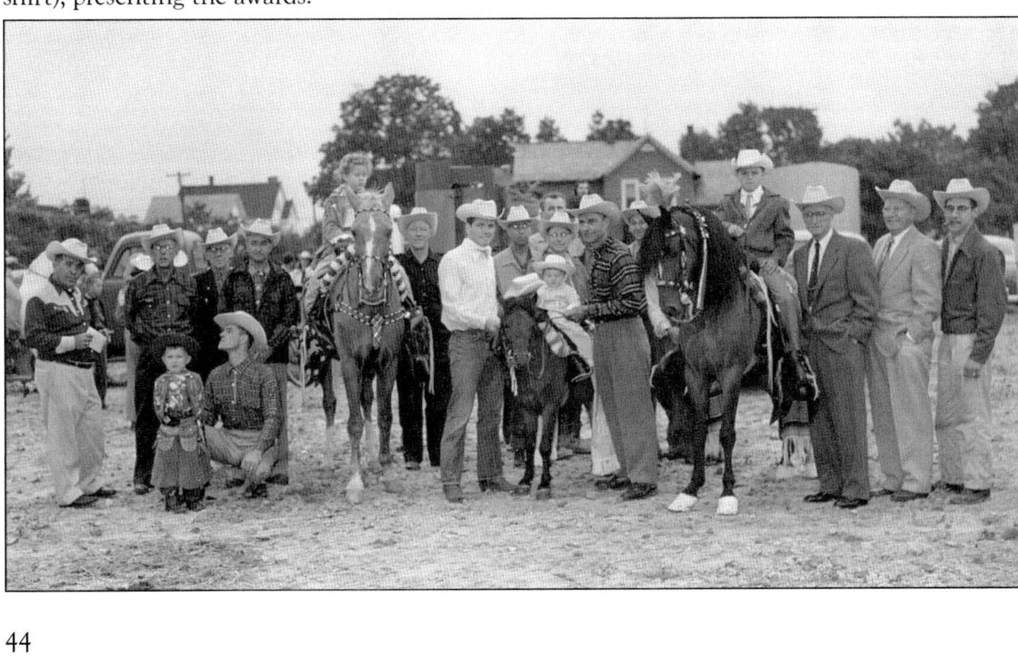

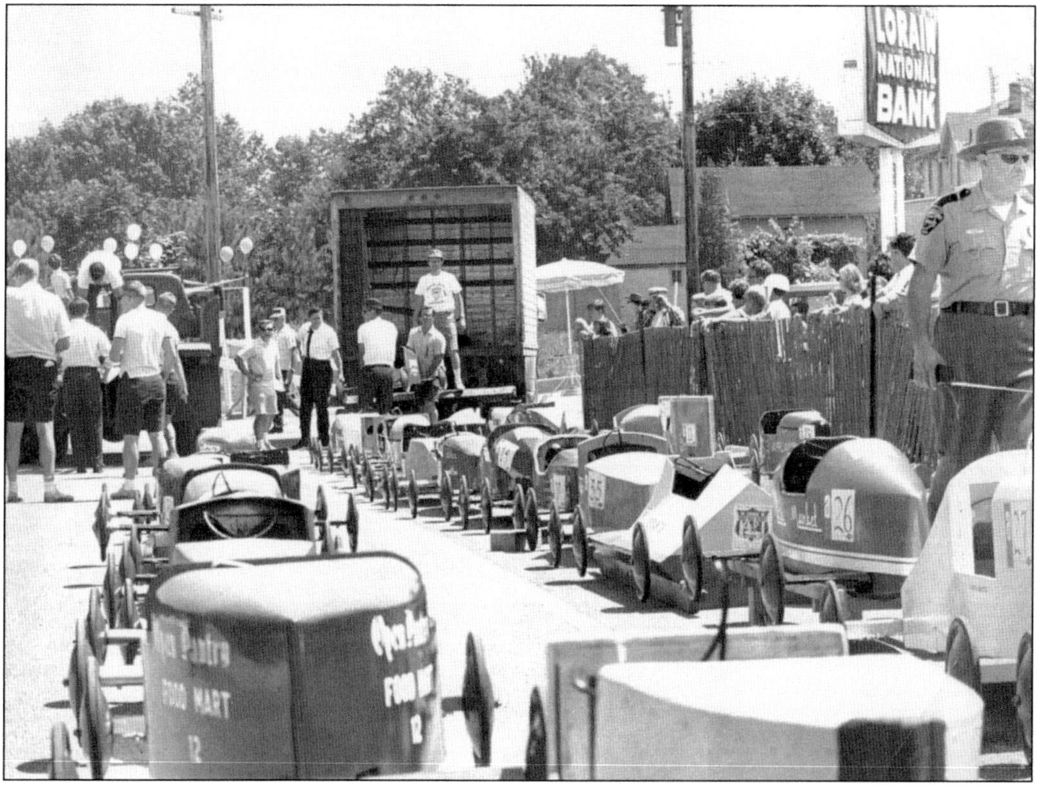

Soap Box Derby. Amherst was the site of the annual Lorain County Soap Box Derby for a number of years in the late 1960s and early 1970s. Local officials (above), with cooperation from the Ohio Department of Transportation, blocked off Leavitt Road (State Route 58), starting at Cleveland Avenue, north to state route 2, for the racetrack. Participants from across the county competed in their individually constructed vehicles for the chance to participate in the All American Soap Box Derby Finals in Akron. Event sponsors included the Amherst Jaycees, the *Elyria Chronicle-Telegram*, and area Chevrolet dealerships. Bob Pallante (right) oversees the construction efforts of several local participants.

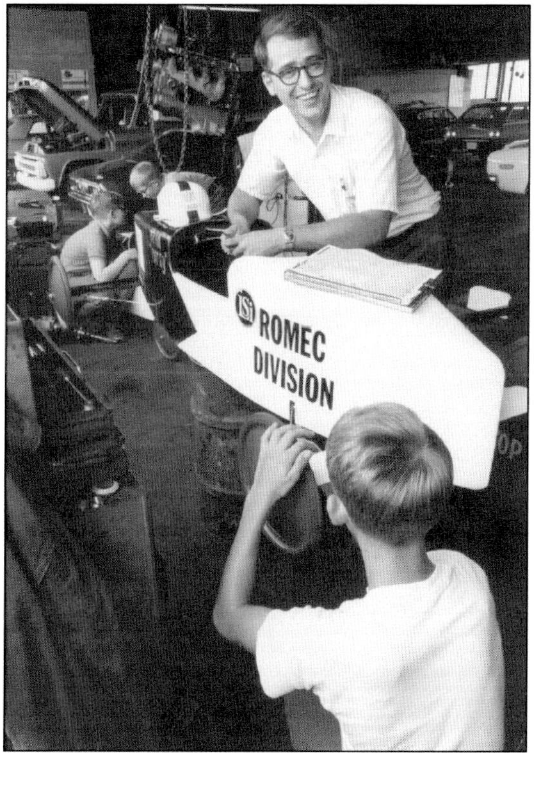

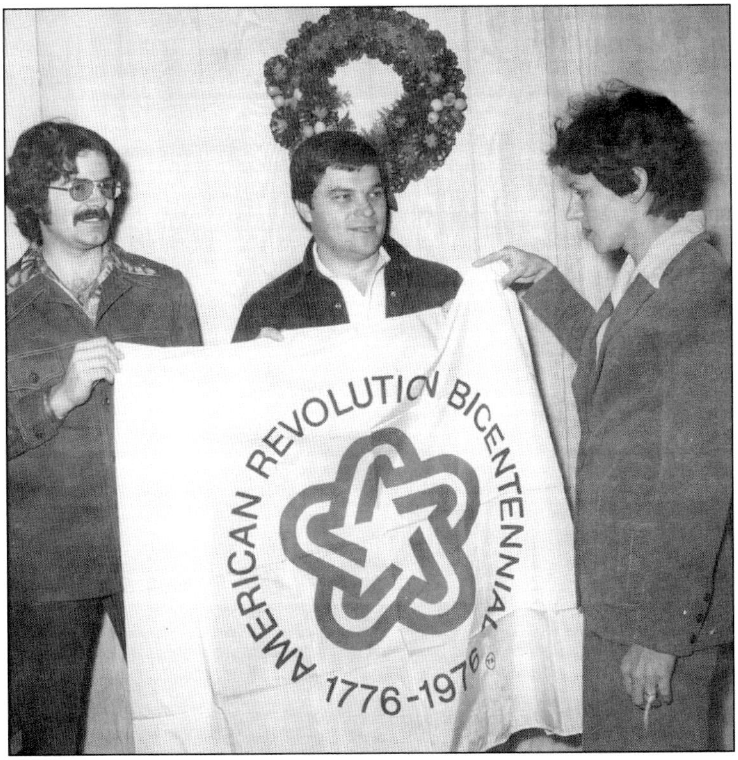

American Revolution Bicentennial, 1976. In preparation for the 200th birthday of the United States, the Amherst Sandstone Bicentennial Committee invited local residents to fly their flags each Sunday and to join them for a parade held in honor of the event. Larry Dobos (left), Joe Druga (center), and Judy Rosenkranz display the bicentennial flag. Below, volunteer firemen march in the Fourth of July parade with the "Live Oak" fire apparatus built in 1833. The fire truck was hand pulled and hand pumped.

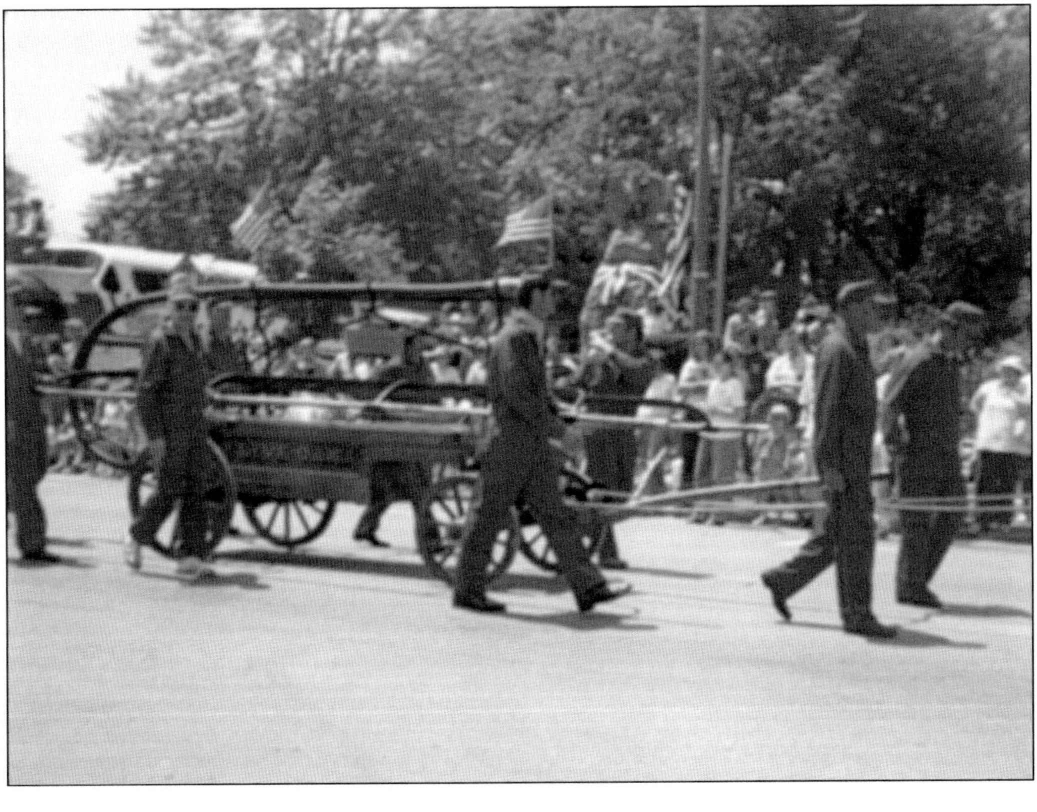

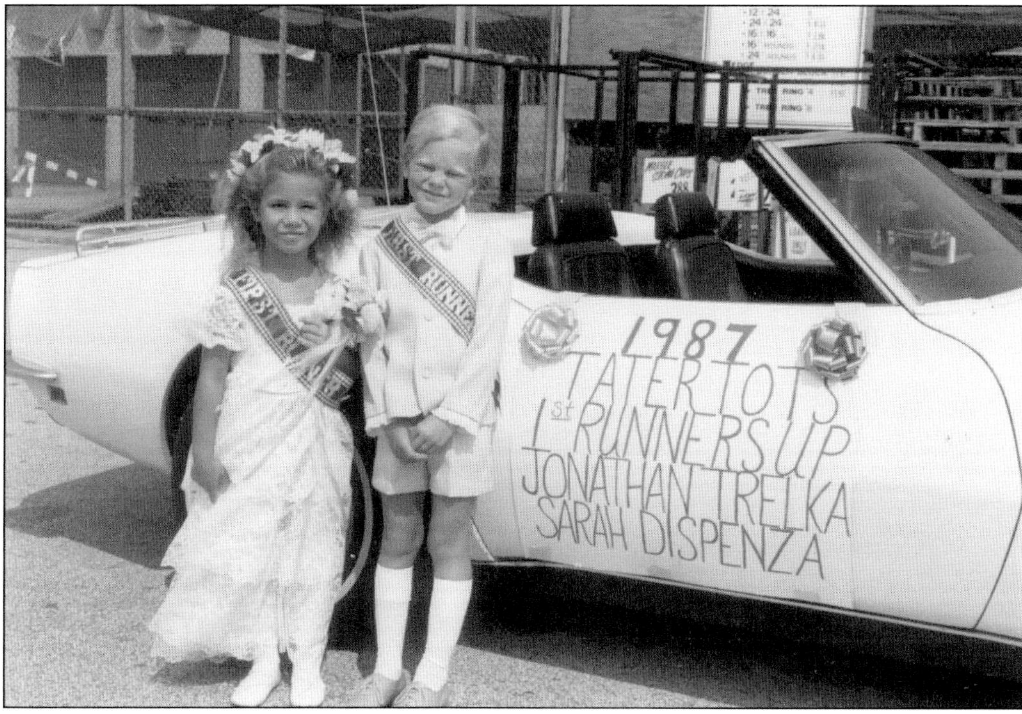

POTATO FESTIVAL. In 1984, the Amherst Area Chamber of Commerce developed a concept that eventually became the Potato Festival. When asked why, they cited three reasons: (1) local farming practices, (2) flexibility, and (3) originality; theirs was the only potato-themed festival in the entire state of Ohio. Above, features of the "a-peeling" event included the selection of its first runners-up, the 1987 Tater Tots Jonathan Trelka, right, and Sarah Dispenza. Another element of the festival was the participation of Marie Robinson (right) and her Potato Pal dolls.

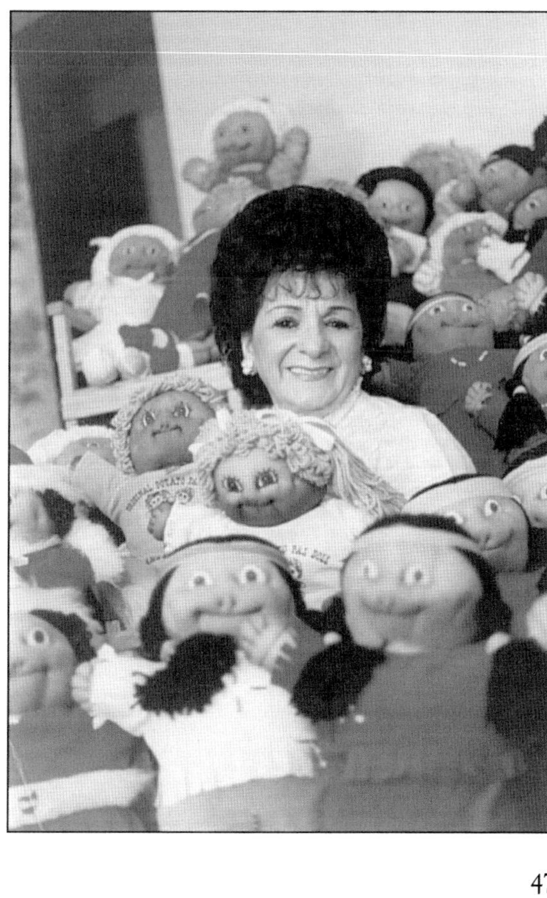

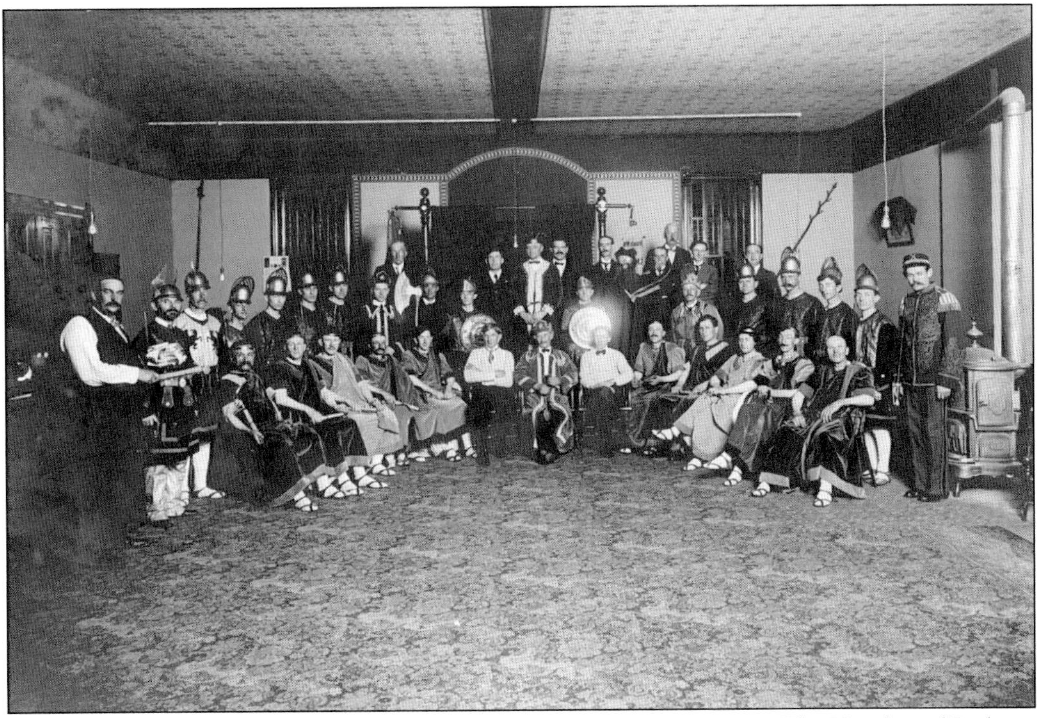

ORDER OF THE KNIGHTS OF PYTHIAS, AMHERST LODGE NO. 74, C. 1900. The Knights of Pythias, organized in 1874, met in the Odd Fellows Hall over O. H. Baker's store. The Knights of Pythias eventually purchased their own hall, located next door. Their ritual, originally performed in German, was changed to English in Amherst in 1878. Here they meet in full regalia.

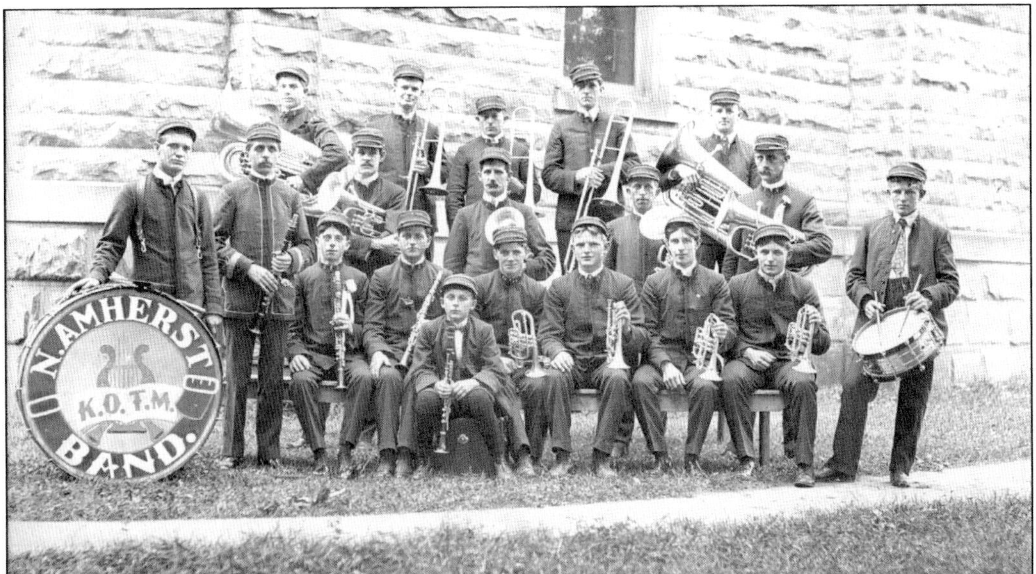

KNIGHTS OF THE MACABEE BAND, C. 1900. The Knights of the Macabee was an insurance organization that also gathered for business and social purposes. They also eventually established a ladies' auxiliary.

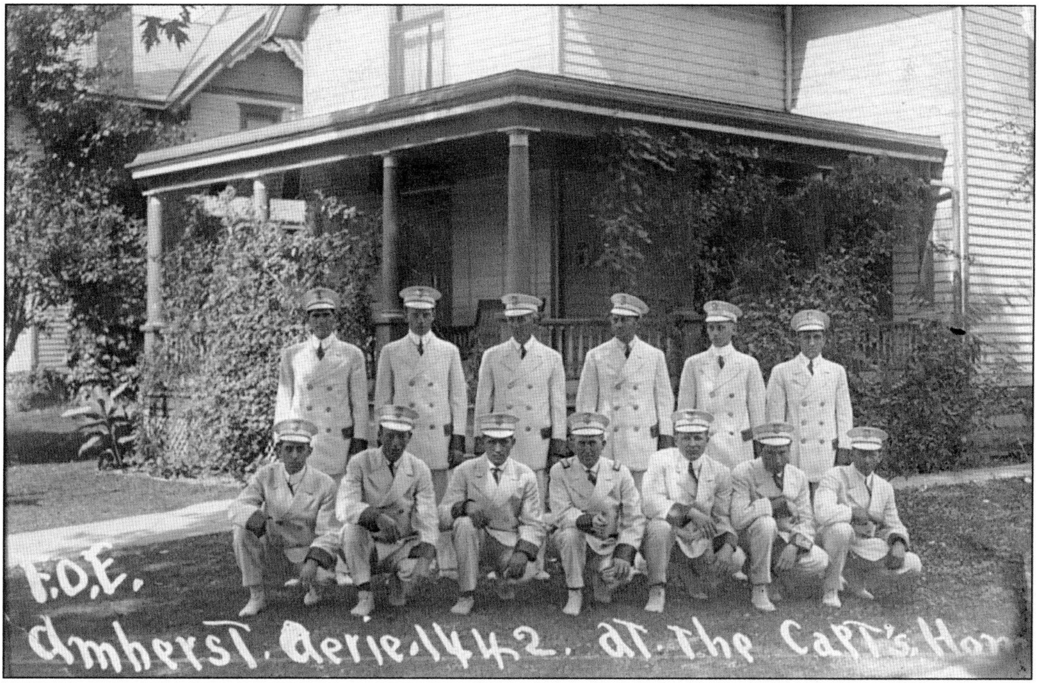

AMHERST FRATERNAL ORDER OF EAGLES. The Amherst Eagles Aerie No. 1442 was established in 1906 and quickly grew to over 200 members. In 1914 (above), their competitive drill team, in white uniforms trimmed in red and blue and under the leadership of Capt. R. E. McMasters, took first prize. They are pictured in front of the captain's house during Old Home week that year. The Amherst Ladies Auxiliary Drill Team (below) marches in a 1933 parade, sporting white satin dresses and scarlet velvet capes. They took a second-place award for the "best appearing team" and a third prize in competitive drill.

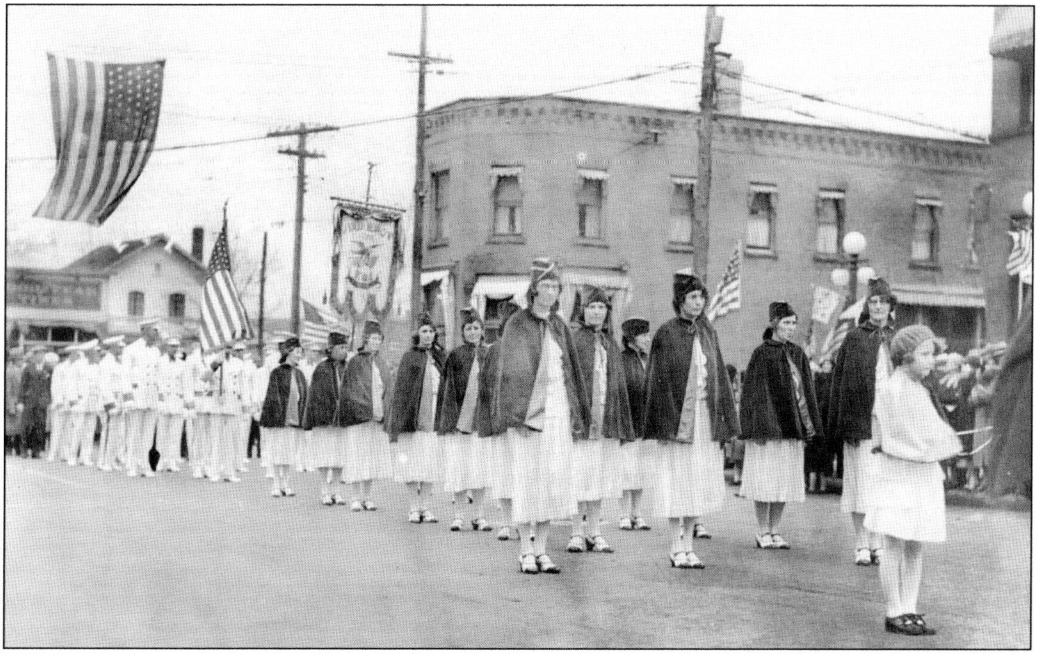

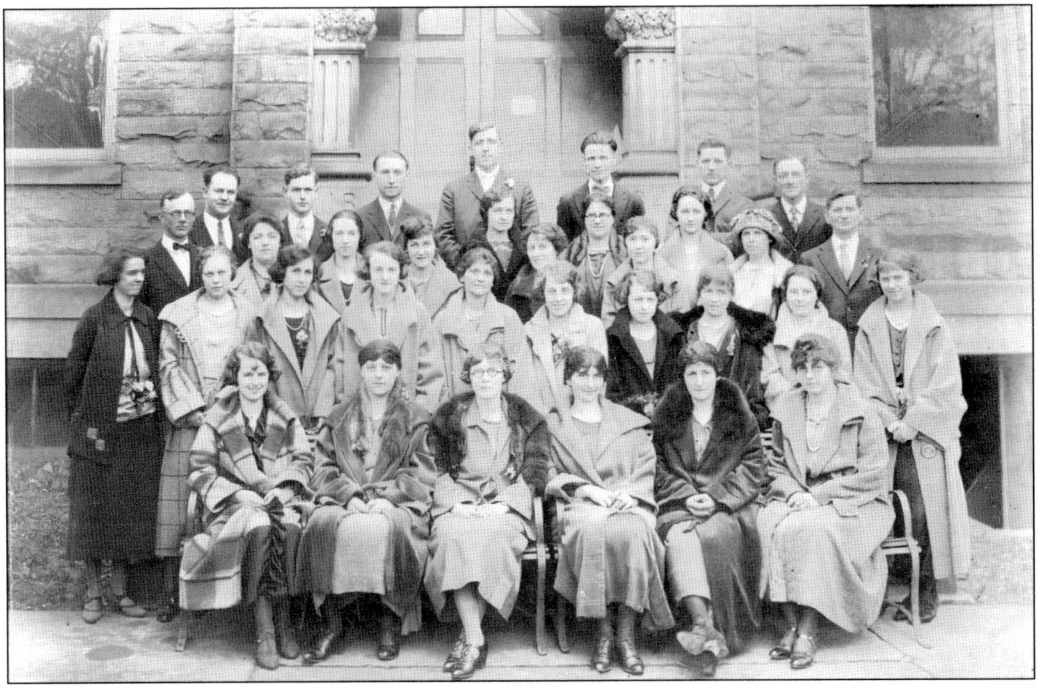

AMHERST CHORAL UNION, C. 1925. The Amherst Coral Union consisted of businessmen and women, teachers, musicians, and homemakers. They performed at significant community events and annual concerts. Captioned "people who enjoy singing together," this group met regularly for their own enjoyment and to entertain the community at large.

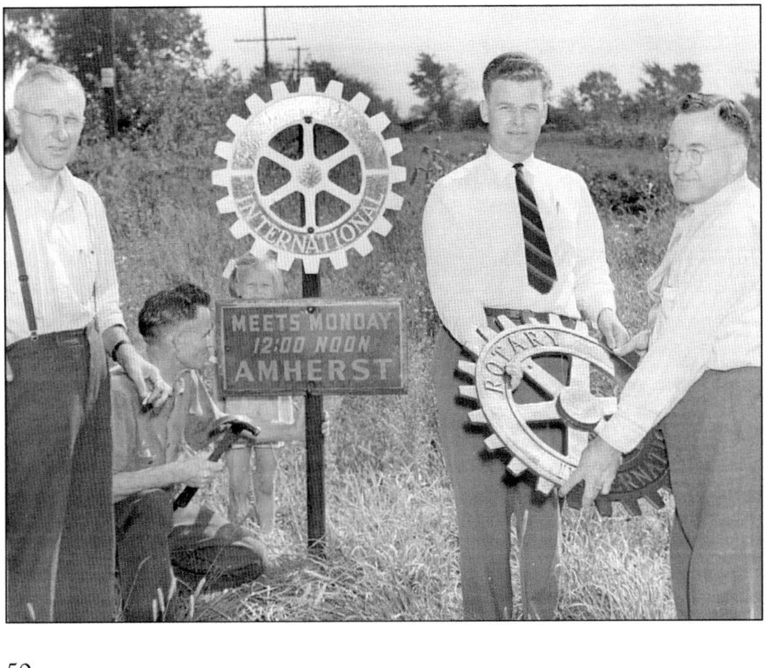

AMHERST ROTARY CLUB, C. 1945. The Amherst Rotary Club was established on January 17, 1938, as a chapter of the Rotary Club International, whose motto is "service above self." From left to right, Amherst Rotary Club members Raymond Wasem, George Cox, Bob Mulford, and Conrad Zilch are seen erecting the club's sign with notice of their weekly Monday meetings.

Four

AMHERST SCHOOL DAYS

One of the primary institutions a region develops as it moves from frontier settlement to established community is a school. As migrants from the east made their way westward, they carried with them a deep respect for education. An educated population made for a wise citizenry. The organizers of the Western Reserve confirmed that sentiment by requiring that one section of each township be set aside for the support of local schools. Amherst Township was no different. The structures that housed the schools mirrored Amherst's growth and needs. The first schools, built in 1823, were simple one-room log cabins. These institutions were ungraded, and the students, ages 5 to 20, advanced grade levels at their own speed. As Amherst grew in population, the original structures were deemed inadequate, and local leaders replaced them with a frame building located on Milan Avenue near the old spring in 1832. The first brick structure, a three room, two-story edifice, was erected on Church Street in 1856 on land donated by local leader Josiah Harris. After the school burnt in 1893, it was replaced with a more substantial building of locally quarried Amherst sandstone. It too succumbed to fire in March 1907, but by 1908, the community rallied and constructed the new Central School. During the years that followed, Amherst's officials and its citizens have maintained a school system that continues to reflect the values and needs of the community.

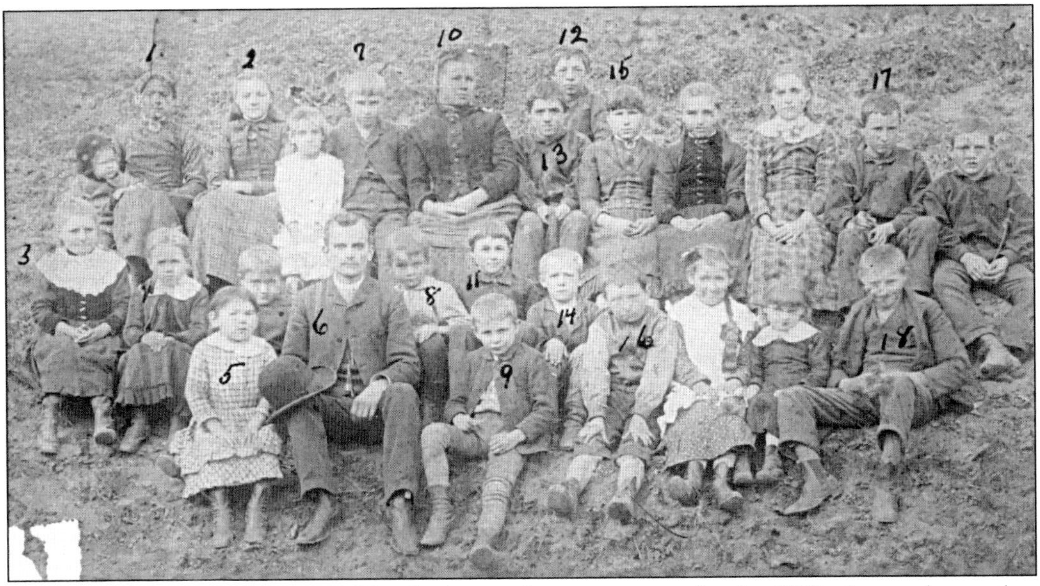

East Quarry School, c. 1887. The Amherst education system, by the 1880s, featured a number of small, more conveniently located grammar schools. One such structure was the East Quarry School. Pictured here is teacher F. B. Rupp (No. 6) with his students of various ages. Rupp worked for Amherst schools during the 1887–1888 school year and earned $45 per pay period for an annual salary of $112.50.

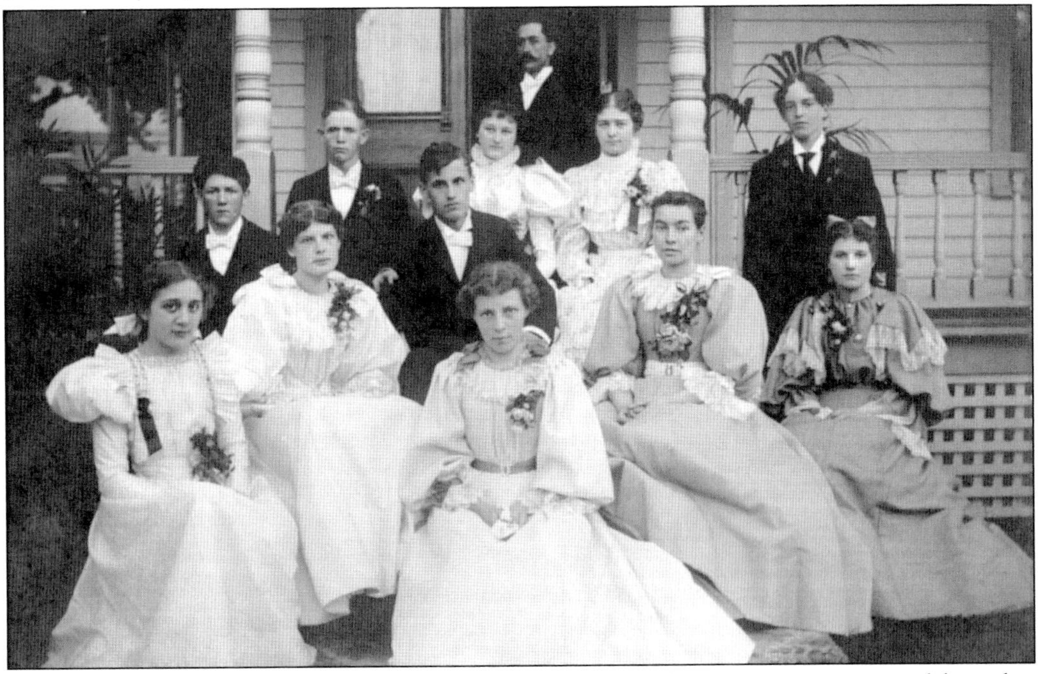

Graduating Class, Amherst High School, 1897. In May 1897, commencement was celebrated in the auditorium of the Amherst Town Hall. By that year, a single high school served the community. Superintendent E. E. Rayman (top of photograph) had established a rigorous two-year preparatory program that included English, mathematics, physiology, bookkeeping, and history. Rayman was also instrumental in making the high school a four-year rather than a three-year program.

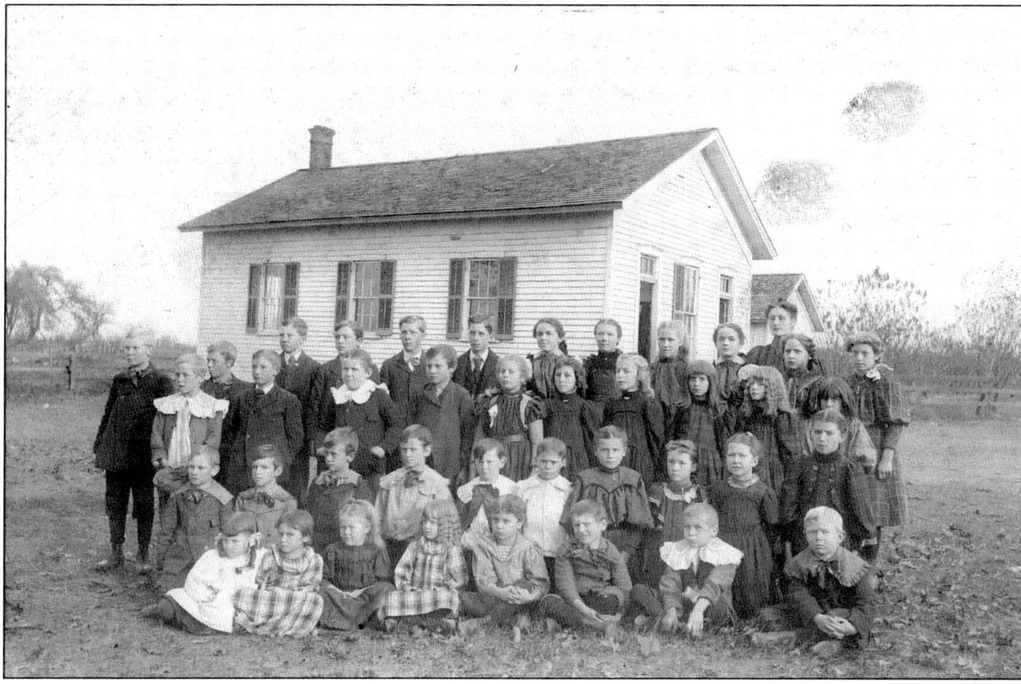

Middle Ridge School. Middle Ridge Road East was the site of an Amherst school from the 1870s on. The frame building (above) was a one-room schoolhouse, constructed in 1876. In 1884, it was replaced by the brick structure (below) that served as a school well into the 20th century. Beral Kuss Powers (standing, right) taught there through World War I and the Spanish influenza epidemic of 1918.

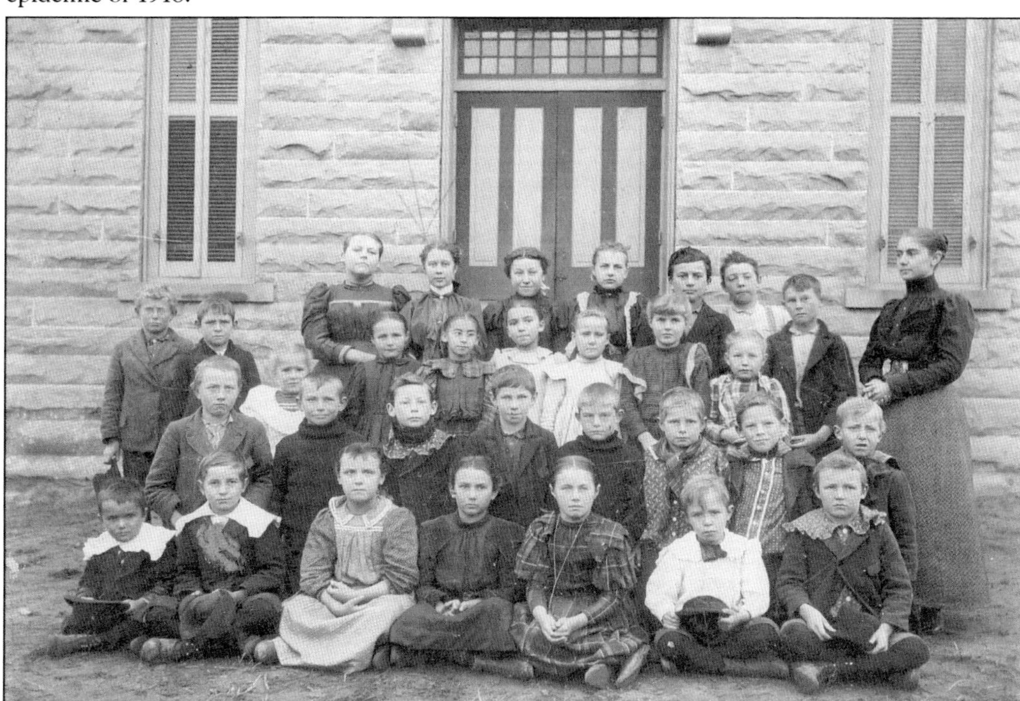

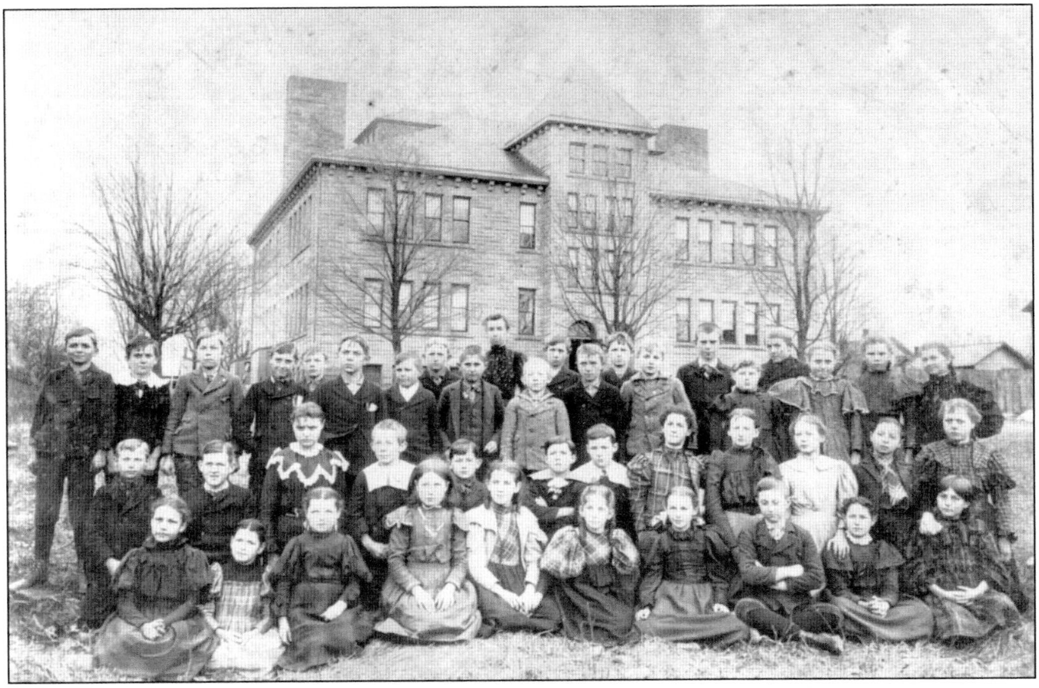

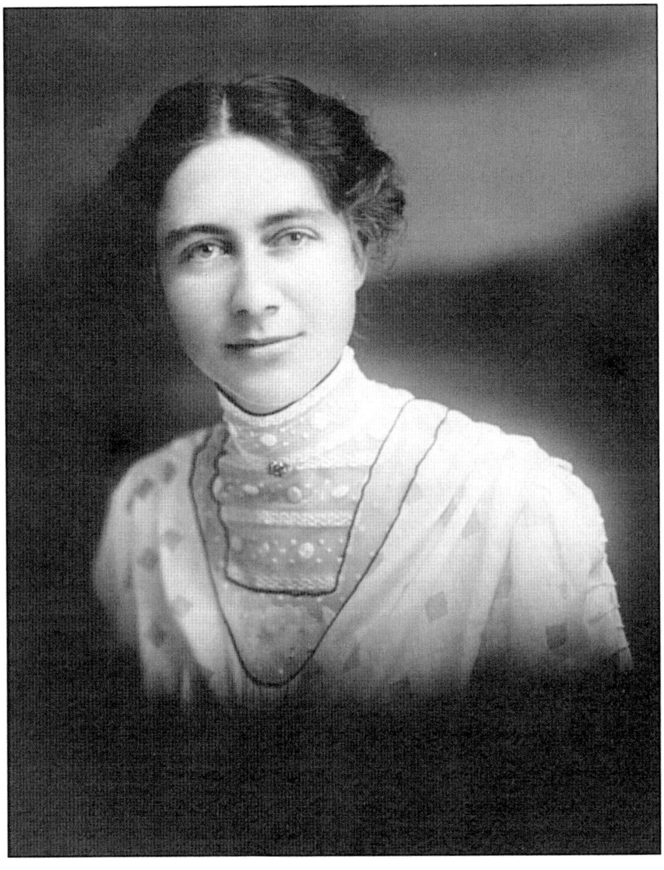

CENTRAL SCHOOL. In 1884, Amherst Township schools undertook a major construction program, resulting in Central School, located on Church Street. Also referred to as Union School, it represented Amherst's adoption of the Akron or Union Plan passed by the Ohio legislature in 1850. This law decreed that property taxes be used for the support of local schools and also required that each school district hire a superintendent.

ELIZABETH HAHN. Elizabeth Hahn was an eighth-grade teacher at Central School in 1904. She had attended the East Quarry School in the late 1880s and at some point finished her Normal School training, a program for teacher preparation, to qualify as a professional educator.

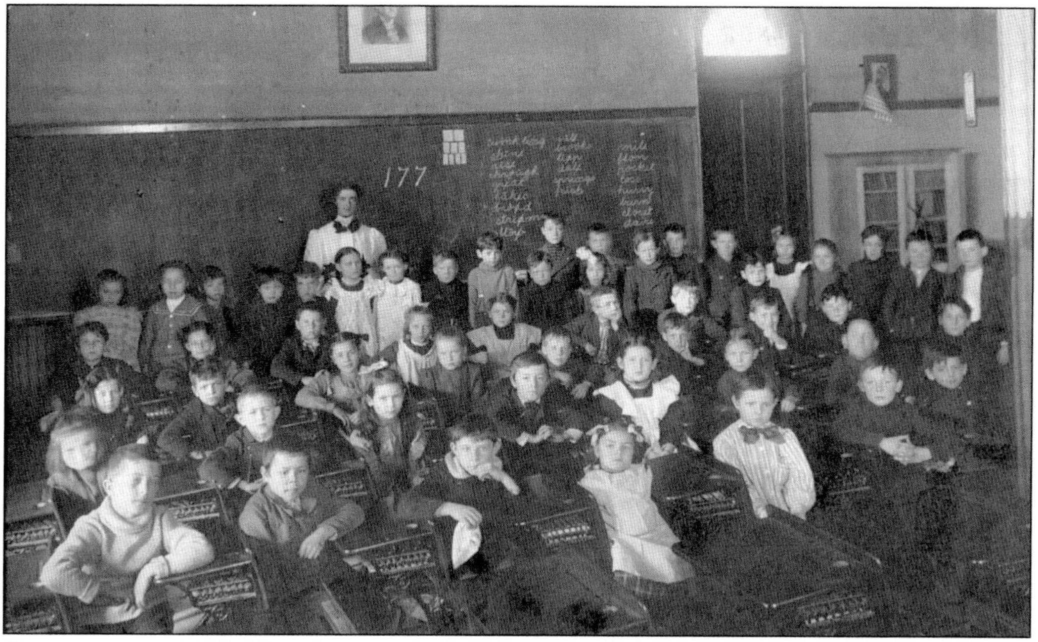

CLASSROOM, C. 1905. This photograph depicts a typical classroom interior at the dawn of the 20th century. Symbols of citizenship, a U.S. flag and an image of George Washington, are prominently displayed. The teacher stands before the chalkboard upon which the week's spelling lesson appears.

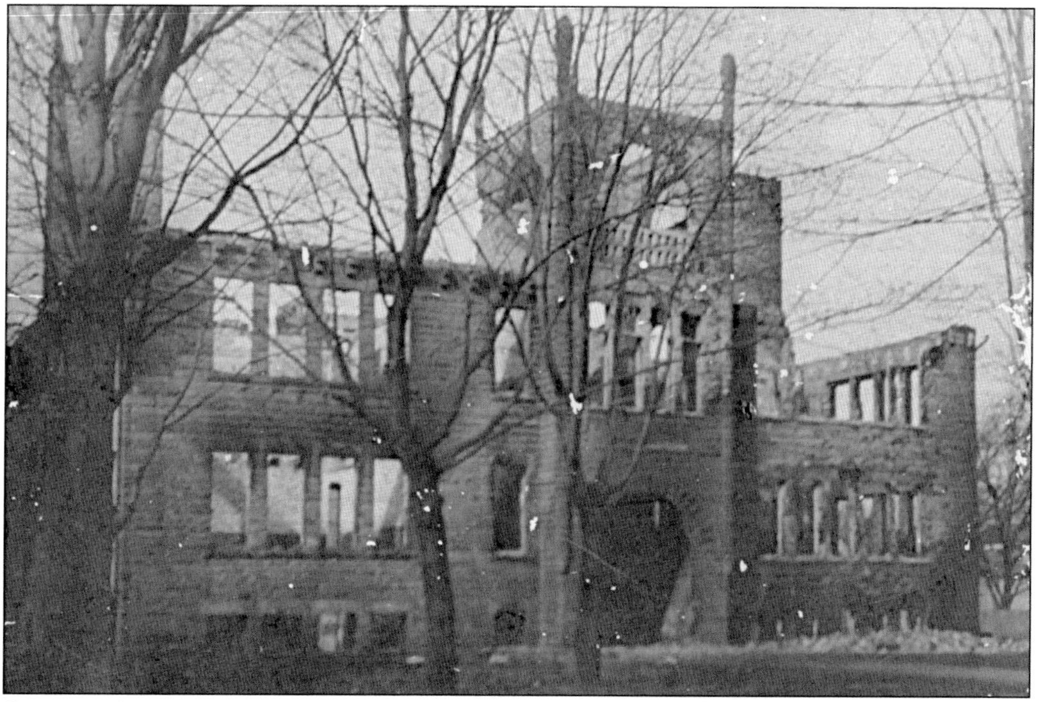

CENTRAL SCHOOL FIRE, 1907. On March 3, 1907, fire once again rocked the Amherst school system. Central School, the jewel of the community, burnt with the loss of all its contents. The community rallied and replaced it by the following year.

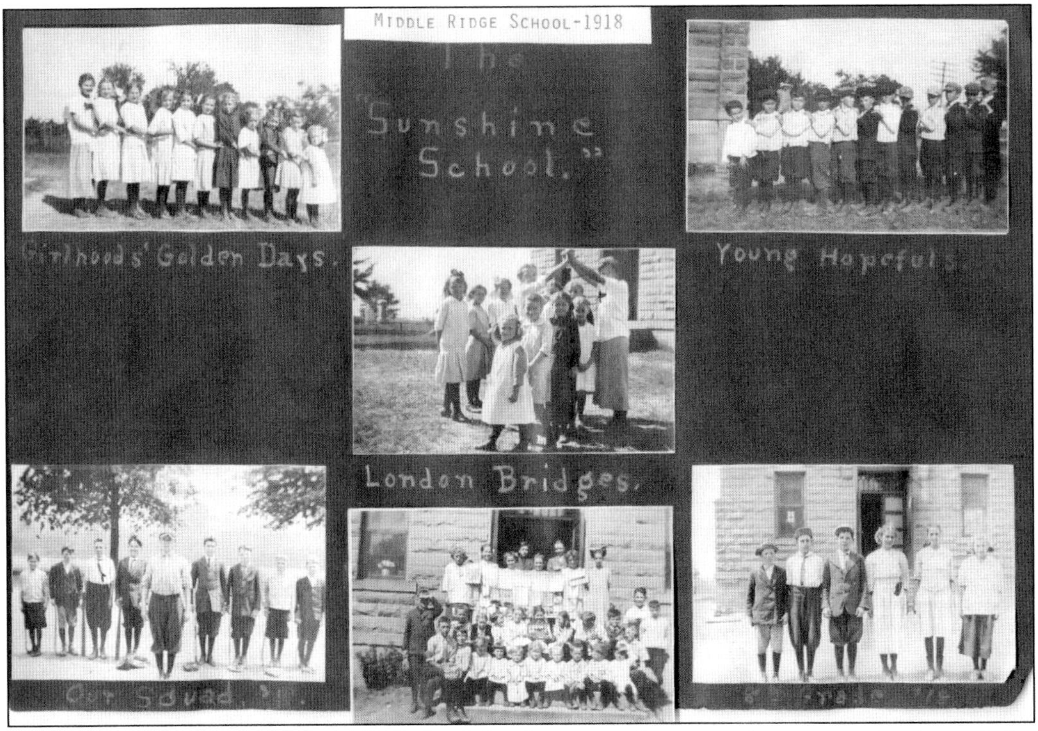

MIDDLE RIDGE SCHOOL. The Middle Ridge School continued to serve the community through the 1920s. Affectionately called "Sunshine School," its pupils engaged in a variety of activities. From left to right, top to bottom, one student's fond memories are captured in this collage: "Girlhood's Golden Days," "Young Hopefuls," "London Bridges," "Our Squad," "Proud Display of Work," and "Eighth Grade Class."

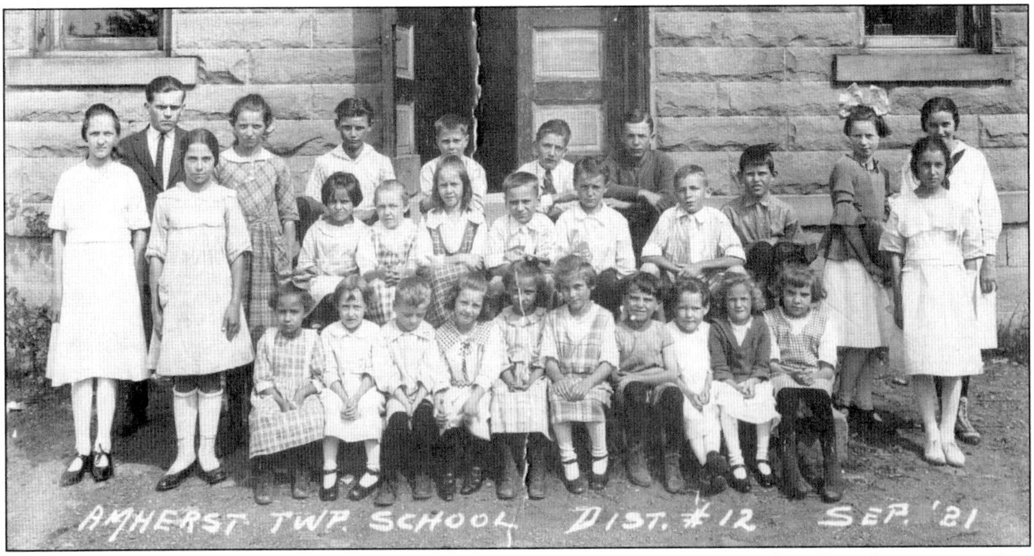

DISTRICT 12 SCHOOL, SEPTEMBER 1921. Students at Middle Ridge School, with its township designation as No. 12, pose before the structure's main doors. Note that the schoolchildren, like their adult counterparts, were conscious of changing fashion trends. The school closed in the fall of 1952, and the building became the Sandstone Players Theater.

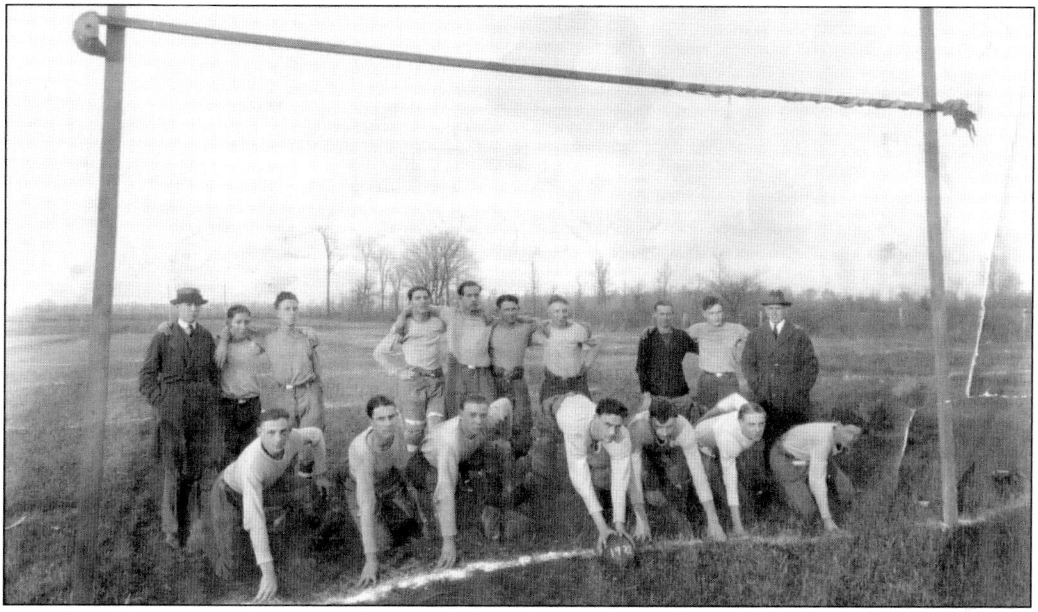

Amherst High School Athletics, 1920s. Amherst public schools reflected the growing interest in organized athletics so prominent in the 1920s. Typical of that emphasis were the Amherst High School football team (above) in 1923. From left to right (first row) are W. Leinhos, H. Marshall, M. Gishman, H. Krause, J. Justin, E. Menz, J. F. Frederick; (second row) K. Tolhurst, L. Baumhardt, J. Wohlever, T. Guiselman, L. Neumeister, D. Leimbach, W. Wilford, C. Bobel, E. Eastman, and Coach William J. Darling. Ahead of the curve, Amherst schools encouraged women's athletics, as exemplified by the girls' 1924 basketball team (below). With a perfect record of 1-0, they sported high tops and bloomers. Members from left to right are Coach Iona Kaiser Maxwell, M. Delbridge, D. Zilch, H. Orcutt, D. Schofield, H. Baker, D. Menz, and M. Sharp.

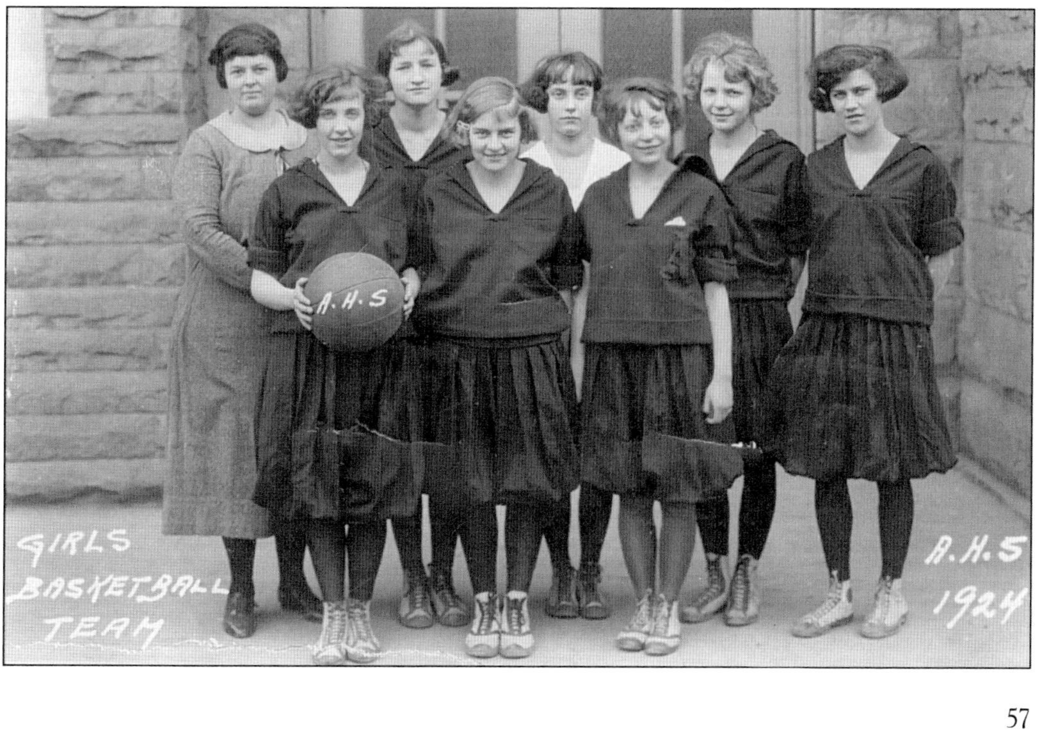

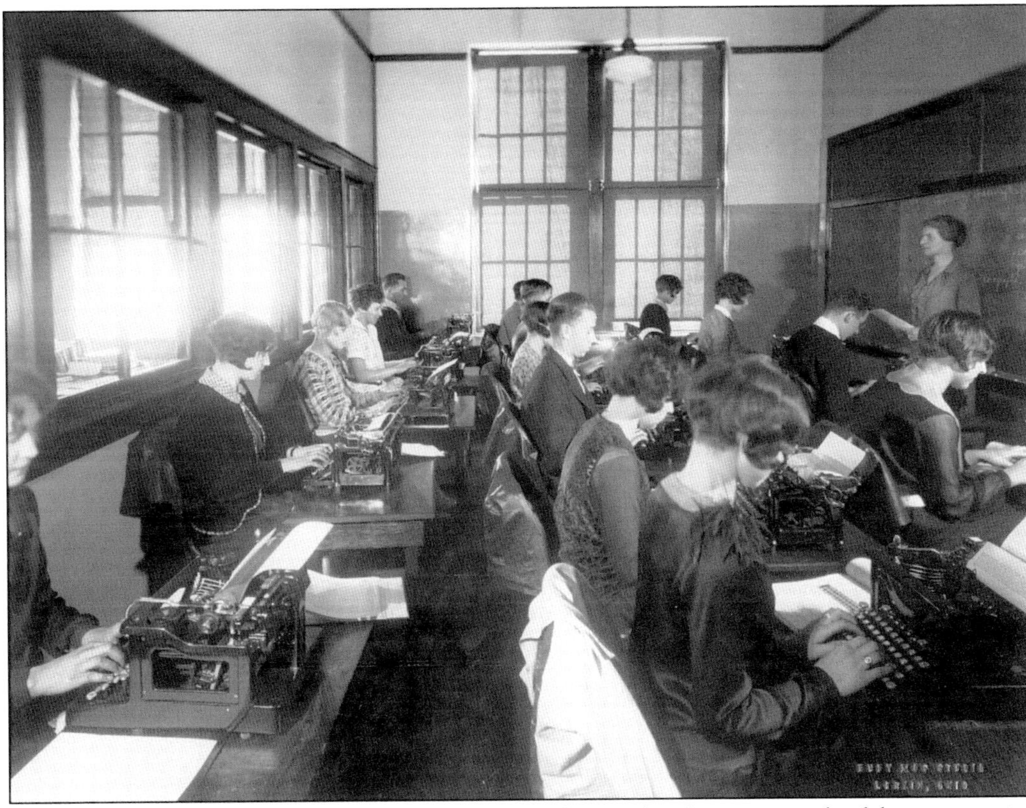

CHANGING CURRICULUM, 1930S. Once again responding to the changing needs of the community, Amherst schools' curriculum aimed at preparing students for the world of work and a healthier life. By 1930, a commercial curriculum had been adopted at Amherst High School (above). Teacher Mattie Driver (Kunkle) emphasized both speed and accuracy in her typing class. Note the stylish 1930s hair bobs. Physical education (below) also became an integral part of the school day. This boys' calisthenics class, pictured around 1933, was led by coach Wilbur Braun.

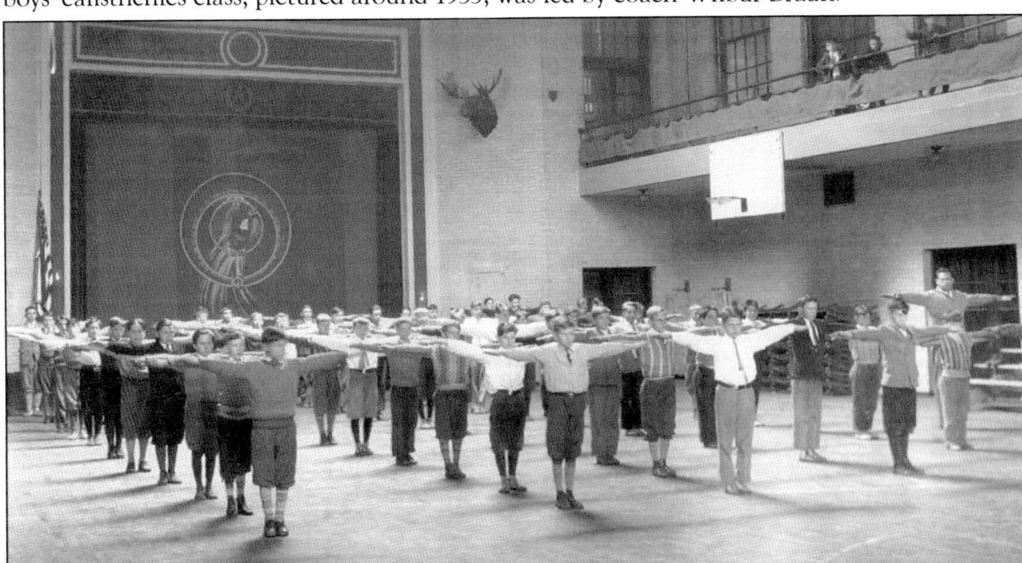

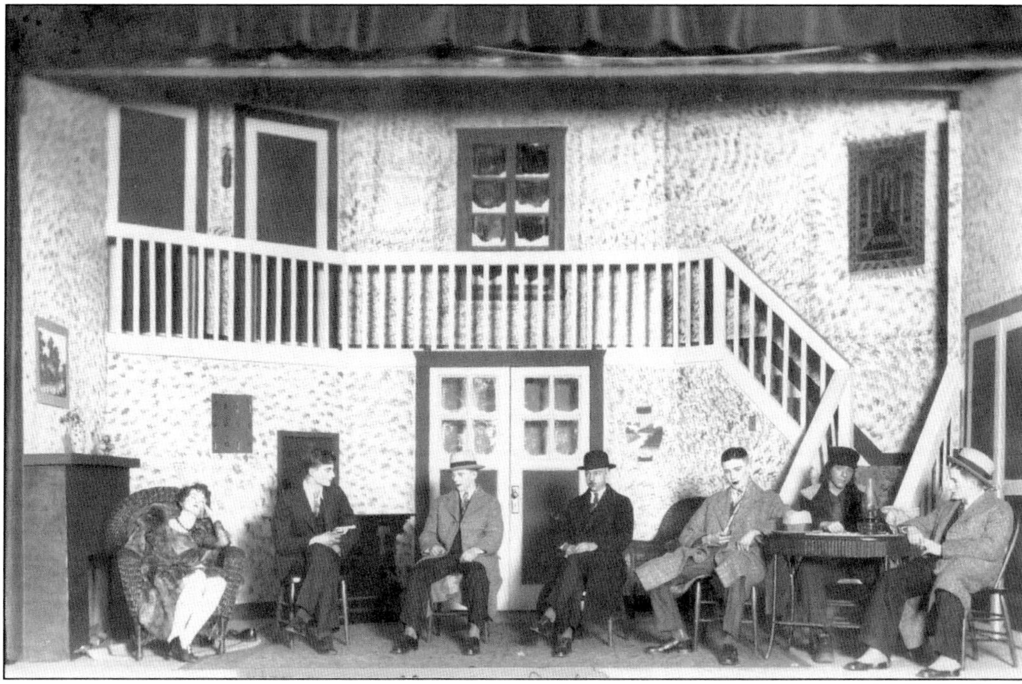

THEATRICAL PERFORMANCES. Theatrical performances constituted another important facet of community life. Pictured above on March 7 or 8, 1929, students from Amherst High School presented *Seven Keys to Baldpate*. From left to right are Ruth Zilch, Lewis Richert, Lloyd Nickel, Robert Standen, Earl Kane, Howard Nalley, and Bob Zilch. In 1953, another student group (below) performed *I Remember Mama*. From left to right are (seated, floor) Mary Washka and Laura Whitman; (seated, table) Honey Lou Olson, Arthur Engle, Kathleen Finnegan, Don Zuspan, and Darwin Colman.

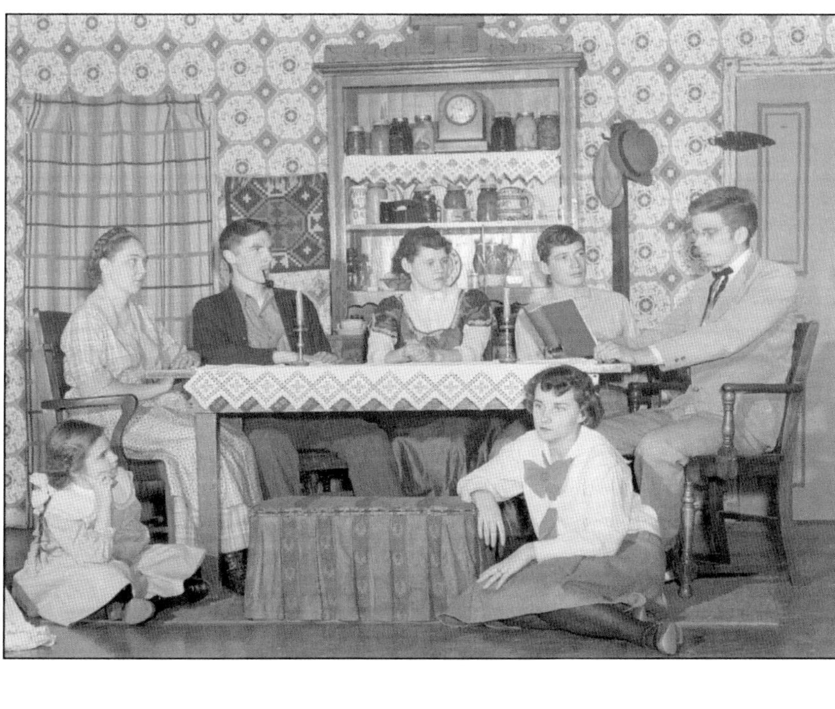

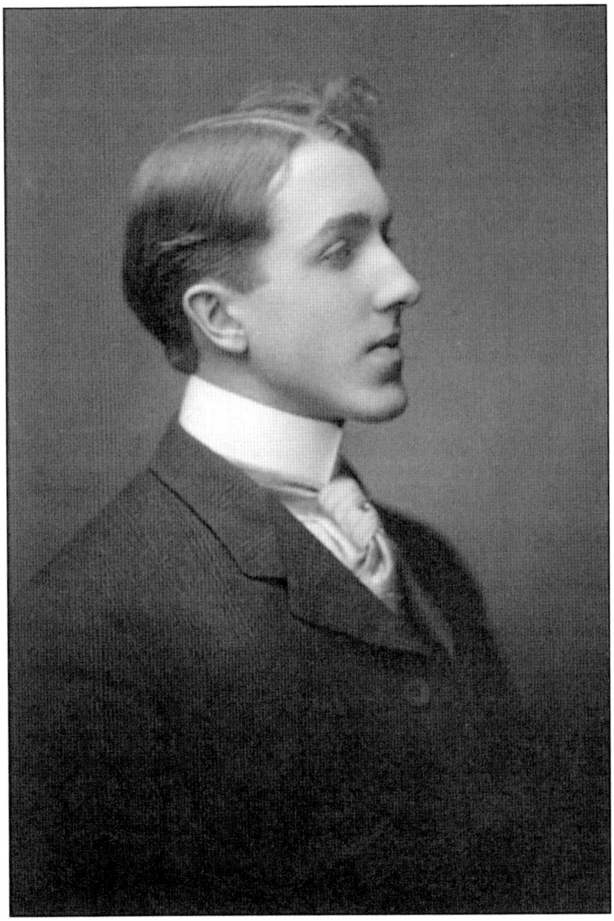

POWERS ELEMENTARY SCHOOL. To meet the needs of a growing population, Amherst citizens funded the construction of Powers Elementary in 1952. The school was named for longtime educator Fred Powers, father of the Amherst school system. Powers completed school in Amherst before attending the College of Wooster and graduating from Oberlin College in 1913 (left). He earned a master's degree from Columbia University, and he started teaching in South Amherst in 1908 and served as superintendent of the Amherst Schools from 1918 through his retirement in 1956. Powers then became principal of the school named for him until 1962. He died in 1983 at the age of 95. Bertine Foster's fifth-grade class (below) presented the first performance on the new school stage, honoring the 150th anniversary of Ohio's statehood in 1953. Foster's production featured highlights from the state's history.

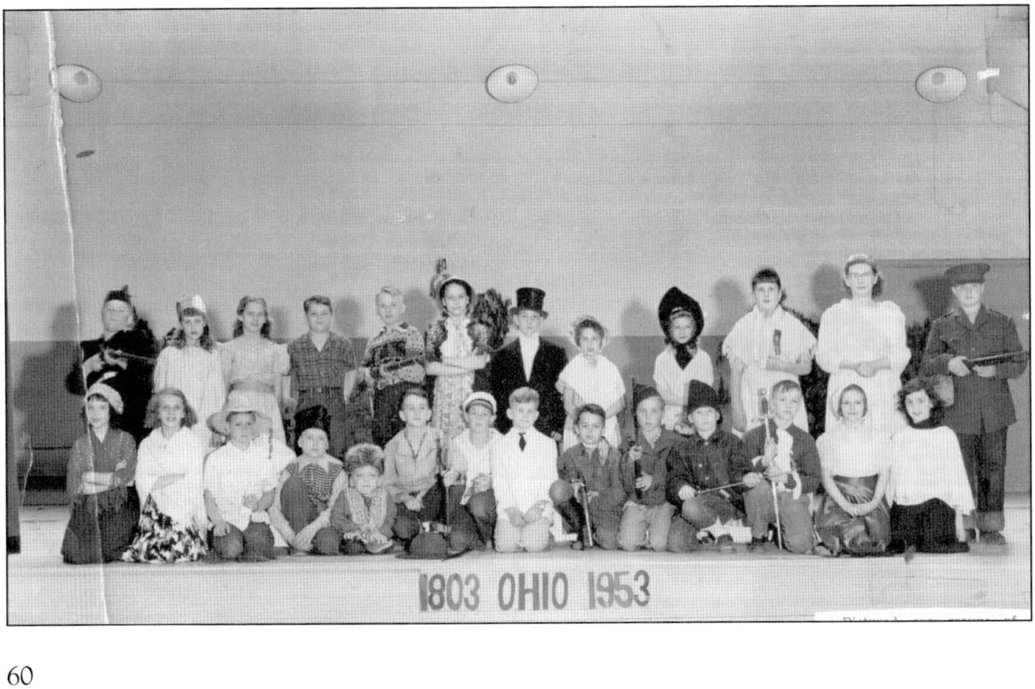

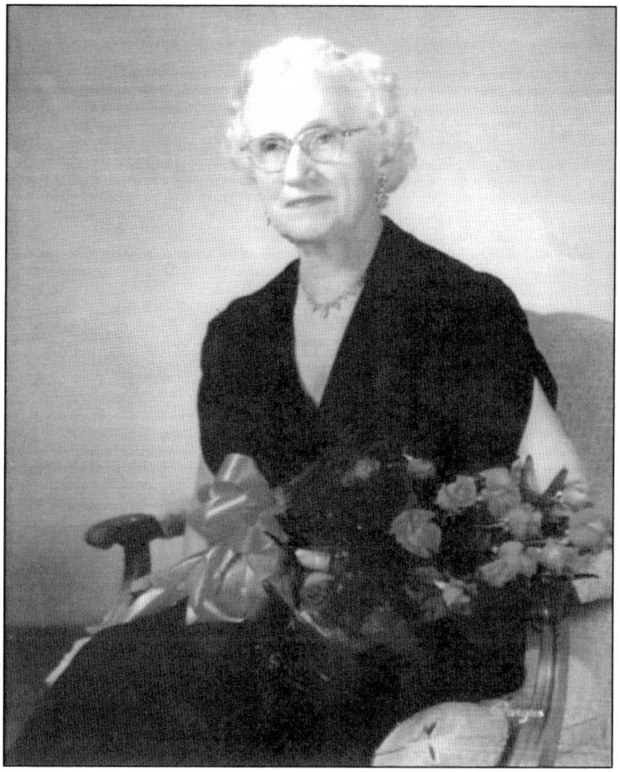

Marion L. Steele High School. Named in honor of longtime educator Marion L. Steele, the district built a new high school in 1957 (below), replacing Central School, which became the district's junior high school. Steele (right) dedicated herself to the education of Amherst's young. A product of Amherst Central School, she graduated from Oberlin Academy and Oberlin College. Soon after, she began teaching English and French in Amherst schools. Three years later, she was named principal of the high school and remained until her retirement in 1957.

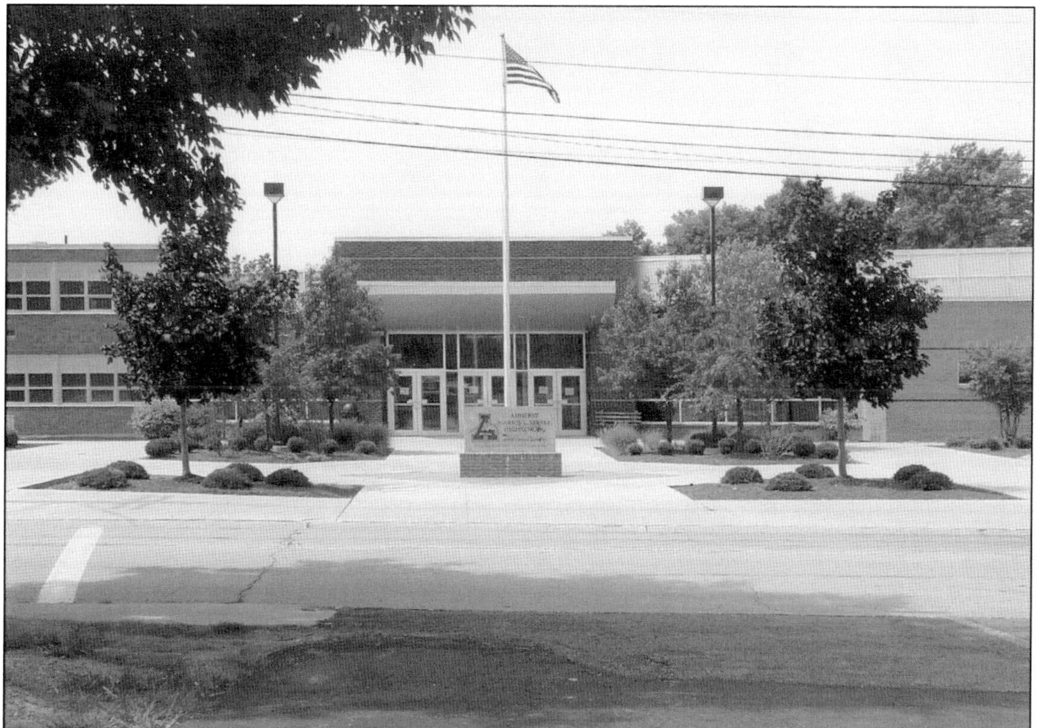

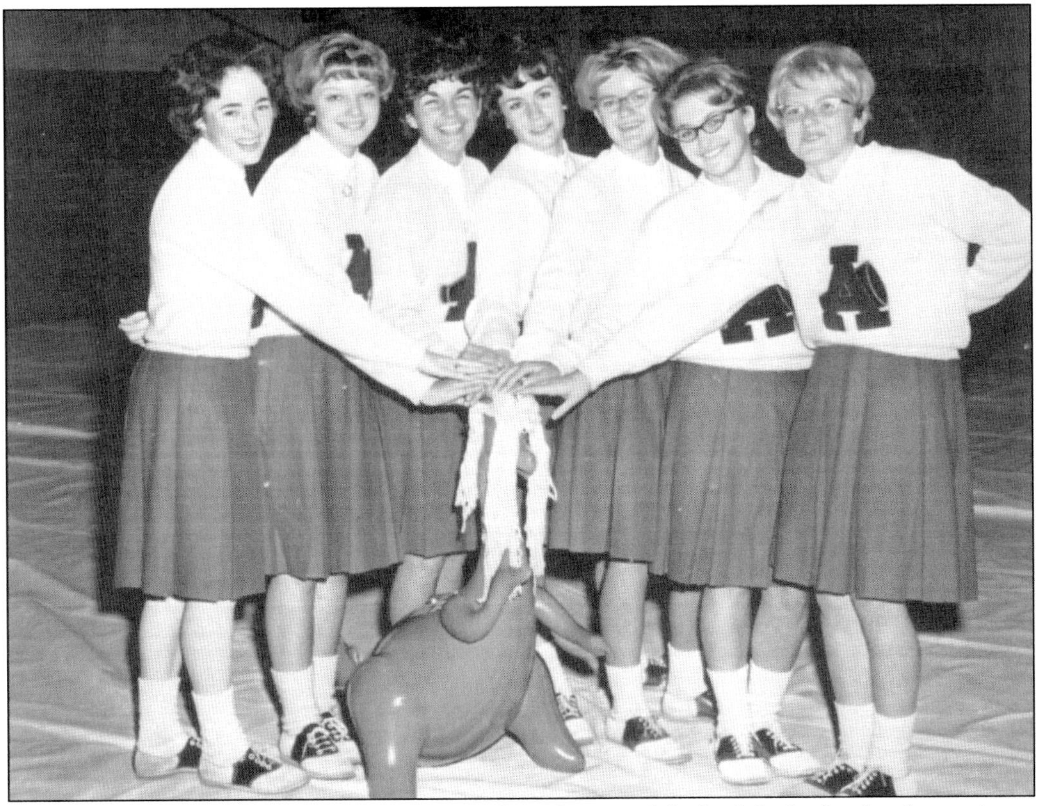

EXTRACURRICULAR ACTIVITIES AT AMHERST HIGH SCHOOL. Much of the high school experience takes place outside of the traditional classroom. Above, cheerleaders prepare for the big game in 1963. Members of the varsity squad from left to right are Debbie Young, Carolyn Brandies, Sue Ryan, Linda Joyce, Sandy Reichert, Cookie Towne, and Bonnie Reichert. An integral part of football games, the marching band (below) performed exuberant shows during half time. The photograph depicts the marching Comets in their banana hats in the early 1970s.

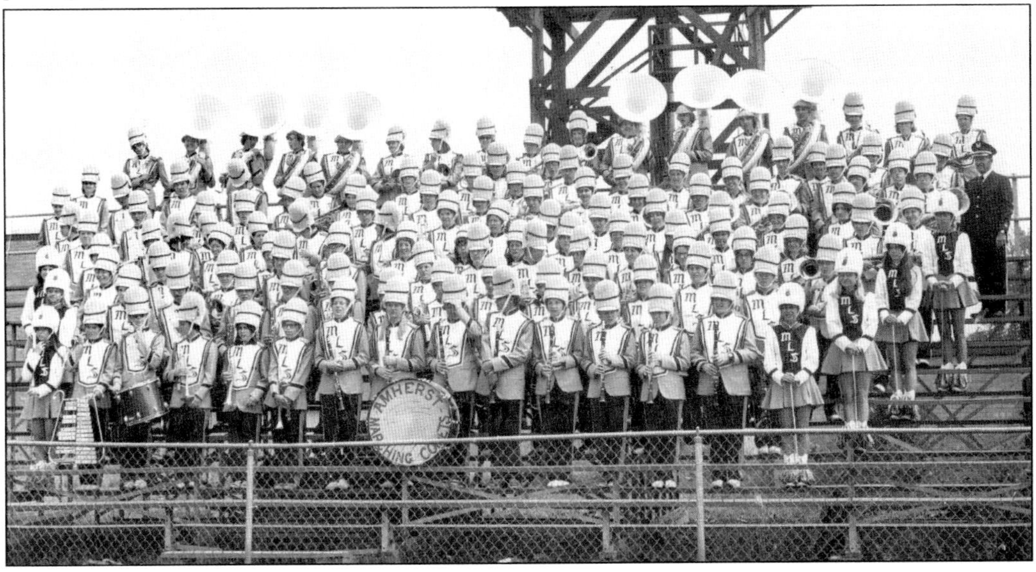

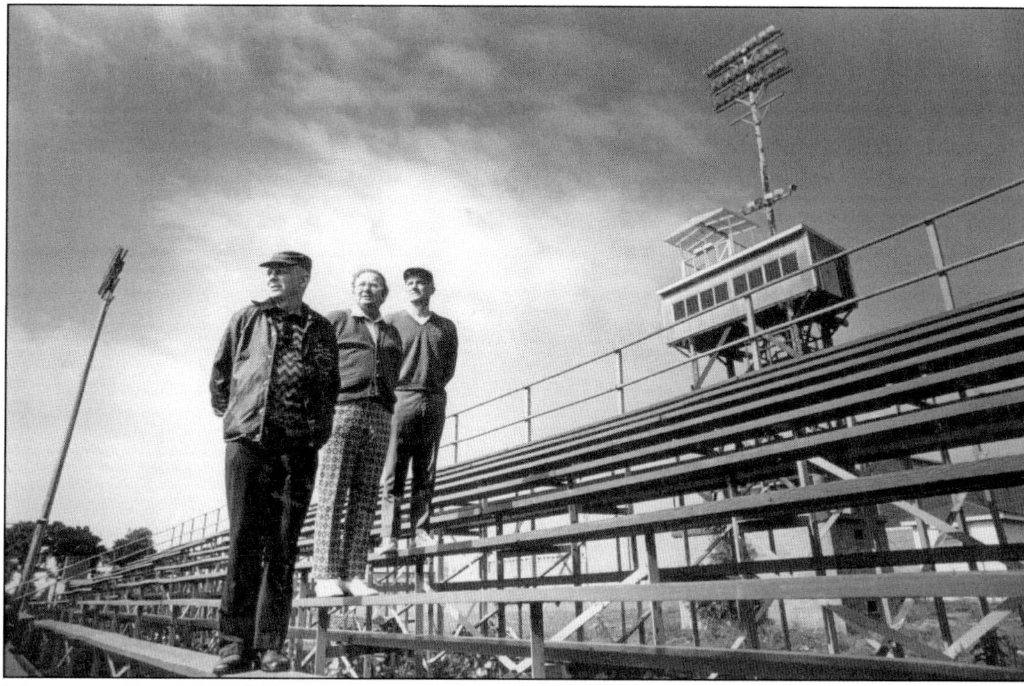

Memorial Field. In 1973, the Amherst band and athletic boosters spearheaded a campaign to rebuild the stadium and its surrounding track. Memorial Field was erected and dedicated as a permanent memorial to Amherst's World War II veterans. From left to right, Jessie Schwartz, Clint Reph, and Dick Malin led the campaign. In time-honored tradition, 1973 graduates (right) of Marion L. Steele High School toss their caps in the air at the conclusion of commencement festivities held at the school's football field.

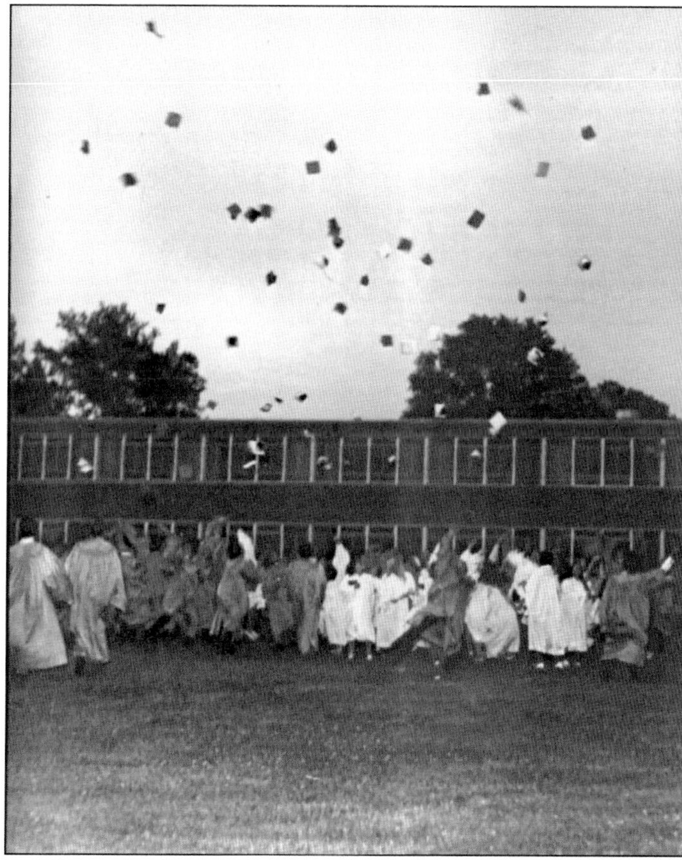

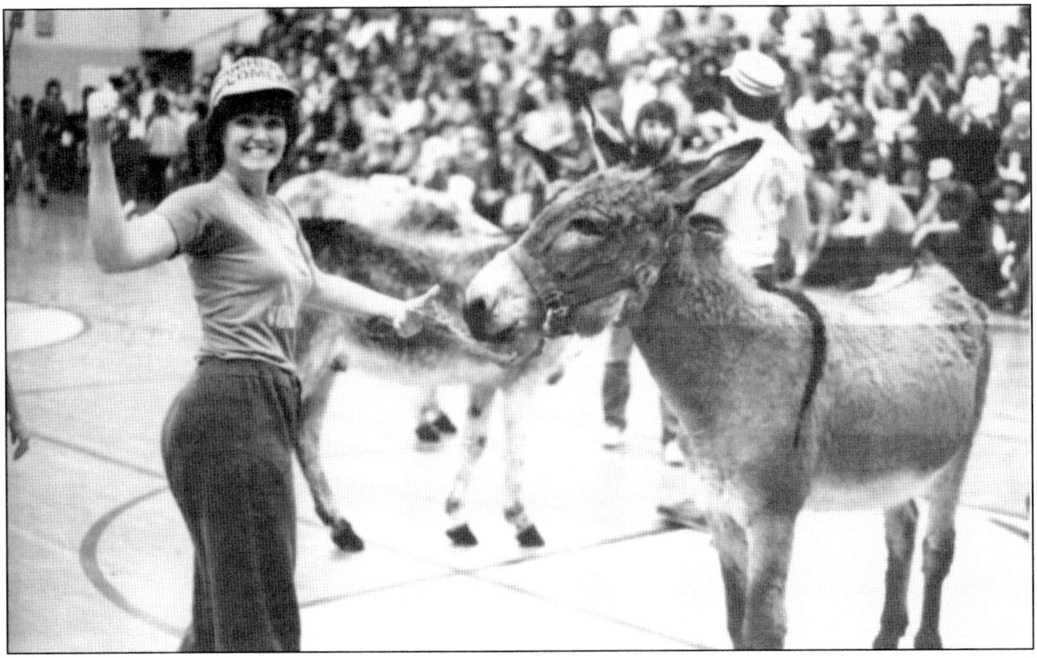

Donkey Basketball. An annual event during the 1980s, the donkey basketball game pitted seniors against teachers in a heated contest. The donkeys had no partisan alliances and treated all players equally. The 1983 event resulted in a victory for the teachers, their first in four years. The final score was 24-20.

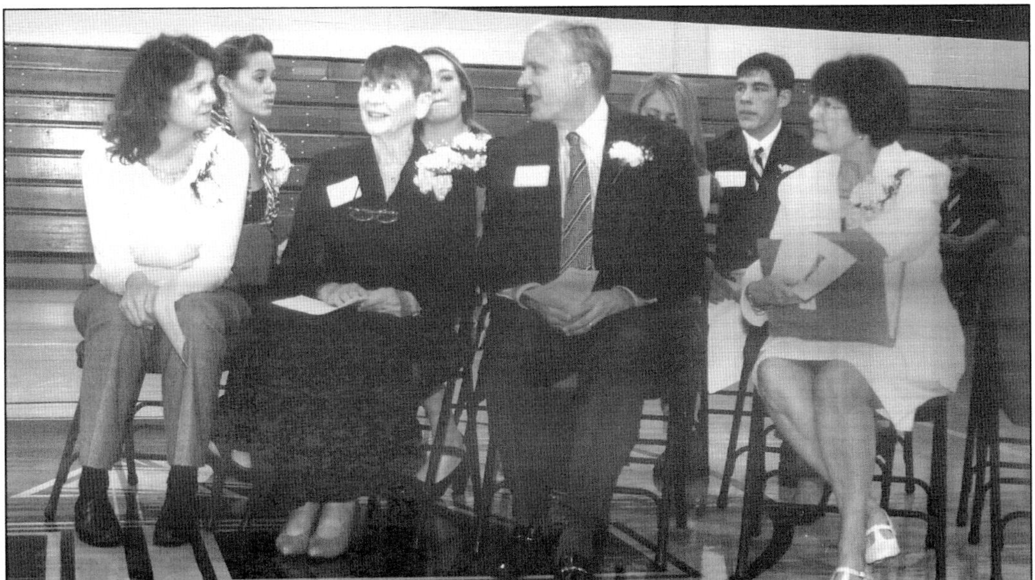

Gallery of Success. In 1986, as part of Amherst High School's centennial celebration, Amherst public schools dedicated its Distinguished Alumni Gallery of Success. Honorees were chosen in recognition of their accomplishments in hopes that they would serve as an inspiration to students. The 2007 honorees included Teresa Tarnowski Goddell, David Allyn Drake, Elizabeth Higgens Horner, and Alexander Karl Kummant. Pictured from left to right are Goodell, Doris Lyle representing Drake Kummant and Joan Rosenbusch representing Horner.

Five

BUILDINGS OF AMHERST

Nowhere are the uses of Amherst's native product, sandstone, better displayed than in the city itself. From the mid-19th century, residents began to harvest local stone for their construction projects. By the beginning of the 20th century, they constructed buildings of local stone for commercial, as well as domestic purposes. In Amherst, the uses of sandstone for utilitarian and decorative functions are quite evident. The city demonstrates the vast array of sandstone applications in a microcosm.

The dignity and solidity that sandstone masonry construction provides is nowhere more evident than in Amherst's public buildings. From its landmark city hall to the public library and the schools, the city's most basic institutions attest to the beauty and permanence of this local product. These structures also illustrate the adaptability of their sandstone to changing architectural styles. It works as well in the sleek and spare modernist style of Powers Elementary School as it does in the massive Romanesque Revival city hall.

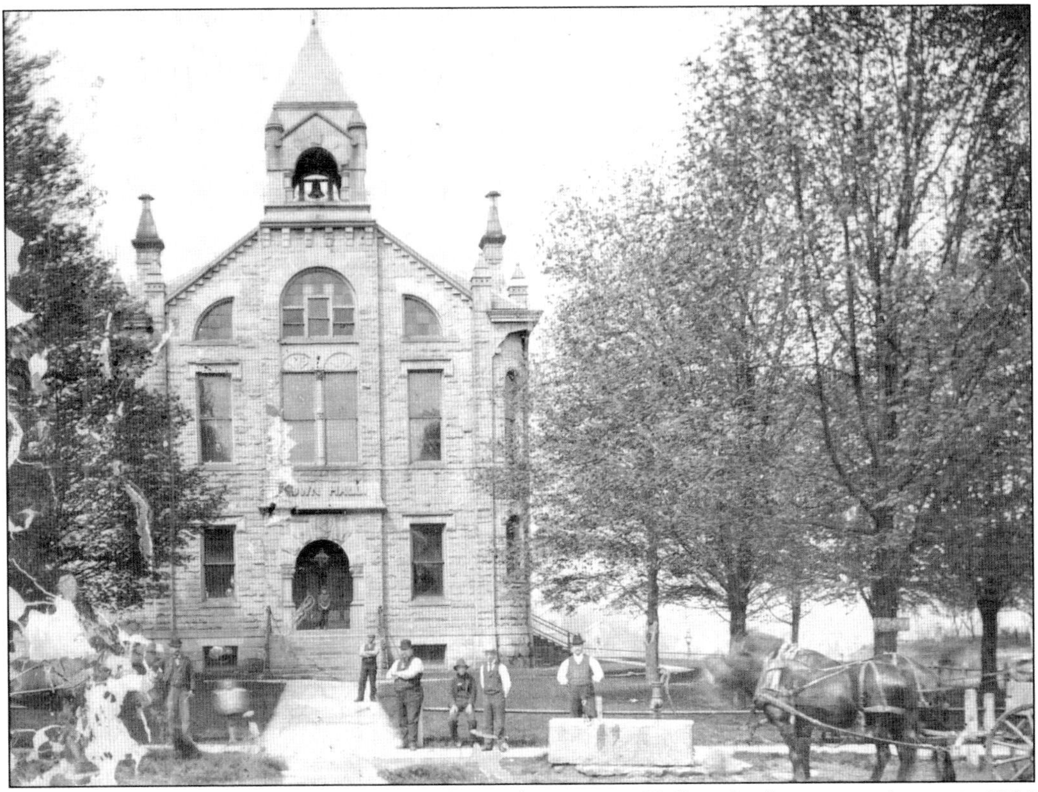

AMHERST TOWN HALL. Construction on the Amherst Town Hall at the five corners began in 1884 (above) for a cost between \$2,000 and \$3,000. The Romanesque Revival structure of Amherst sandstone houses the town government to the present day. The second floor (below) was dedicated to public assembly and served as a theater and opera house. For many years, it also functioned as a school auditorium, as seen here, decorated for the 1910 commencement ceremonies.

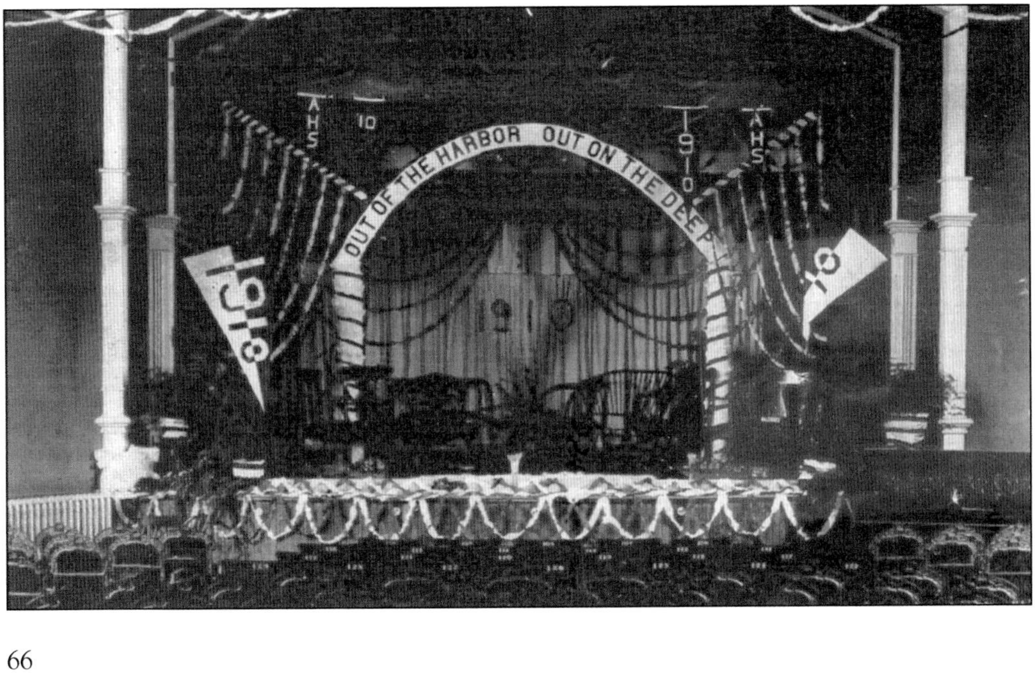

Town Hall Grounds. In 1915, the citizens of Amherst constructed a comfort station and bandstand (right) on the northwest corner in front of town hall. Its cornerstone reads, "This building dedicated to Amherst through the generous spirit and labor of the citizens, stonecutters, cut stone co.'s and quarries, 1915." On the southwest corner is the memorial (below) to those who died in the "Great War" (World War I). It was erected by the Amherst Eagles Aerie No. 1442 and dedicated in June 1924.

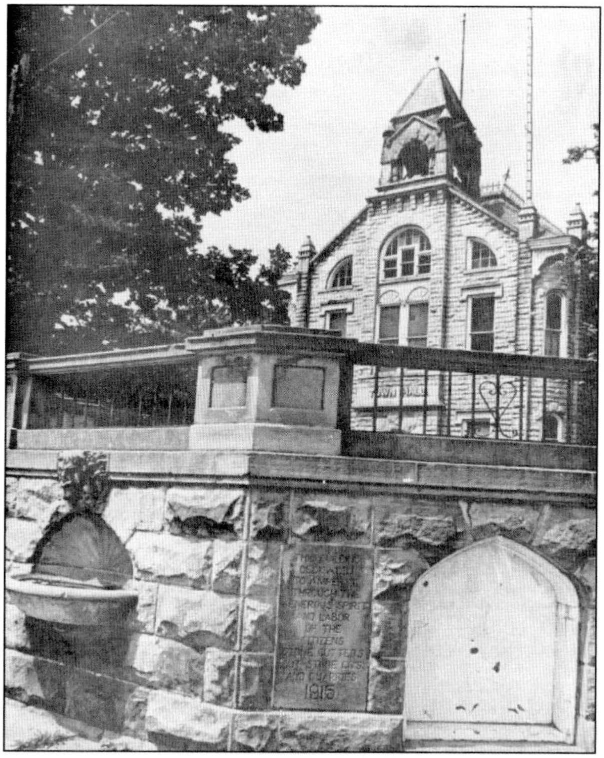

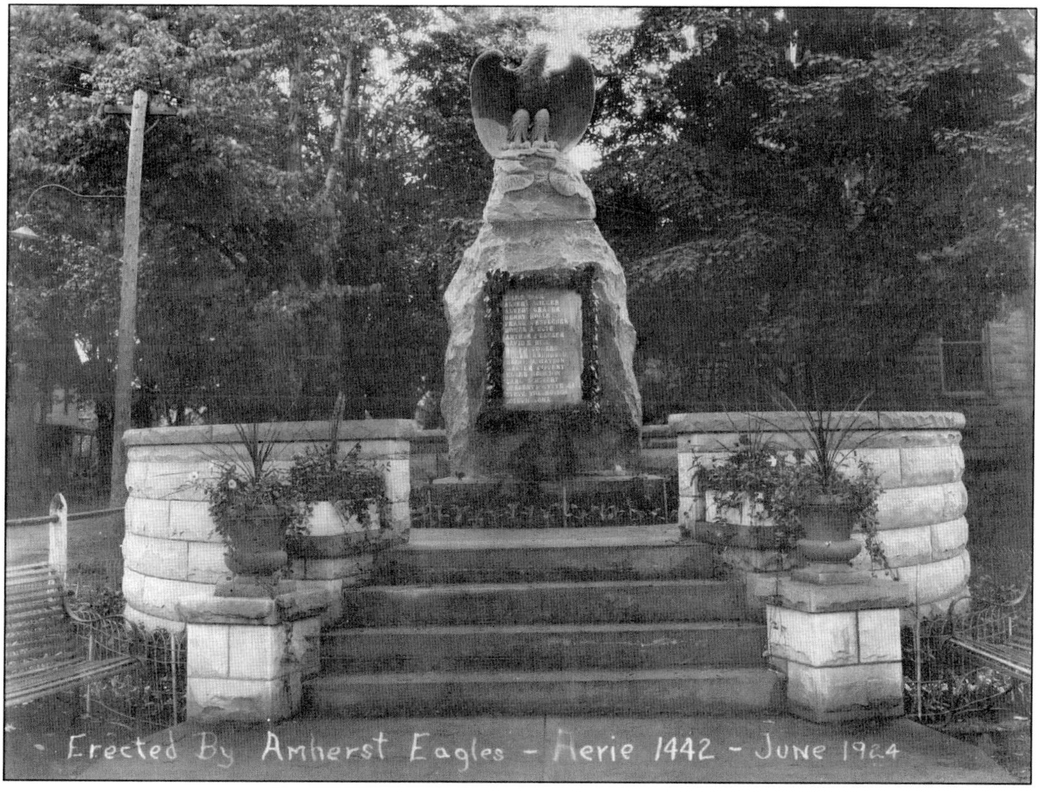

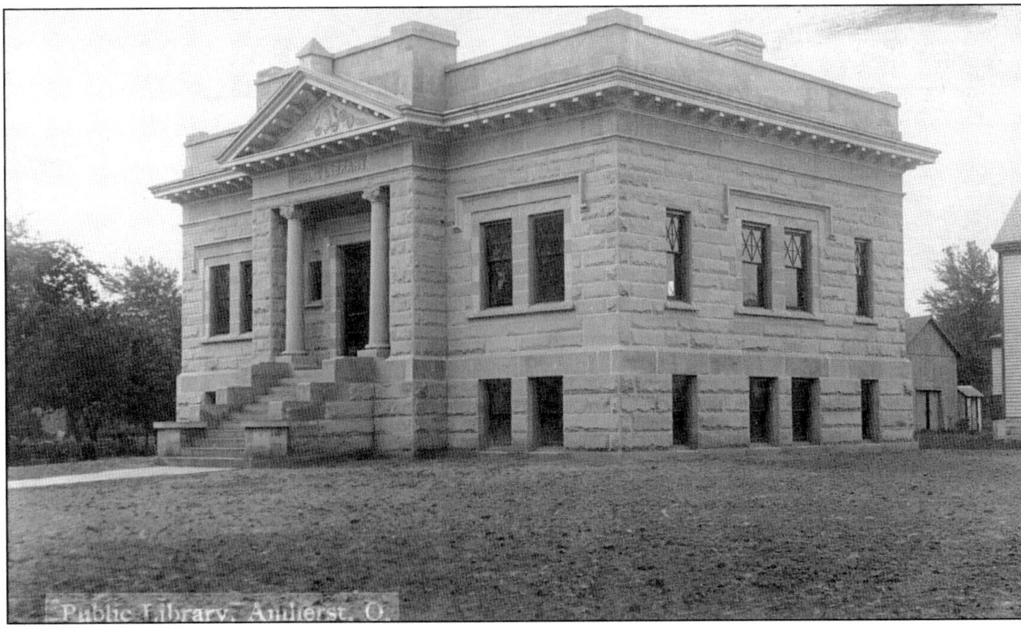

AMHERST PUBLIC LIBRARY. The Amherst Public Library, located at 428 Park Avenue, remains another community icon. Built in 1906, the structure is the result of the fund-raising efforts of A. Baker, a local businessman and one-time postmaster for the village. The library raised $10,000 in Carnegie library grants. An addition was constructed in 1975.

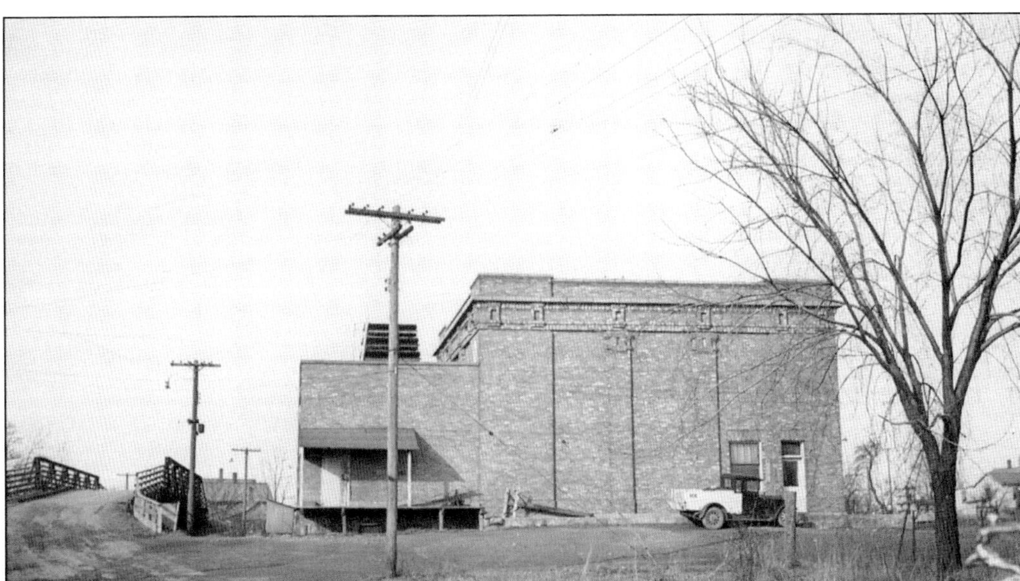

AMHERST COLD STORAGE, c. 1915. Amherst Cold Storage, located next to the Jackson Street bridge, was started by U.S. Automatic in 1908. The company was a frozen foods center that processed meats, frozen fruits, and vegetables for wholesale and retail markets. It also leased space for bulk cold storage. The building was demolished in 1991 during an expansion of Nordson Company.

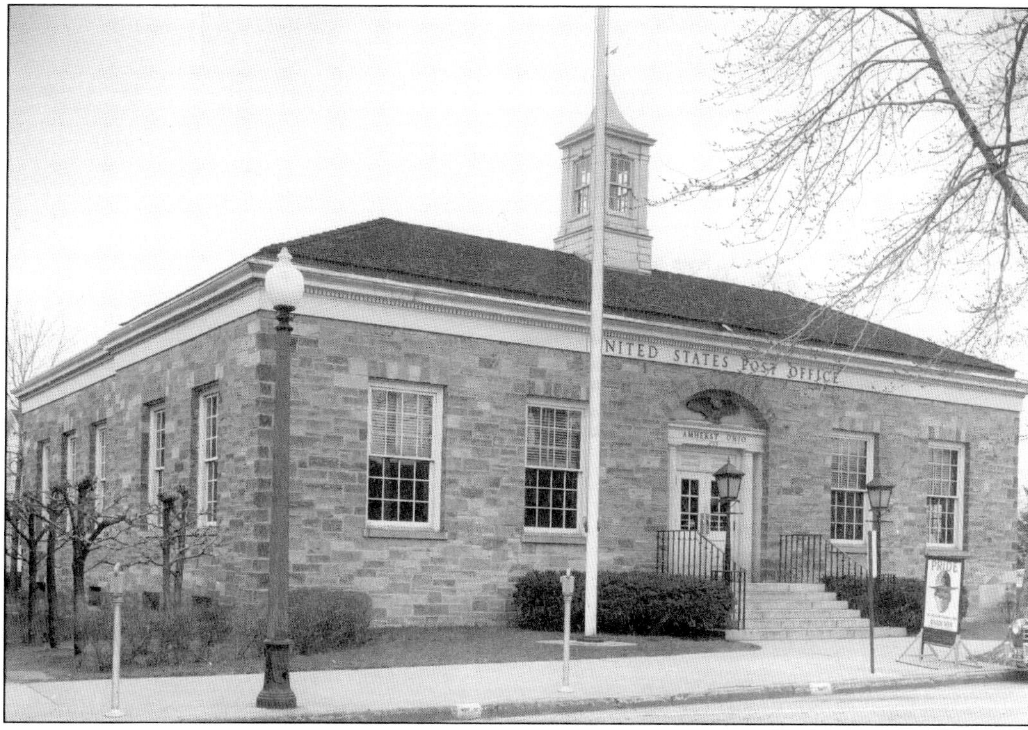

Post Office and Mural. Finished in 1940, Amherst's post office (above) was one of the last federal projects completed before the United States entered World War II. The Georgian Revival building cost $70,000 to construct out of Amherst Gray sandstone. The architect was LeRoy Barton of Washington, D.C., and the general contractor was Mutual Construction Company of Youngstown. Located on Park Avenue, it now houses Amherst's Main Street program. One of the outstanding features of the building is a 1941 Works Projects Administration (WPA) mural (below). Artist Michael Loew of New York completed the painting, titled, *Pioneers Crossing the Ohio River* as one of the last projects of this New Deal program. Of the mural, Loew stated he wished to capture the spirit of "scores of families in search of new land."

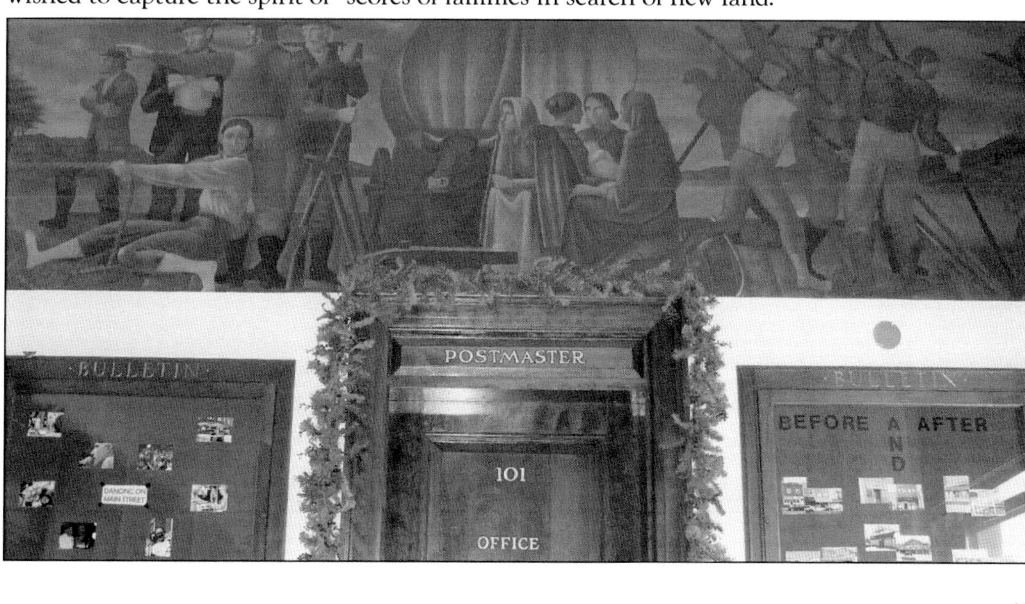

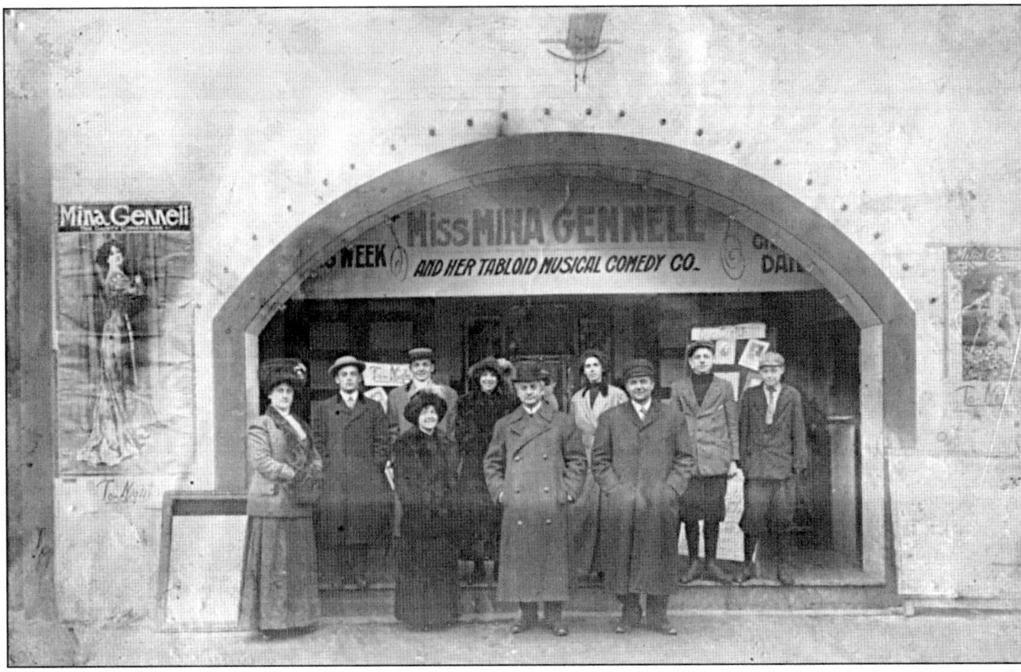

The Empire Theater, c. 1912. The Empire Theater, located at 257 Church Street, was the first motion picture theater in Amherst. Owned by V. E. McGhee, it featured a variety of silent movies and vaudeville performances—in this case, Mira Gennell and her Tabloid Musical Comedy Company.

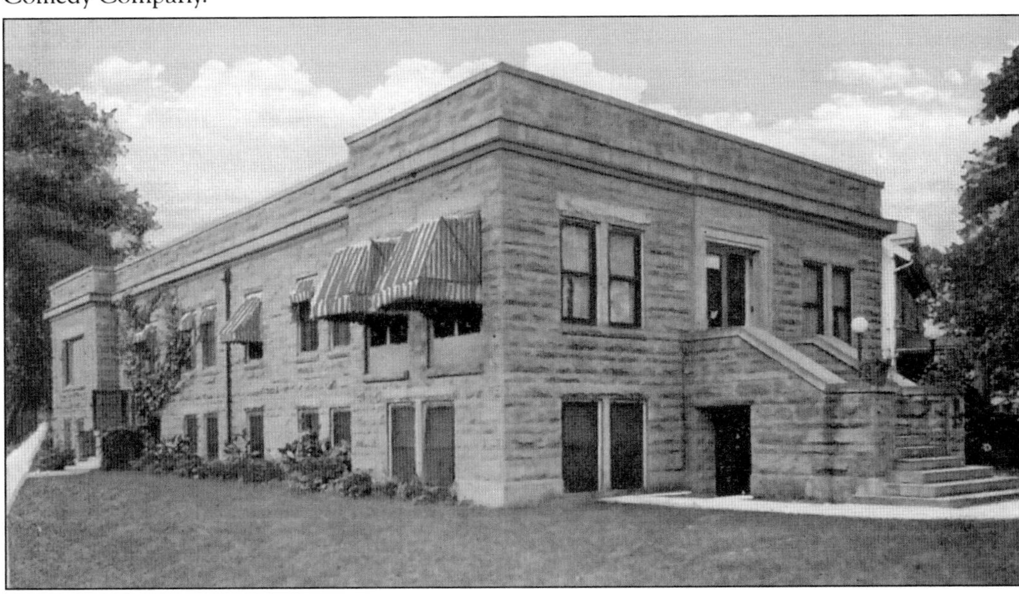

Amherst Hospital. Another local landmark is Amherst Hospital. A fund-raising drive for the building of the hospital began in October 1915, and by the summer of 1916, construction on the corner of Cleveland Avenue and Prospect Street was underway. Its doors opened in February 1917. At a total cost of $20,450, the one-story building of Amherst sandstone provided much needed services for the community. A number of later additions have the changed the look but not the importance of the facility.

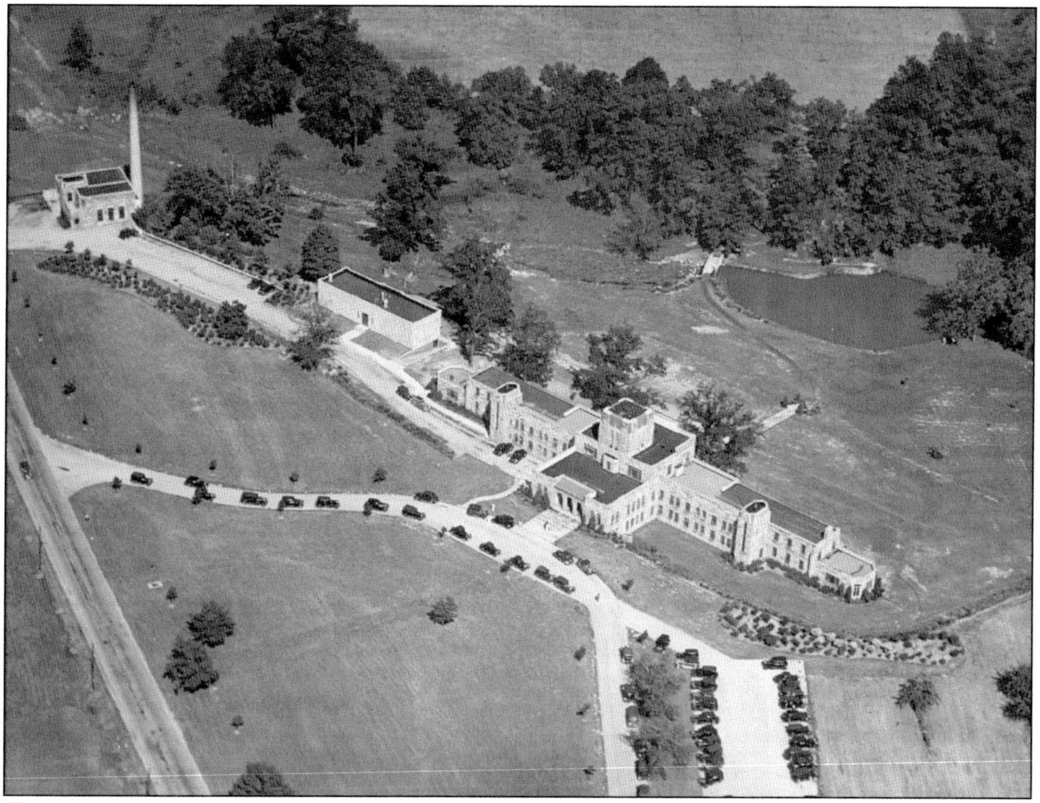

Tuberculosis Sanitarium. In 1931, construction began on the brick structure with sandstone trim (above), originally known as Lorain County Tuberculosis Sanitarium. The building, at a cost of over $270,000, was built by T. J. Hume of Lorain County. The stone for the building came from Nichol's Quarry at Kipton. By World War II, the facility was known as Pleasant View Sanitorium (below). Having outlived its usefulness, the structure was later converted to a county-operated nursing home known as Golden Acres.

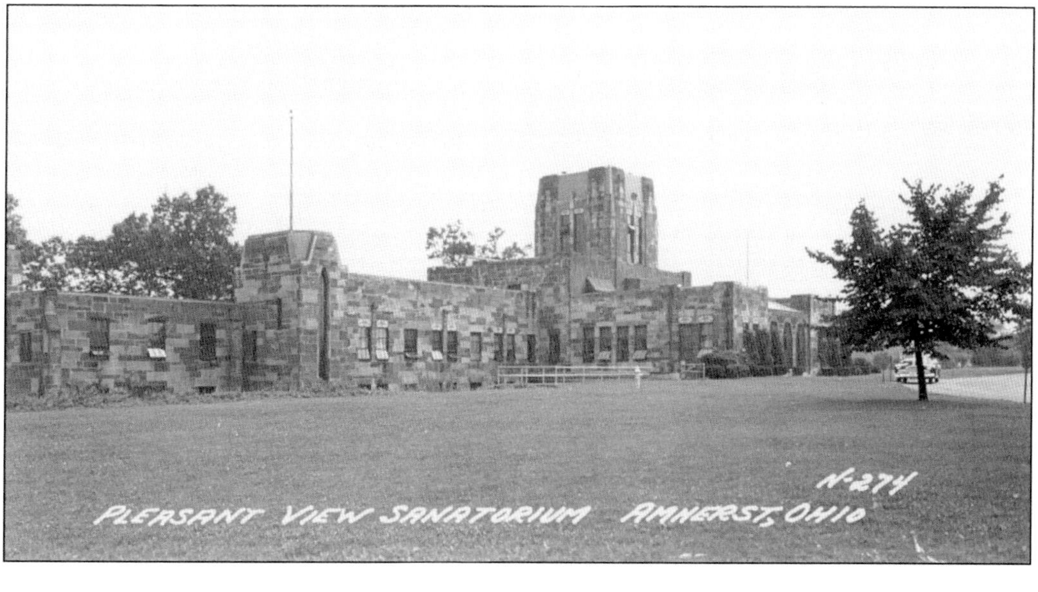

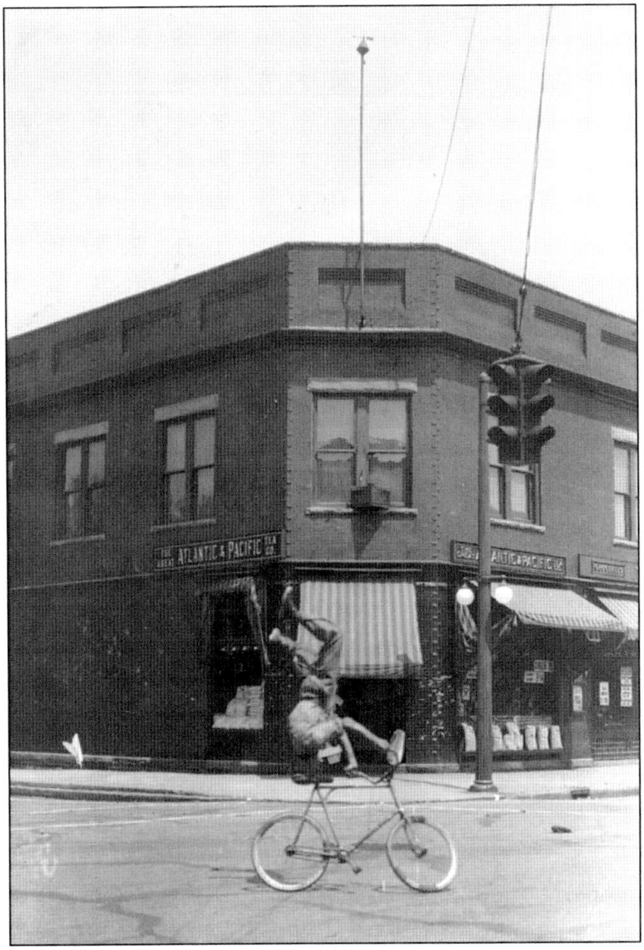

PARK AVENUE COMMERCIAL BUILDING, C. 1930. Built at the dawn of the 20th century, this particular building housed the local Great Atlantic and Pacific Tea Company (A&P) store. Out front, a young man demonstrates his extreme bicycle skills.

THE OLD CATHOLIC SCHOOL. The first school associated with St. Joseph's Catholic Church was located on Forest Street behind the church. The small frame building was constructed in 1883; it closed 10 years later due to the lack of teachers. It was eventually sold and the structure was moved to Spring Street.

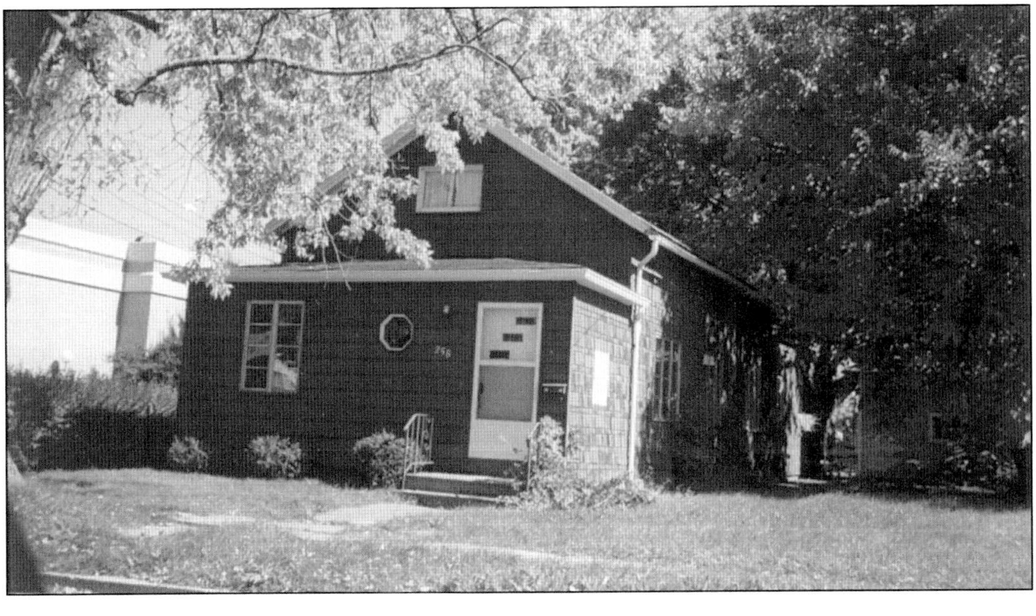

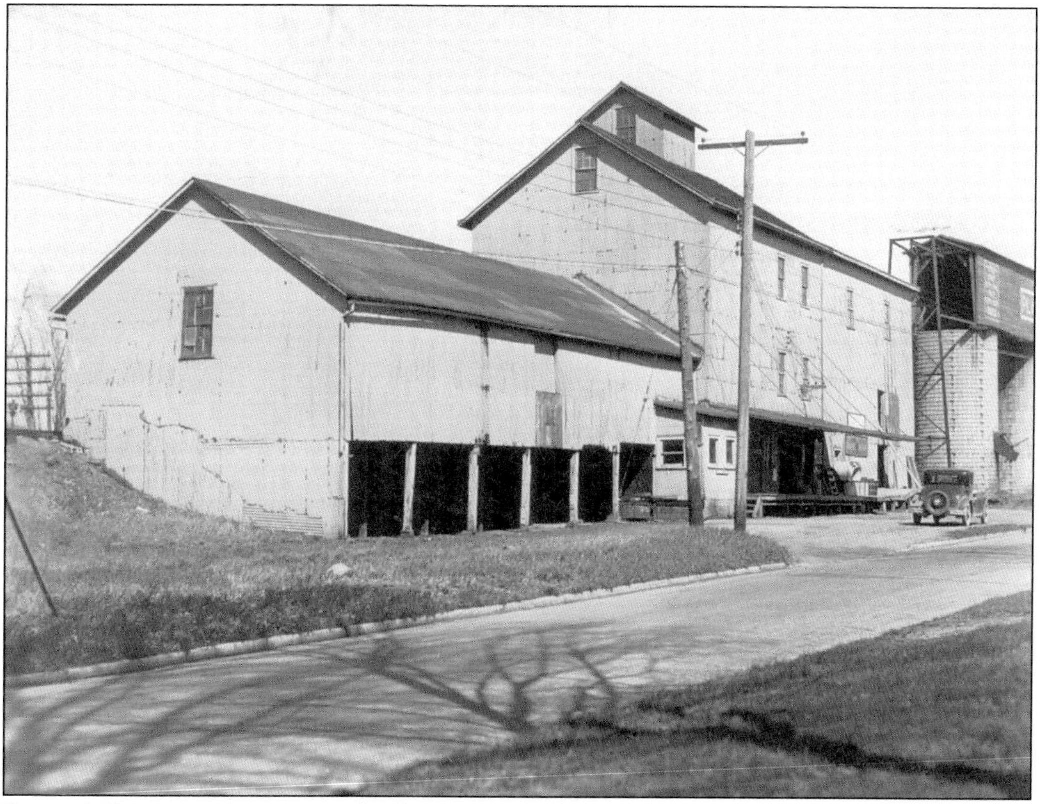

Farmer's Elevator. Among its other businesses, Amherst boasted a grain elevator on Maple Street near the end of East Street. The Farmer's Elevator stored grain for local farmers until it could be sold and shipped. It also supplied feed, flour, coal, builders' supplies, and farm implements. The structured was demolished around 1960.

Carrot Canning Factory. The Carrot Canning Factory provided another outlet for farm produce. This business exemplified attempts at diversification in the early 20th century. Other such enterprises included nut and bolt, tin can, and furniture factories. A fire may have hastened the company's demise. A building at the site later housed the Amherst City utilities office.

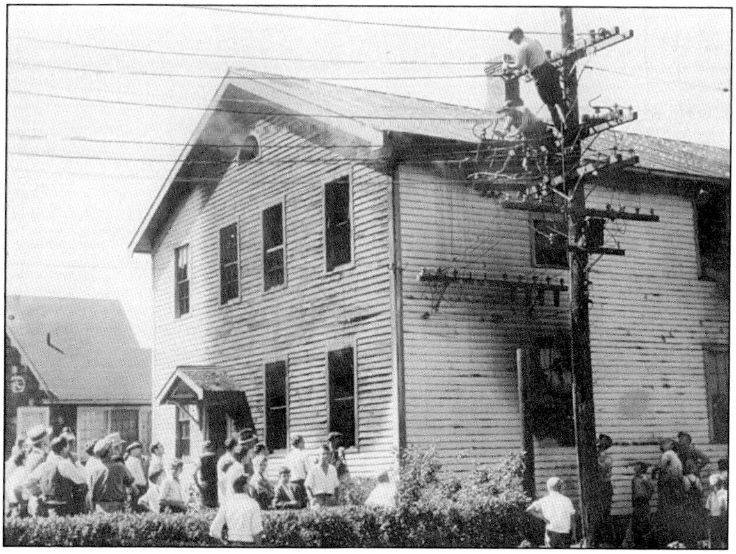

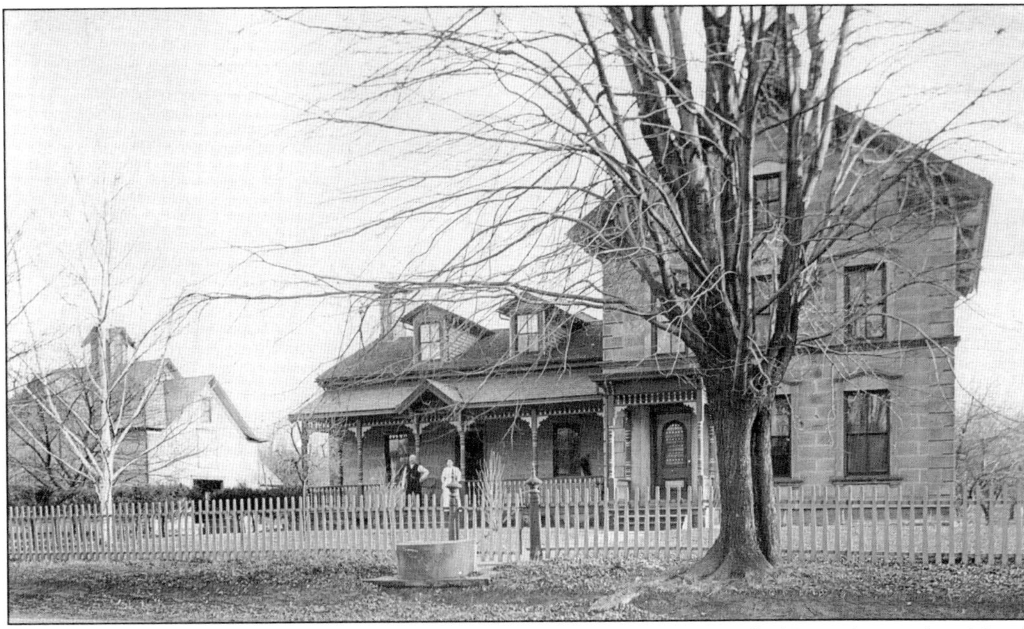

NICHOL HOUSE, NORTH RIDGE ROAD. The original home of James Nichol I was located on North Ridge Road. Built of sandstone taken from the Nichol Quarry, the *c.* 1870 house exhibits Greek Revival and Italianate design elements. Because of its stone construction, the residence is unusual, as most structures in these styles were wood frame rather than masonry.

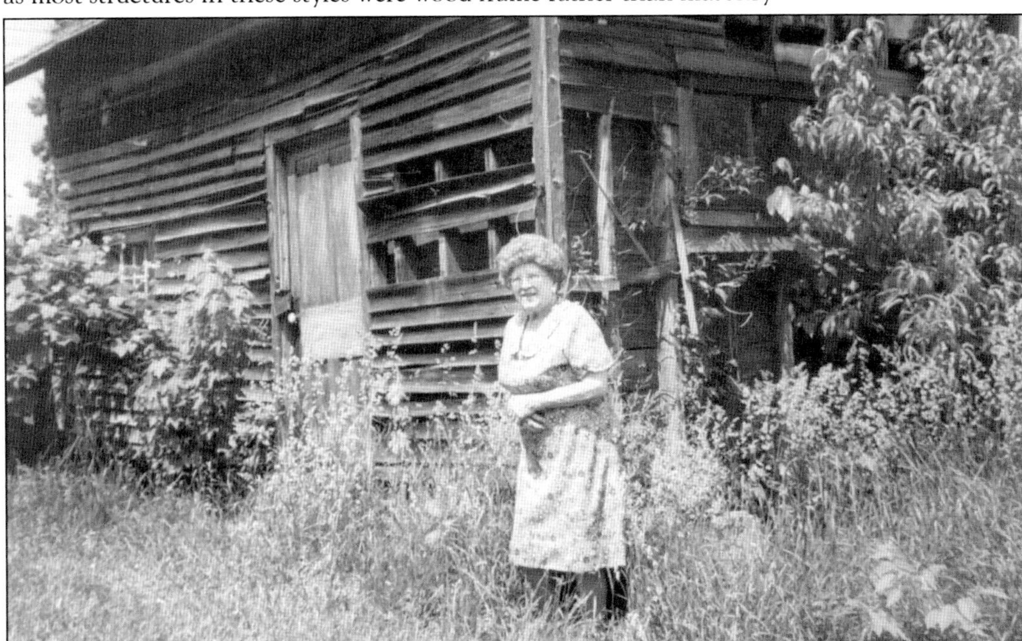

RUTH HERMAN HOUSE. Ruth Herman moved to 6031 Oberlin Road in Amherst with her parents. There are two structures on that property, the oldest of which was constructed in the mid-1800s. The simple, timber-framed building with clapboard siding was a small structure of the hall and parlor type with stairs to a sleeping loft above. There was also an outdoor pump and privy like most houses of its era had.

Six

Amherst Sandstone around the World

Amherst's sandstone is found in remarkable structures both in the United States and Canada that represent a range of architectural styles from public buildings to residences. Sandstone is particularly well suited for the Richardsonian Romanesque, an architectural style named after its originator, architect Henry Hobson Richardson. This style is marked by heavy massing, rock-faced stone, and dramatic, round arches. In the second half of the 19th century and the beginning of the 20th century, American architecture consisted mainly of revivals of earlier architectural styles. For example, because of the Philadelphia Centennial Exposition in 1876, Americans gained a renewed interest in all things colonial, including architecture. One of the nation's premiere architectural firms, McKim, Mead and White, started a fad for the Colonial Revival, which has never really gone out of fashion.

Concurrent with the Colonial Revival was also a new interest in classicism. Many American architects began going to the École des Beaux-Arts in Paris to study their profession. The school emphasized the importance of studying the architecture of ancient Greece and Rome, as well as that of the Italian Renaissance. The American students brought these ideas home with them and implemented their training by producing structures dubbed "Neoclassical Revival" and "Second Renaissance Revival." These styles, which emphasized symmetry, classical columns, and other embellishments, blended elements of Greek, Roman, and Renaissance architecture. Classicism was particularly well suited to large public buildings as opposed to domestic structures. By the 1920s, influenced by the desire to develop new architectural forms, other styles emerged. One of the most popular was art deco, which takes its name from the 1925 Exposition des Arts Decoratifs et Industriel held in Paris. Art deco is an eclectic style, utilizing geometric patterns and stylized floral motifs, as well as borrowing decorative elements from ancient Egyptian and Mayan cultures. Art deco is one of the first truly modern styles and a precursor to the more streamlined and simpler lines of later styles, such as the international style, art moderne, and even brutalism.

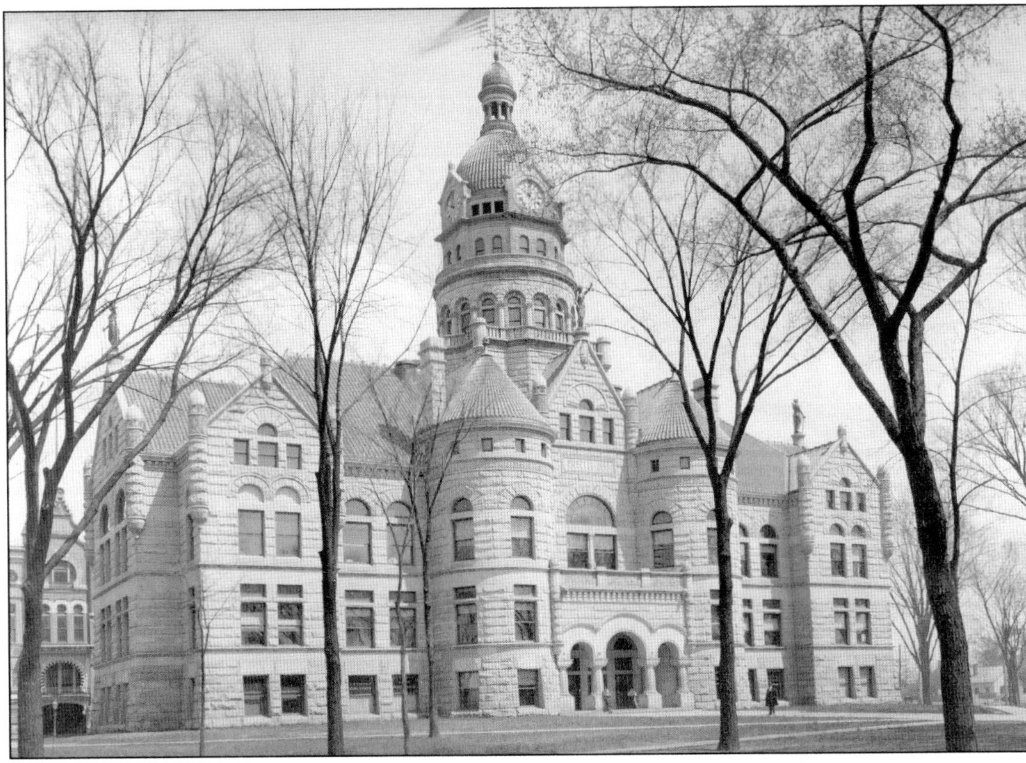

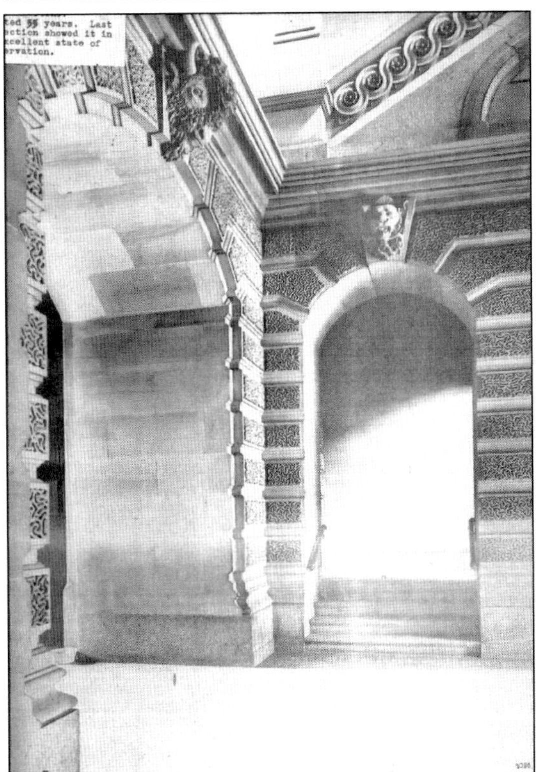

TRUMBULL COUNTY COURTHOUSE, WARREN. The Trumbull County Courthouse (1897), an example of Richardsonian Romanesque, was designed by architects LaBelle and French of Marion, Indiana, and constructed by E. M. Campfield of Findley. The sandstone was shipped to the courthouse site and cut to size. Clarence Darrow, the defense attorney in the 1925 Scopes trial, participated in trials at the courthouse. The building was listed in the National Register of Historic Places on December 31, 1974.

INTERIOR OF PHILADELPHIA CITY HALL, PHILADELPHIA, PENNSYLVANIA. Designed by John McArthur Jr. in the Second Empire style, Philadelphia City Hall (1871–1901) has interior walls of Amherst Gray sandstone with detailing and sculptures of animals and people representing the characteristics of humankind. Alexander Milne Calder in 1873 created over 250 sculptures, including the statue of William Penn, located on top. It was listed in the National Register of Historic Places on December 8, 1976.

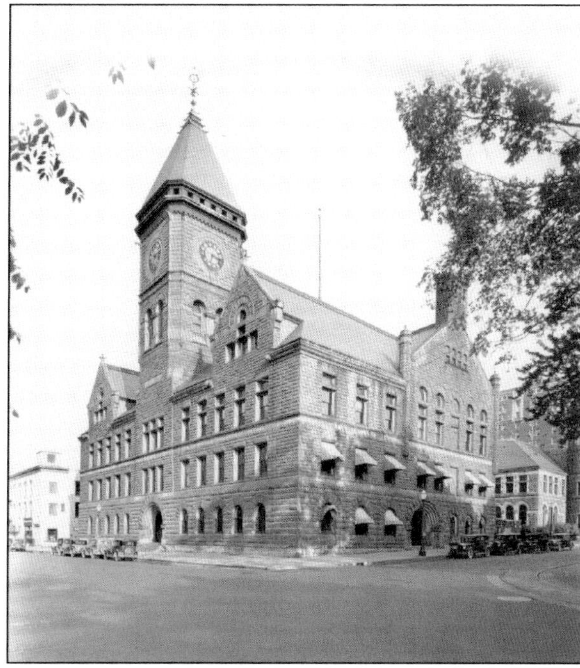

LANSING CITY HALL, LANSING, MICHIGAN. The Lansing City Hall (1897) was designed by Lansing architect Edwyn A. Bowd in the Richardsonian Romanesque style and features a tall central tower with a clock face on all four facades. City administrators constructed the monumental building to lure the county seat from Mason. However, the county seat was not moved, and Bowd built a new courthouse in Mason in 1902. Lansing City Hall was demolished in 1959.

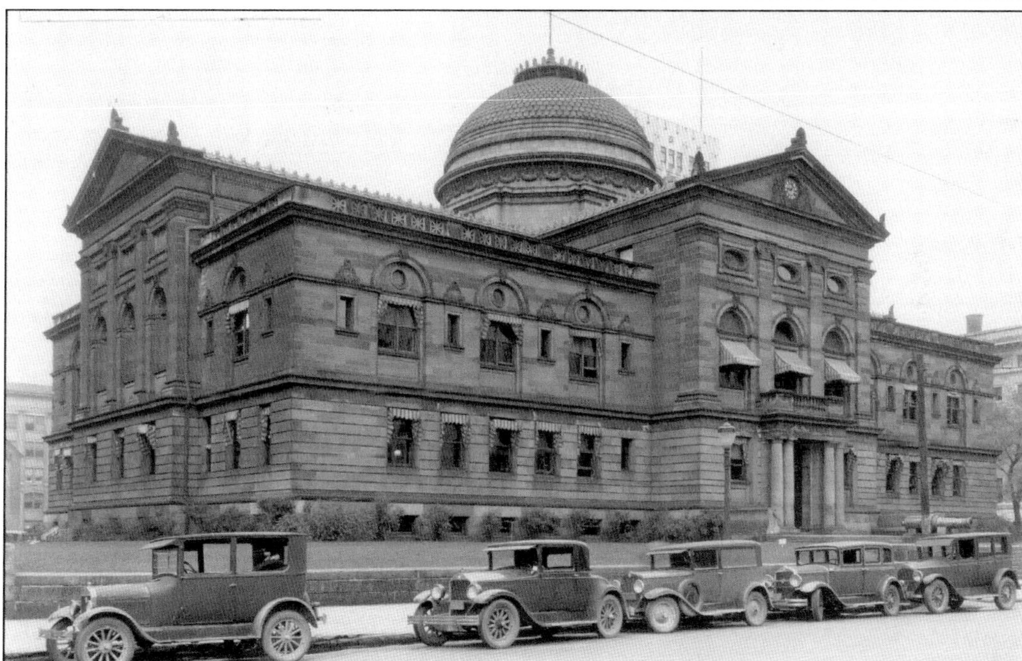

THIRD ST. JOSEPH COUNTY COURTHOUSE. The Third St. Joseph County Courthouse (1898) was designed by the Chicago architectural firm of Shepley, Rutan and Coolidge and constructed by James Stewart and Company in the neoclassical revival style using Amherst Buff sandstone. It replaced the smaller second courthouse, which was moved from its original location and is still standing in South Bend, Indiana. It was listed in the National Register of Historic Places on June 5, 1985.

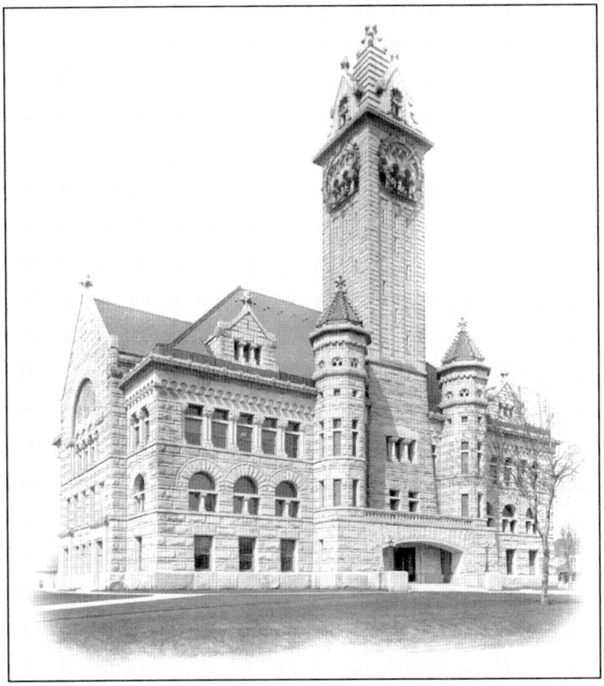

Wood County Courthouse, Bowling Green. The Wood County Courthouse was constructed between 1893 and 1896. The building was designed by Yost and Packard of Columbus in the Richardsonian Romanesque style and constructed by T. B. Townsend of Youngstown. The building features a 185-foot central tower with four separate clock faces built by the Howard Watch and Clock Company. The Wood County Courthouse was listed in the National Register of Historic Places on June 25, 1974.

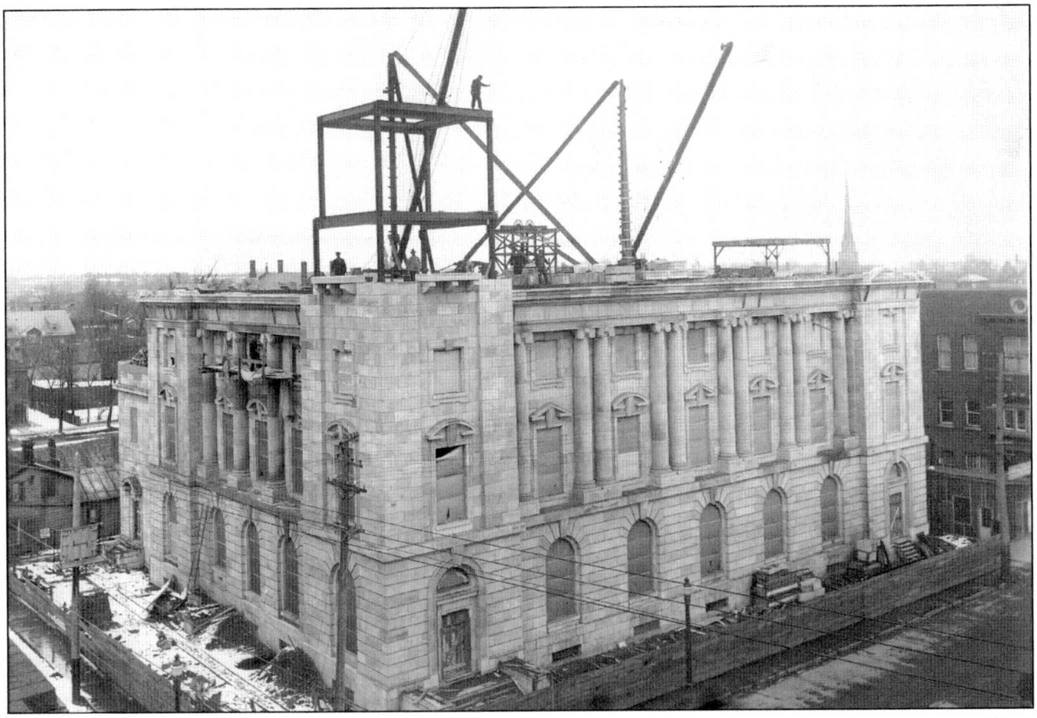

Brantford Post Office, Brantford, Ontario, Canada. The Brantford Federal Post Office and Customs building was constructed in 1913 and designed by Canada federal government's chief architect David Ewart in the Beaux-Arts style. Ewart was known for designing monumental buildings with grand towers, and this building fits that mold. As seen in the picture, it features a six-story tower under construction at the main corner of the two-story building.

BUFFALO CITY HALL, BUFFALO, NEW YORK. Construction of the Buffalo City Hall began in 1929 and was completed in 1932. Designed by architects Dietel, Wade, and Jones, it exemplifies the art deco style. Buckeye Gray sandstone is used throughout the building, as well as for the reliefs and sculptures, which represent industrial themes. It was listed in the National Register of Historic Places on January 15, 1999.

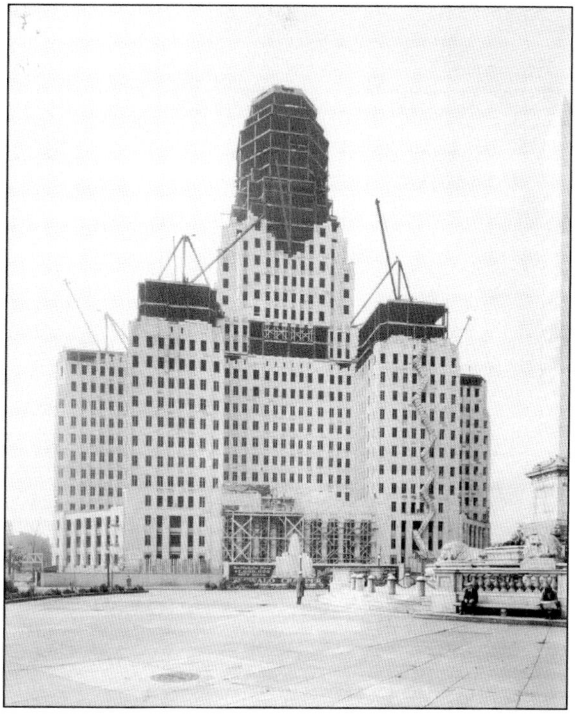

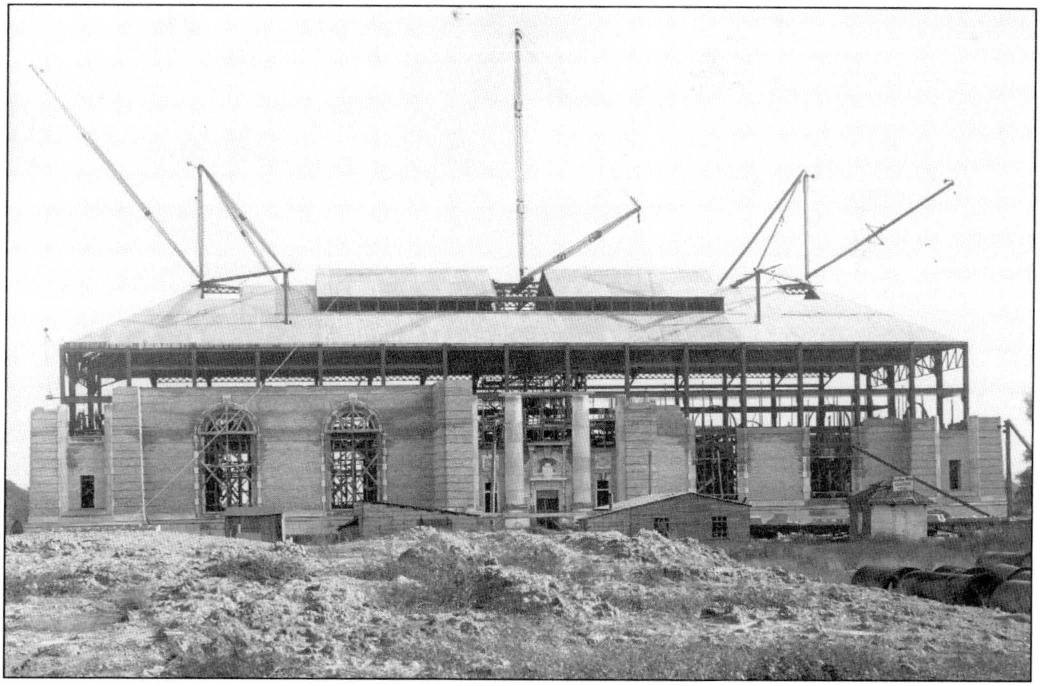

DETROIT PUMPING STATION, DETROIT, MICHIGAN. The City of Detroit started the Detroit Water Works in 1879. In response to rapid population growth in Detroit in the early 20th century, the city constructed several new buildings between 1909 and 1914. The picture above shows a second pumping station built by Blum and Delbridge of Amherst in 1911. Many of the new buildings looked similar to the neoclassical revival pumping station.

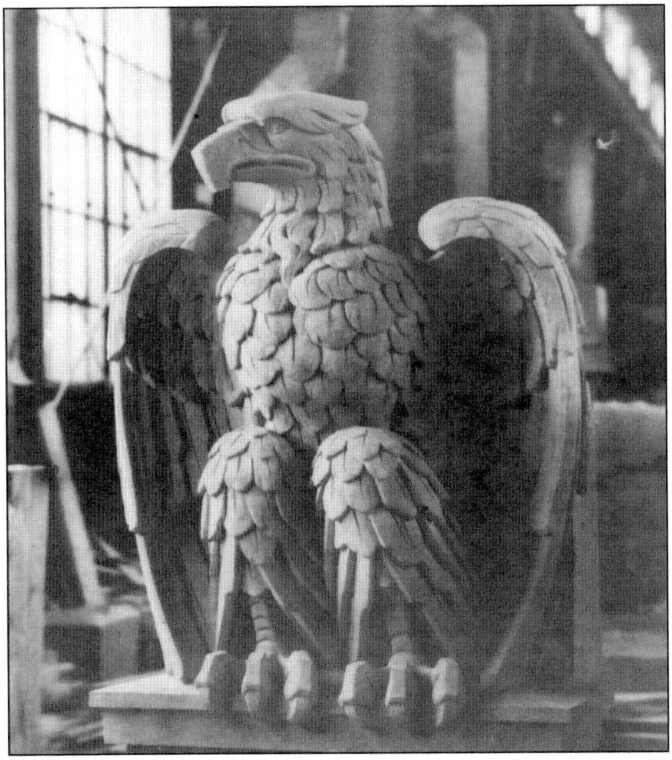

Sandstone Eagle at the Long Beach Municipal Auditorium, Long Beach, California. The Long Beach Municipal Auditorium (1930–1932) was designed by Cleveland architect Harold MacDowell. The architect's works include the public auditorium, also locally known as Public Hall, in downtown Cleveland. The 8,000-seat Long Beach Municipal Auditorium was a popular seaside resort that featured dances and concerts. Demolished in 1975, it was replaced by the Long Beach Convention and Entertainment Center.

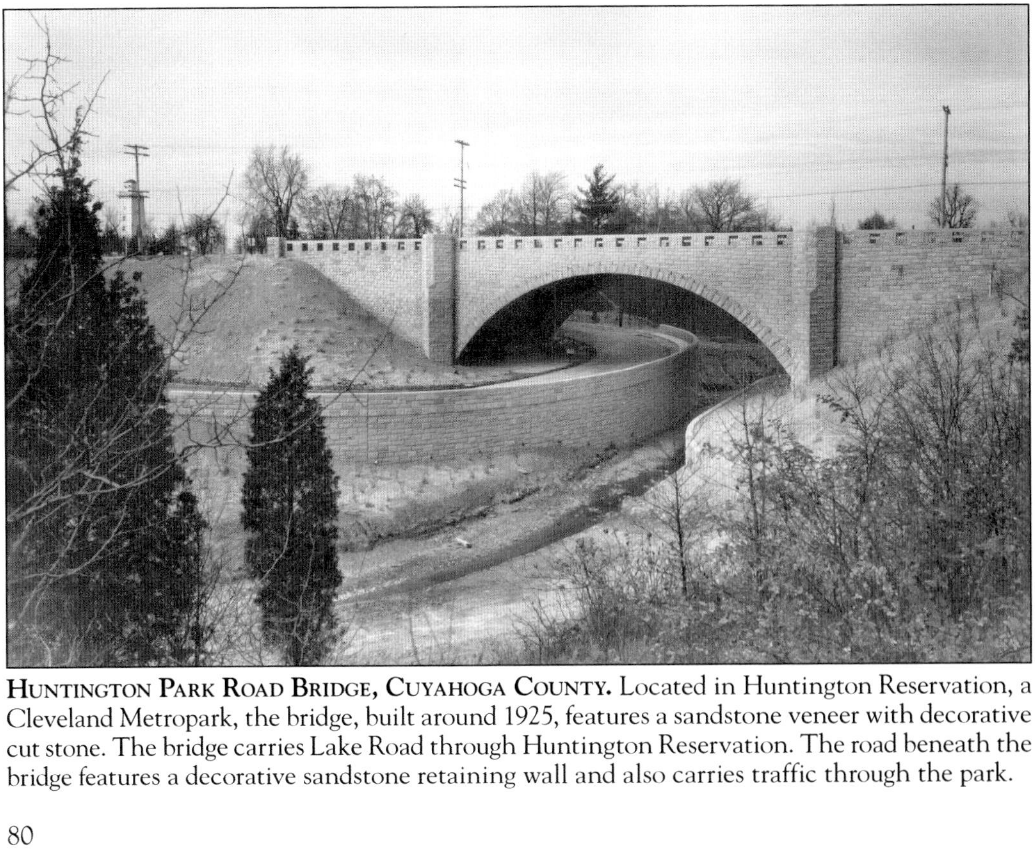

Huntington Park Road Bridge, Cuyahoga County. Located in Huntington Reservation, a Cleveland Metropark, the bridge, built around 1925, features a sandstone veneer with decorative cut stone. The bridge carries Lake Road through Huntington Reservation. The road beneath the bridge features a decorative sandstone retaining wall and also carries traffic through the park.

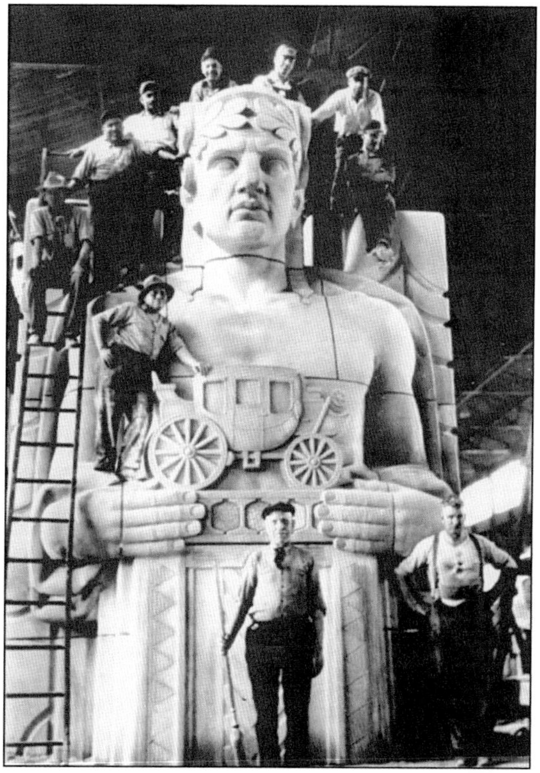

HOPE MEMORIAL BRIDGE, CLEVELAND. The Hope Memorial Bridge (1932), originally the Lorain-Carnegie Bridge, was renamed in 1983 for William Henry Hope, stonemason and father of Bob Hope. It connects Lorain and Carnegie Avenues on Cleveland's west side. This pylon (right) is one of four constructed for the bridge, featuring the Lords of Transportation, which were carved from 43-foot-tall slabs of Amherst sandstone. Each holds vehicles typifying advancements in transportation from covered wagon to truck. Cleveland architect Frank Walker and sculptor Henry Hering of New York City created the figures. The 5,865-foot span (below) features 132- to 299-foot cantilevered trusses. Rising 93 feet above the Cuyahoga River, it was designed by engineers Wilber J. Watson and Associates and Walker in the art deco style. It was listed in the National Register of Historic Places on October 8, 1976.

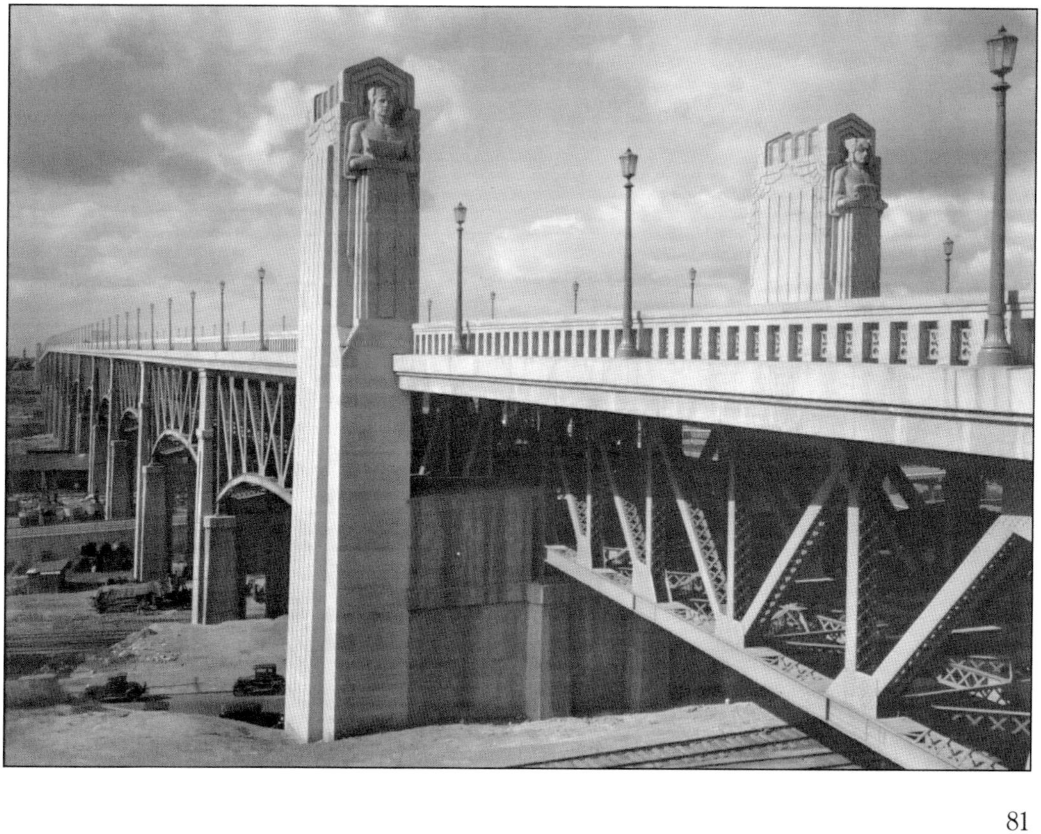

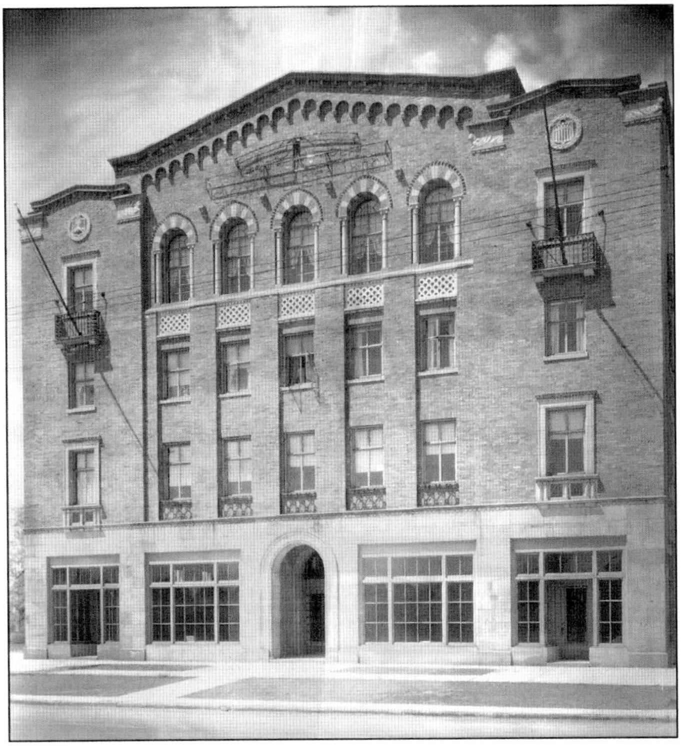

Slovenian Women's Club, Cleveland. The Slovenian Women's Club (above), also known as the Catholic Slovak Ladies Union, was constructed in 1929 and designed by the architectural firm of Fox, Duthie and Foose in the Italian Renaissance style. Before the construction of the building, organizational meetings and records where held in private homes. The building features a smooth finish with Birmingham Warmtone Buff sandstone trim. The general contractor was Crowell and Little Construction, and the cut stone contractor was the Ohio Cut Stone Company. The arched entrance (right) is constructed of Birmingham Warmtone Buff sandstone and features delicate cable molding. In the top of the arch is the phrase "URODOVEN PRVEJ KATOLICKEJ SLOVENSKEJ ZENSKEJ JEDNOTY," which translates to "Office in First Catholic Slovak Ladies Union." Anna Hurban, a Slovakian-born woman from Cleveland, founded the first Catholic Slovak Ladies Union in 1892.

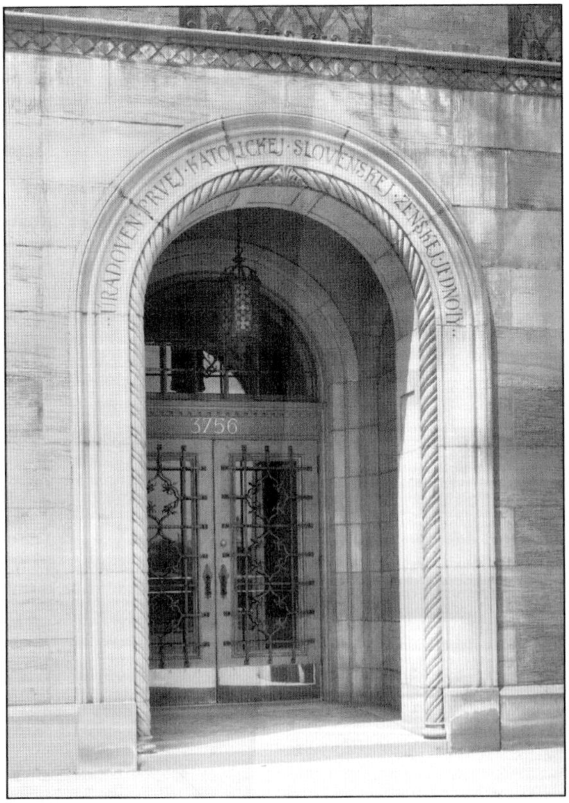

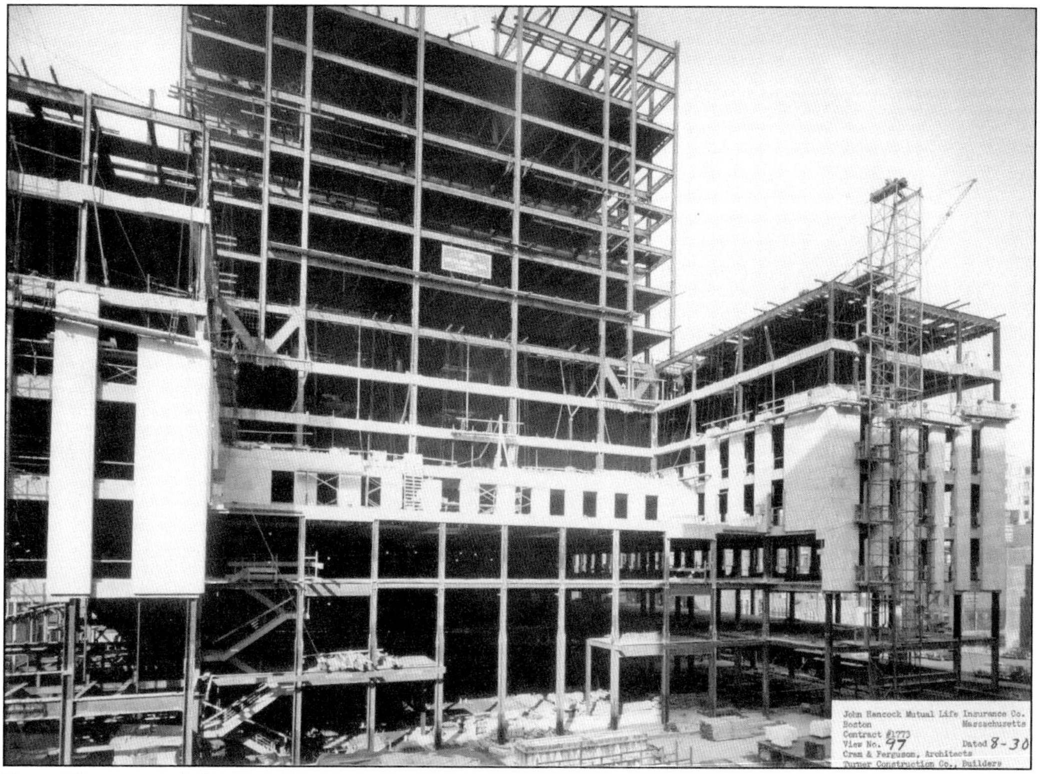

JOHN HANCOCK MUTUAL LIFE INSURANCE COMPANY BUILDING, BOSTON, MASSACHUSETTS. The photograph above shows the early stages of construction of the John Hancock Mutual Life Insurance Company building. The building was designed by the architectural firm of Cram and Ferguson in the art deco style in 1947. Built by the prolific Turner Construction company, it is one of many renowned buildings credited to the firm. The photograph reveals the steel-frame construction that supports the Amherst sandstone exterior. The almost-finished John Hancock Mutual Life Insurance Company building (right) was the second of three John Hancock buildings constructed in Boston. The 36-story building is 495 feet tall. From 1947 until 1964, the old John Hancock building, as it is now called, was the tallest building in Back Bay and second tallest in the city.

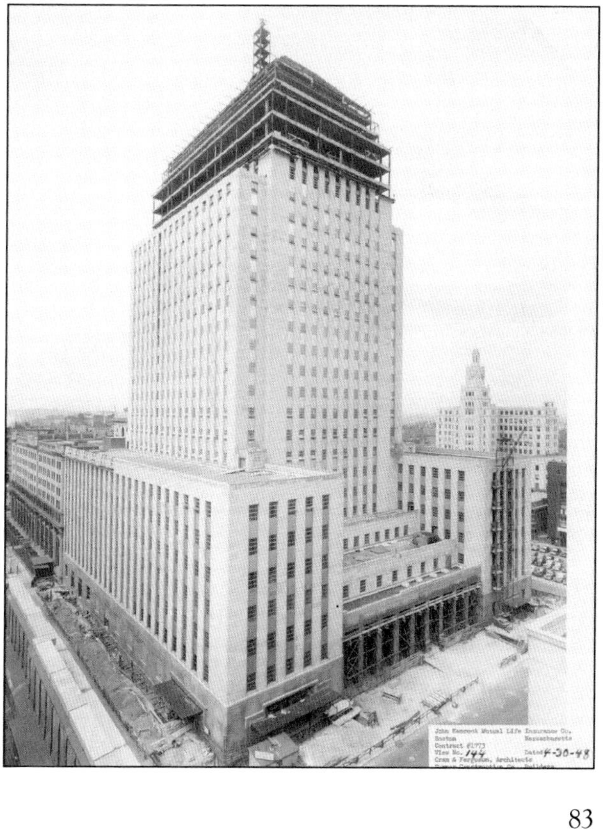

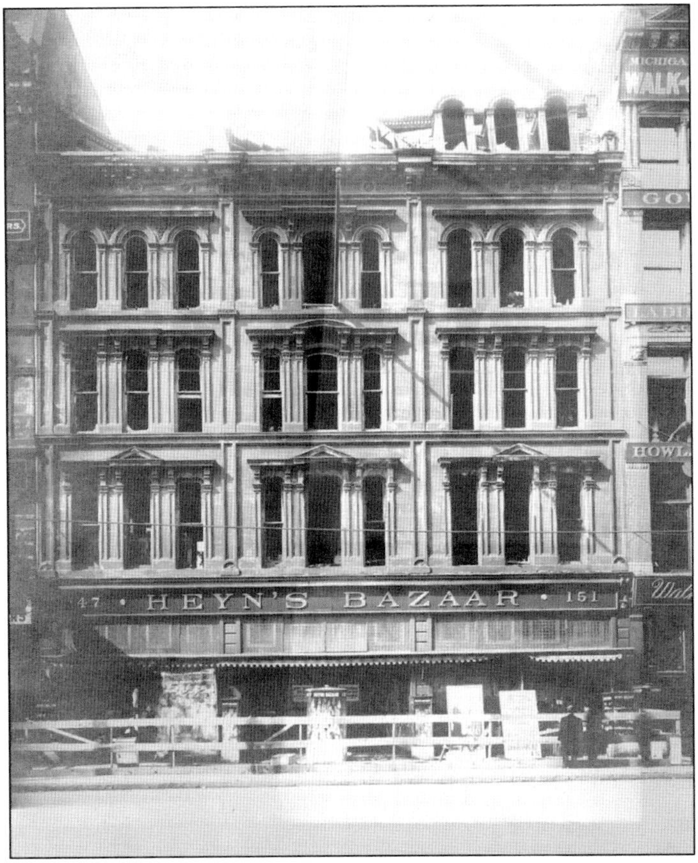

HEYNS BAZAAR, DETROIT, MICHIGAN. The Heynes Bazaar in downtown Detroit, Michigan, was constructed in 1861 and suffered a devastating fire in 1909. The building features Greek Revival and Italianate stylistic elements. The picture to the left shows the collapse of the mansard roof all the way to the ground floor. The building was constructed of Amherst Gray Canyon sandstone.

WISE BUILDING, CLEVELAND. The Wise building was designed by Albert Skeel in 1905. It incorporated decorative brick detailing on the front facade. The ground floor featured smooth stone columns framing three-bay storefronts with large display windows and transoms. The building was located at 6408 Euclid Avenue but has been demolished.

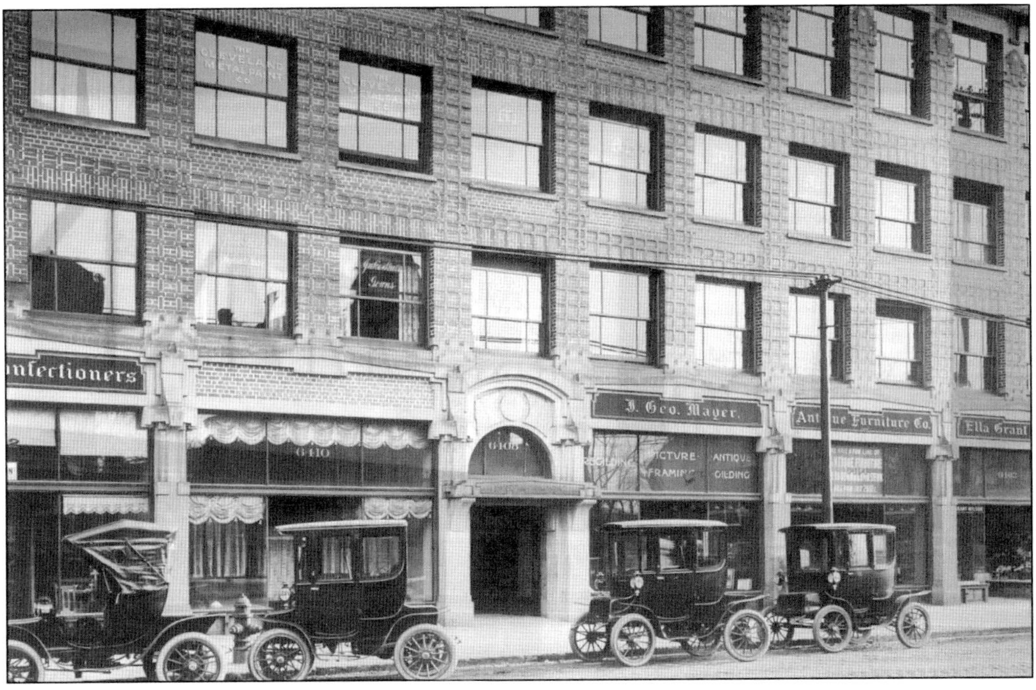

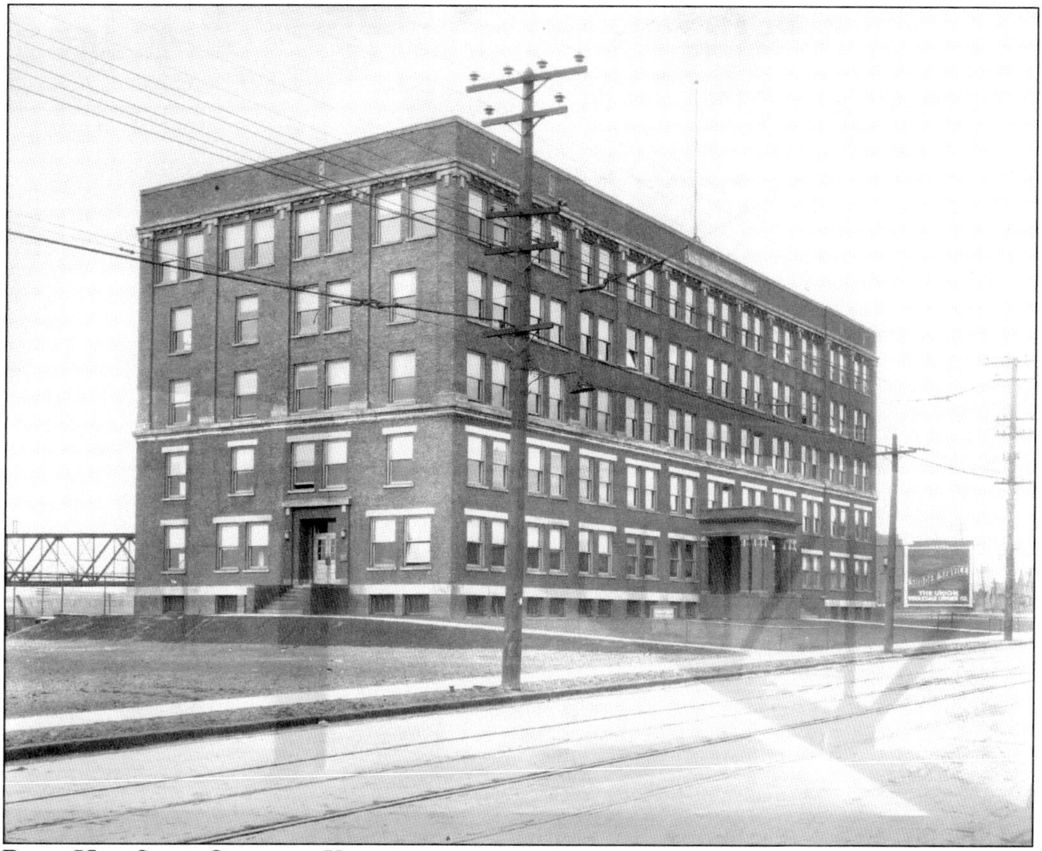

Brier Hill Steel Company, Youngstown, Ohio. The firm that became the Brier Hill Steel Company had its origins in the mid-19th century under the auspices of the Tod family. It was formally reorganized as Brier Hill Steel Company in 1912. The office building was constructed in the neoclassical revival style just prior to the company's purchase by the Youngstown Sheet and Tube Company in 1923. Amherst sandstone was used in the trim, sills, water tables, and lintels.

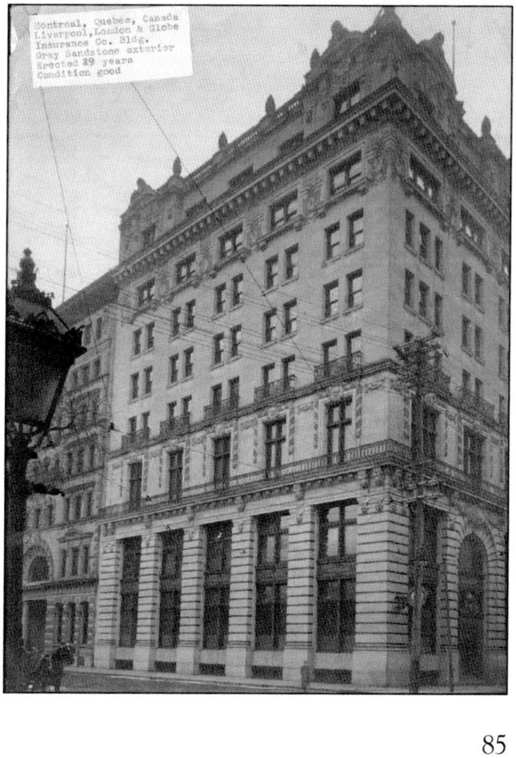

Liverpool, London and Globe Insurance Company Building, Montreal, Quebec, Canada. The ornate Liverpool, London and Globe Insurance Company building was constructed in 1901 by the architectural firm of Nobbs and Hyde in the Beaux-Arts style. The building served as the company's main headquarters. It featured a monumental two-story base with ornate window and door surrounds and wrought-iron balustrades and balconets. The building has been demolished.

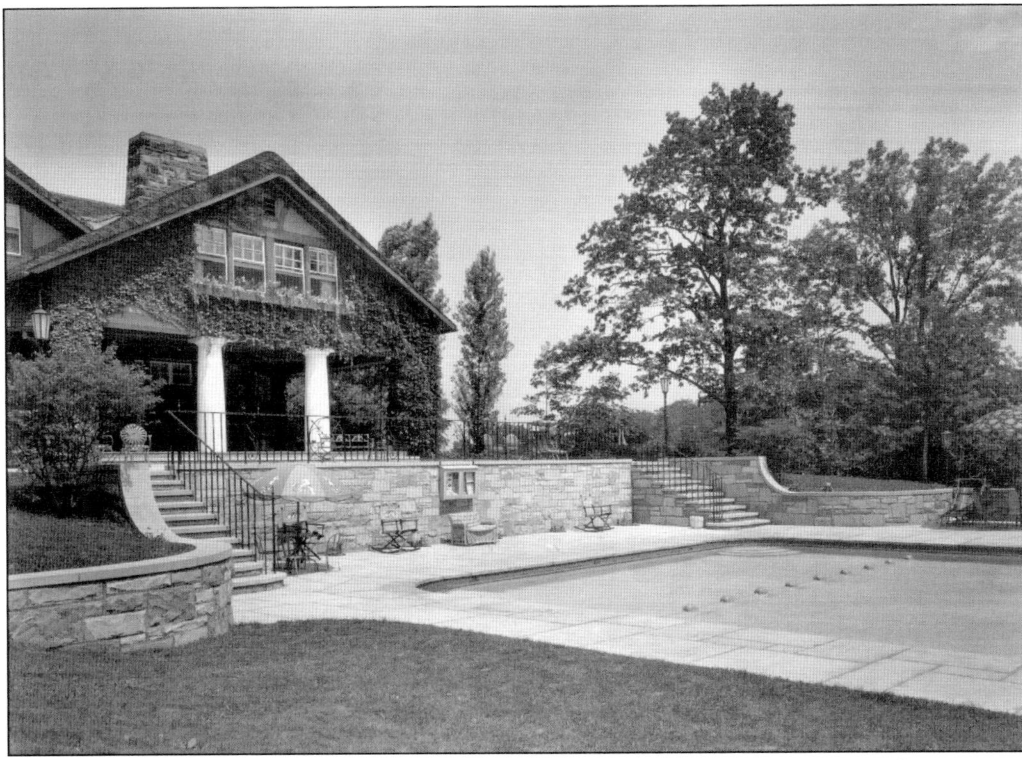

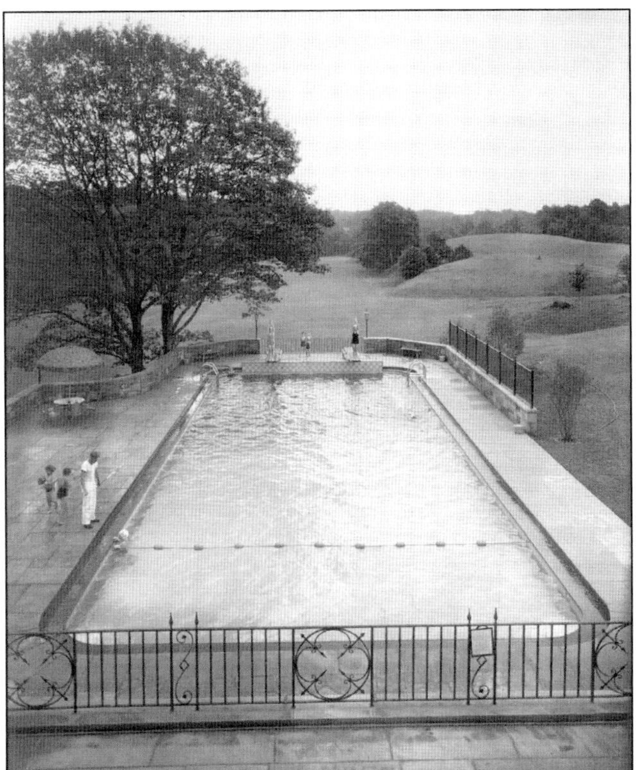

MAYFIELD COUNTRY CLUB SWIMMING POOL, CLEVELAND, OHIO. The Mayfield County Club (above) was established in 1911 and the swimming pool was added in 1931. At that time, few country clubs offered swimming. The Mayfield County Club swimming pool (left) was designed by William Pitkin Jr. and Seward H. Mott, landscape architects. Pitkin and Mott were from Cleveland and designed several swimming pools and bathhouses in that area. The swimming pool was constructed with Birmingham Warmtone Buff sandstone.

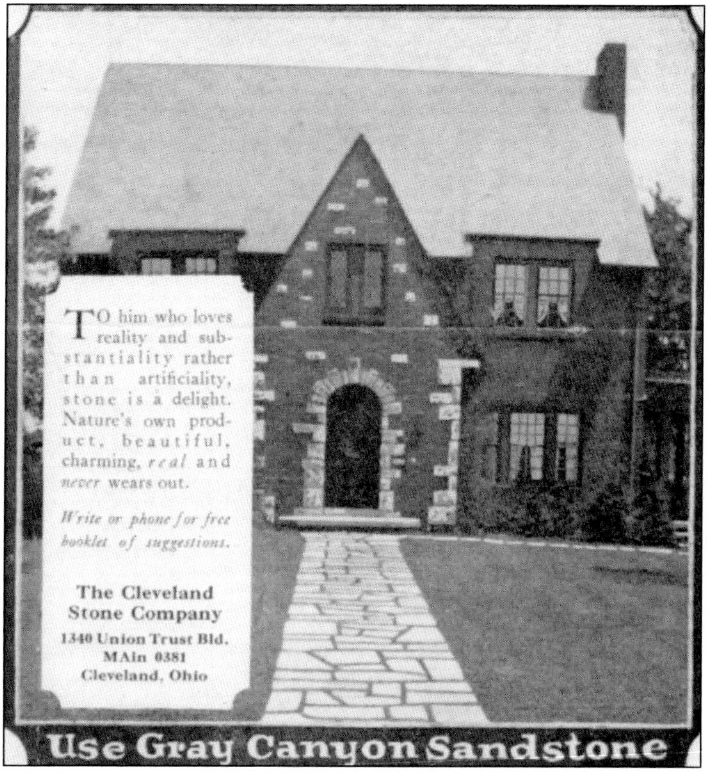

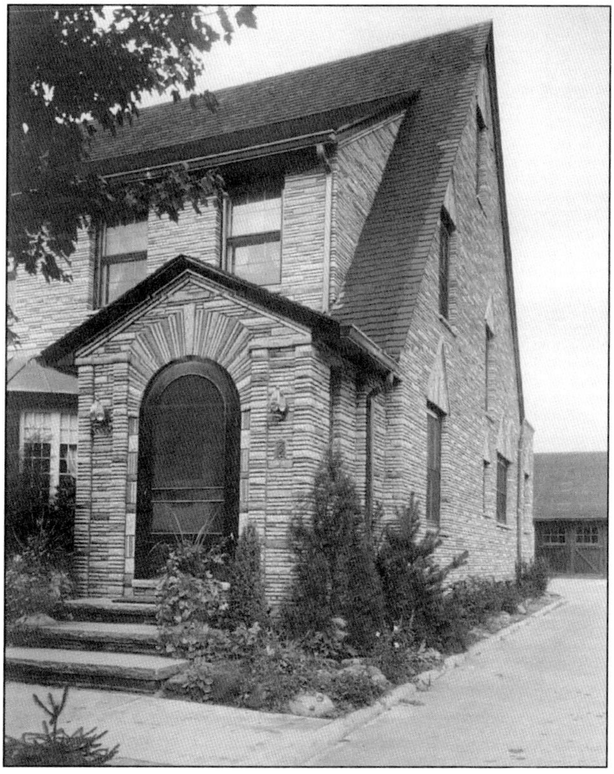

AMHERST STONE IN DOMESTIC ARCHITECTURE. The advertisement (above) for the Cleveland Stone Company was intended for the *Ohio Motorist* in May 1928. It features uses of Amherst sandstone for residential construction and landscaping design. It targeted an audience that "loves reality and substantiality rather than artificiality." The Schloss house in Cleveland Heights (left) exemplifies the use of Amherst sandstone for domestic construction. Built in 1932 during the Great Depression, it illustrates the adaptability of stone to various architectural design elements. While known especially for use in monumental structures like Boston's old John Hancock building, Amherst stone companies also marketed their product for smaller projects.

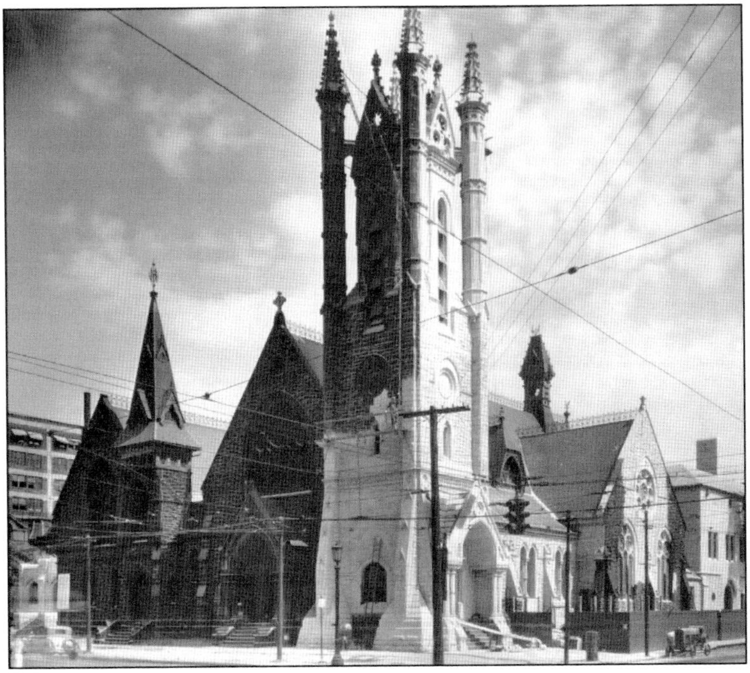

The Church of the Conversion of St. Paul, Cleveland, Ohio. Founded as St. Paul's Episcopal Church, the core was constructed in 1875. Purchased and renamed the Church of the Conversion of St. Paul by the Roman Catholic Church in 1930, it was cleaned and enlarged in 1931. The Amherst Buff sandstone Gothic Revival building features a soaring corner bell tower. It was listed in the National Register of Historic Places on November 25, 1980.

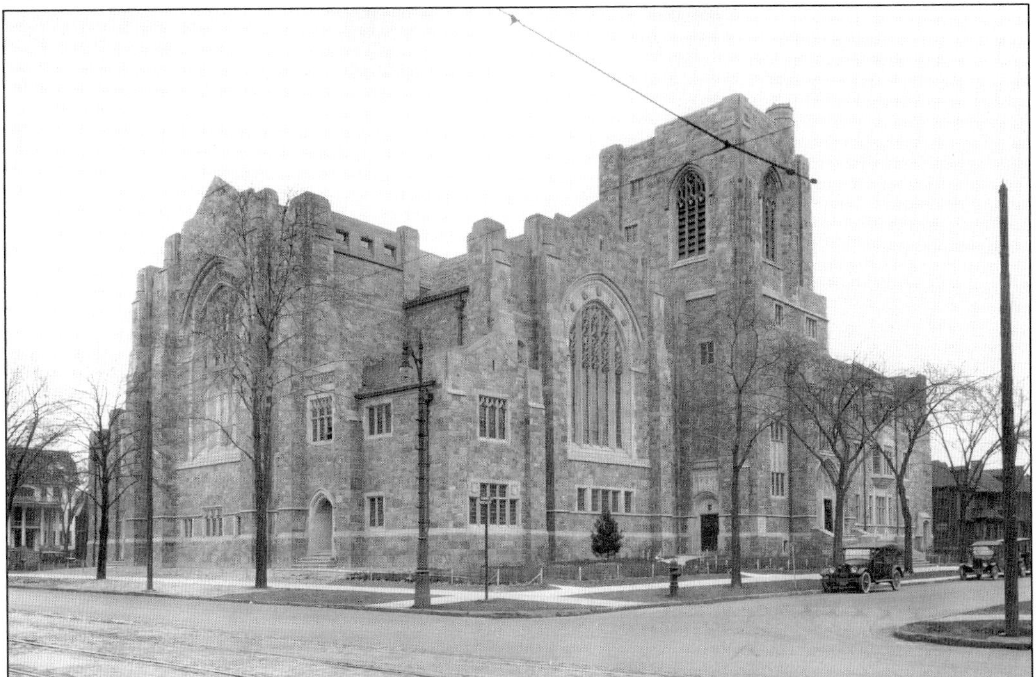

North Woodward Avenue Methodist Episcopal Church, Detroit, Michigan. The North Woodward Avenue Methodist Episcopal Church (1922–1926), now Metropolitan United Methodist Church, is an excellent example of the late Gothic Revival style designed by architect and church member William N. E. Hunter. Its cruciform footprint dominates the city block. The projecting gable ends feature decorative tracery windows. It was listed in the National Register of Historic Places on August 3, 1982.

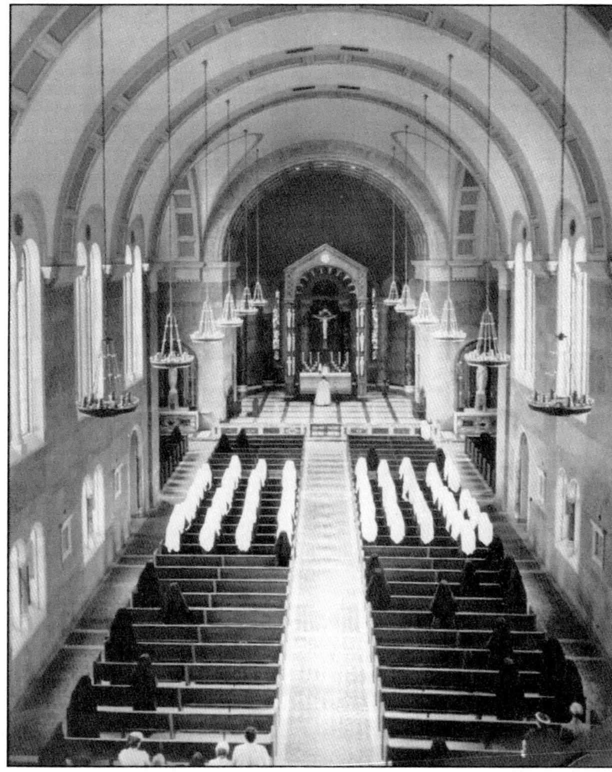

Assisi Heights, Rochester, Minnesota. Assisi Heights, also known as the Mother House, was constructed between 1952 and 1955 by the architectural firm of Maguolo and Quick from St. Louis, Missouri. It was constructed to appear as an older building, representing the Italian Renaissance style, an architectural style popular in the early 20th century. Assisi Heights and its grounds are located on the site of the demolished St. Clare Novitiate School.

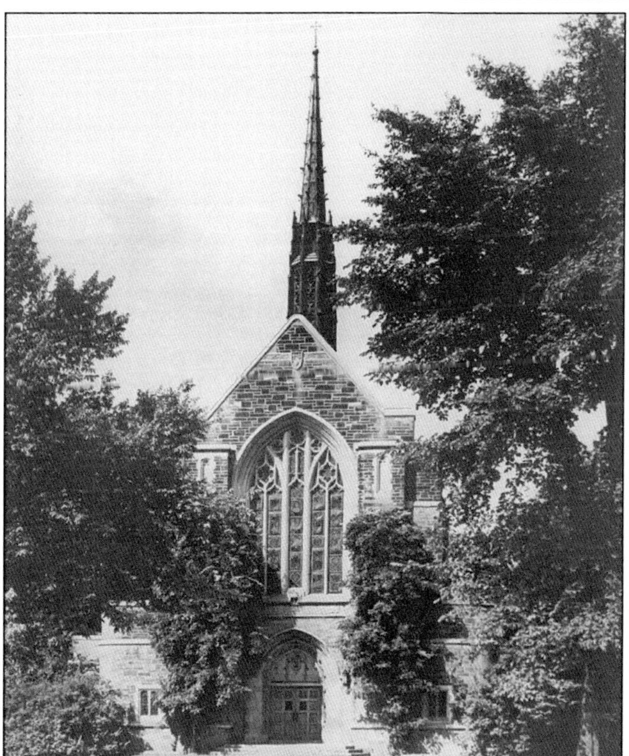

Harbison Chapel, Grove City College, Grove City, Pennsylvania. Harbison Chapel was built between 1929 and 1930 to serve as the religious center of Grove City College. The building is an excellent example of the late Gothic Revival style and conforms to the cruciform plan. The exterior of the building features Amherst Sawn Bed Ashlar cut stone and a large tracery window above the main entrance.

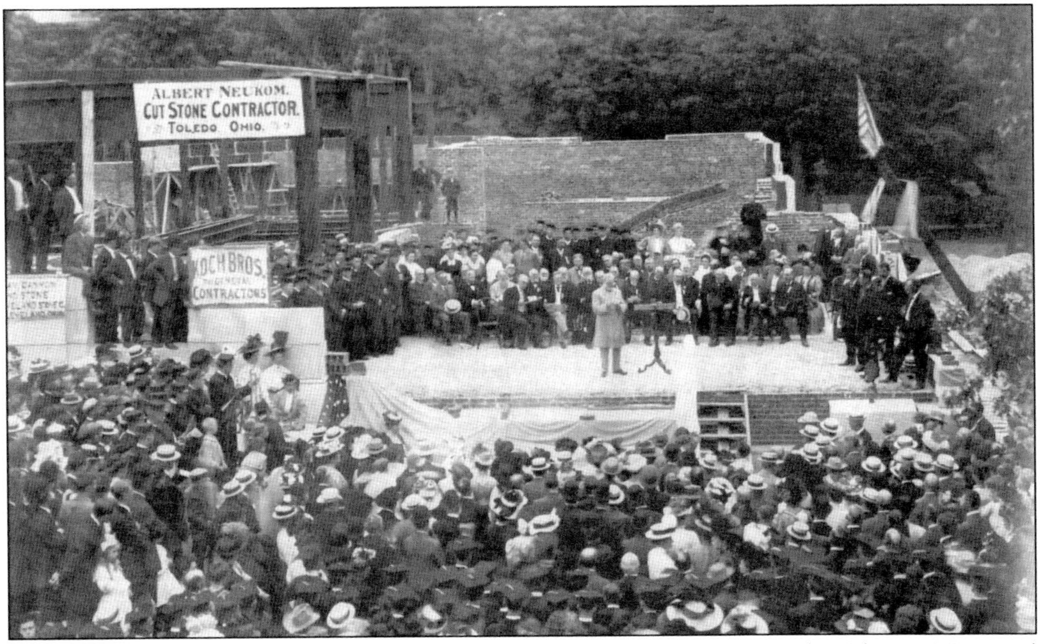

ALUMNI MEMORIAL BUILDING, UNIVERSITY OF MICHIGAN, ANN ARBOR. The Alumni Memorial building was constructed between 1907 and 1910 and designed by the architectural firm of Donaldson and Meier from Detroit in the neoclassical revival style. The building, constructed of Amherst Gray Canyon stone, also functions as a war memorial by featuring a plaque, designed by New York sculptor A. A. Weinmen, commemorating the men from the university killed in armed conflicts.

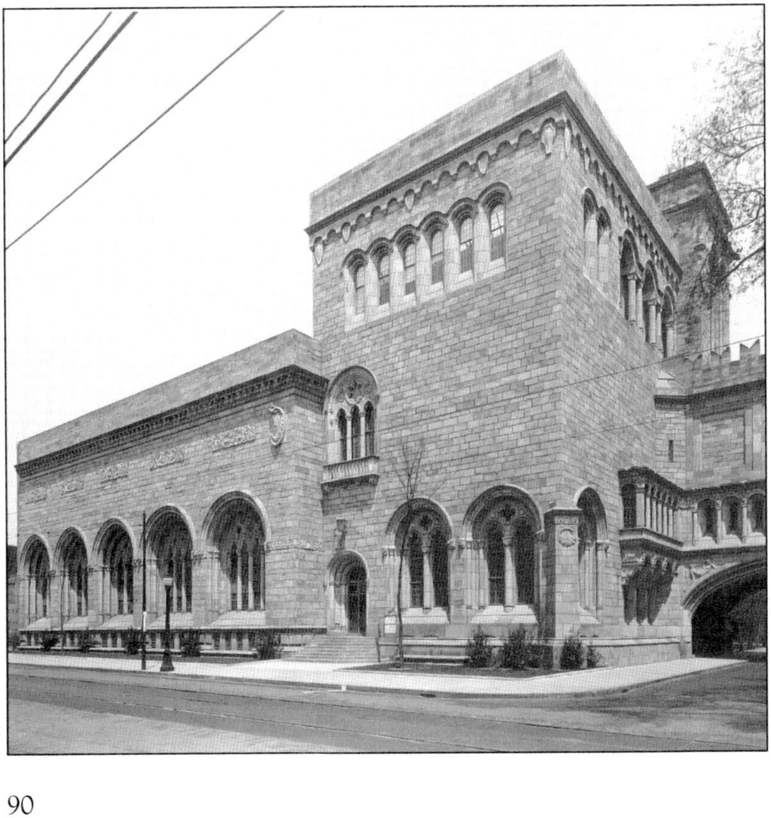

GALLERY OF FINE ARTS BUILDING, YALE UNIVERSITY, NEW HAVEN, CONNECTICUT. The Gallery of Fine Arts building was constructed in 1928 and designed by Egerton Swartwout, a Yale graduate, in the Romanesque Revival style. The building was constructed with Birmingham Buff and Mahogany stone. In 1953, a Modernist-style addition designed by Louis I. Kahn was added to the 1928 building. The addition connects the first and third floors of the two buildings.

Cleveland Heights High School, Ohio. Cleveland Heights High School (1925) was designed by architects Franz Childs Warner and W. R. McCormack in the Jacobethan or Collegiate Gothic style. The building features the use of brick and Buckeye Gray sandstone to create the polychromatic color scheme so prominent on the building. Originally constructed to serve as a combined academic and technical high school, the building has been enlarged with several additions to accommodate the growing student body.

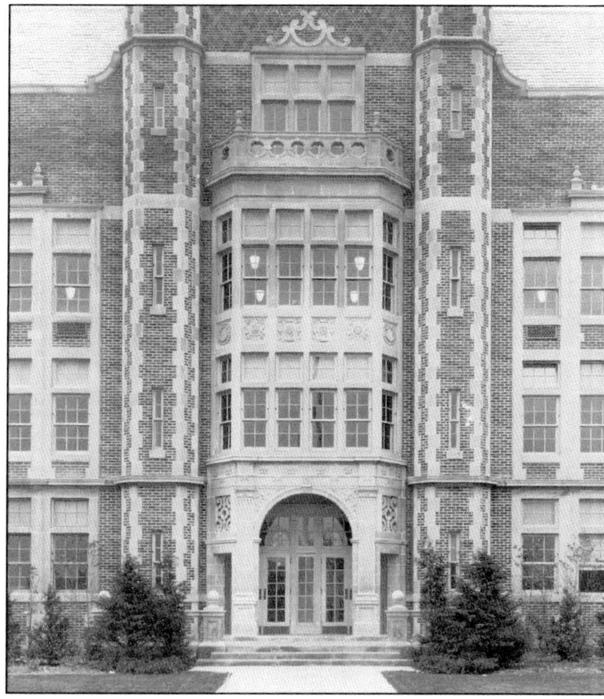

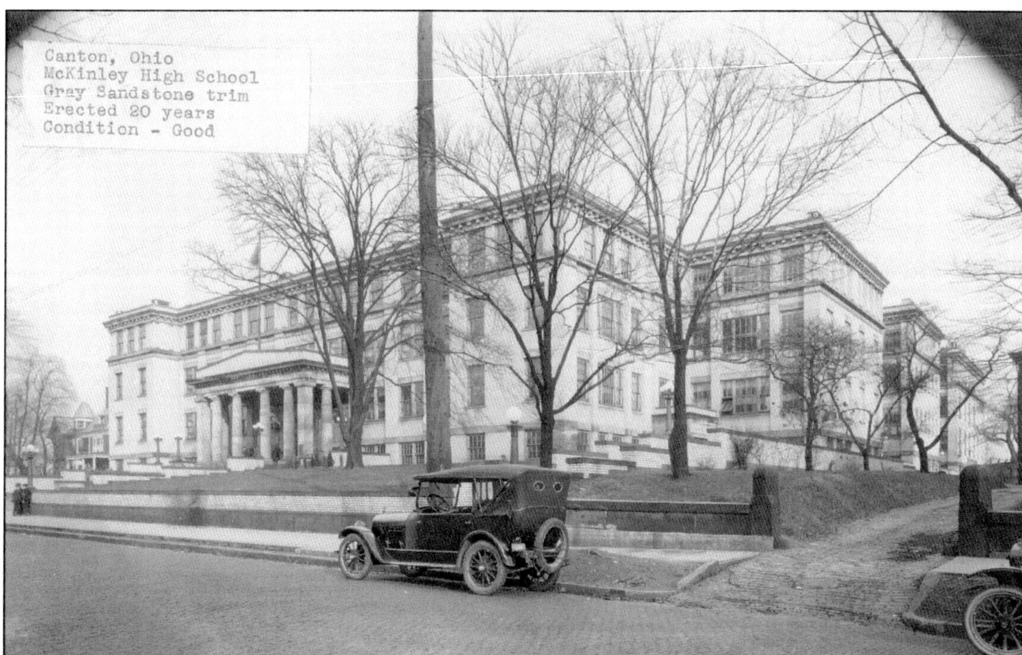

McKinley High School, Canton, Ohio. McKinley High School (1916–1921) was designed by George F. Hammond, a Cleveland architect, in the neoclassical revival style. The school was named after William McKinley, the nation's 25th president, who lived in Canton. The building features a large temple front entrance and Buckeye Gray sandstone trim to create the classical elements of the entablature, dentils, and stone bonding. It was listed in the National Register of Historic Places on July 30, 1982.

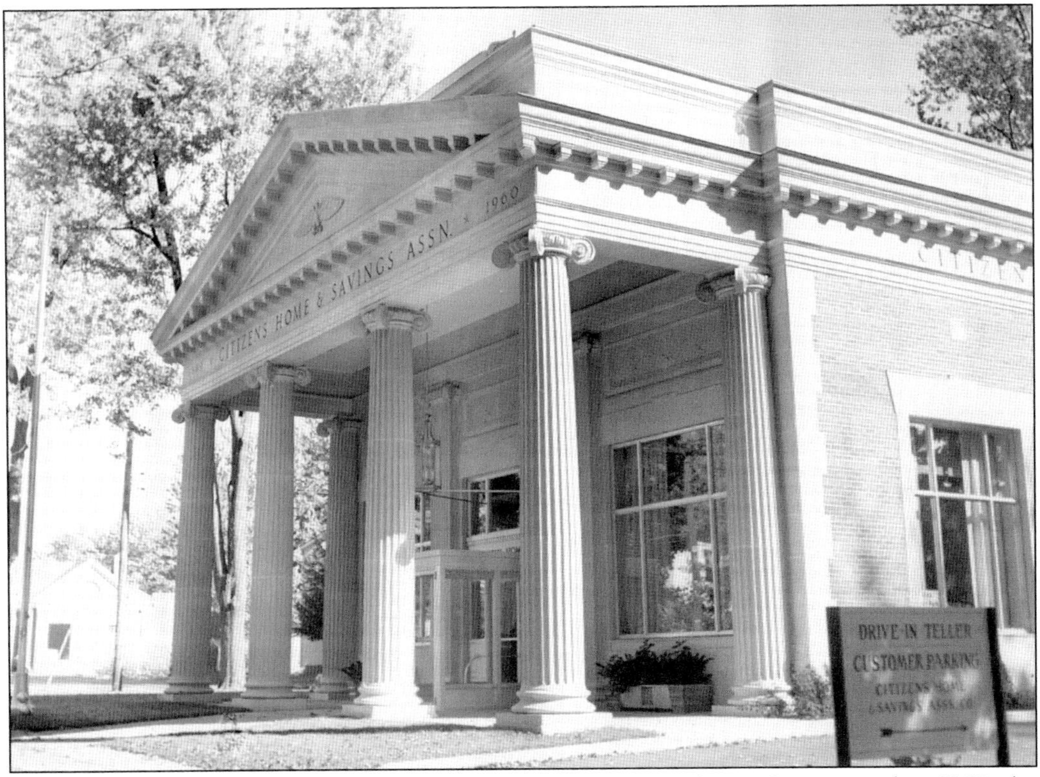

Citizen's Home and Savings Association Bank, Amherst, Ohio. Constructed in 1960, the Citizen's Home and Savings Association Bank replaced an earlier 1922 building, although the corporation itself dates from 1889. Designed by A. C. Lenander of Columbus with T. S. Hume Company of Lorain as the general contractor, the new bank is in the neoclassical revival style and is clad in Amherst Gray sandstone. Citizen's is the oldest savings and loan institution in Lorain County.

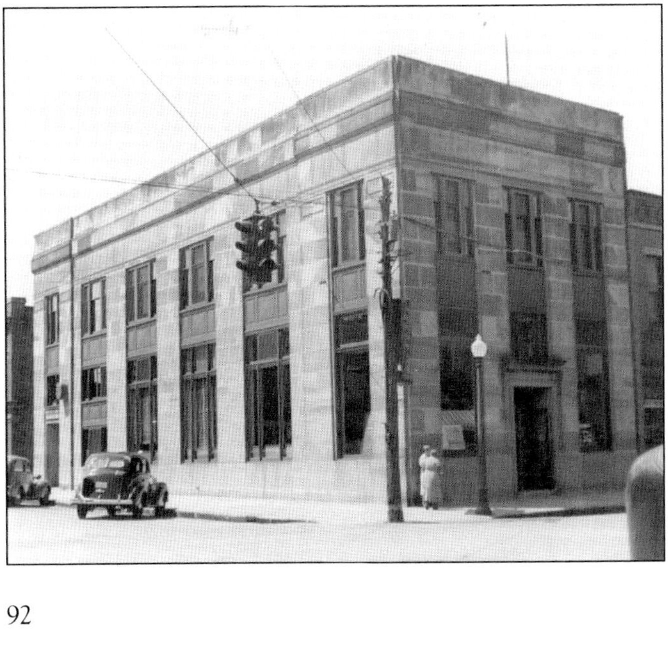

Lorain County Savings and Trust, Amherst, Ohio, Branch. In 1896, the brick Lorain County Savings and Trust building was refaced in Birmingham Hard Gray and Variegated Buff sandstone in the neoclassical revival style. It was designed by Cincinnati architects Webber and Webber, with Lorain contractor Graupner and Ule Construction. Originally called the Amherst Savings and Banking Company, it liquidated in December 1929, a victim of the Great Depression. It reopened in 1933 as Lorain County Savings and Trust.

Seven

A New Era

Amherst, as it nears the bicentennial celebration of its founding, continues to adapt and reflect the needs of its residents. While there are new faces and new enterprises, its focus remains on maintaining the quality of life for its people. Firmly committed to life in 21st century America, the community also sustains a firm connection to its past.

Gone are the one-room schoolhouses, replaced by consolidated schools, well equipped to educate students for the new century. The quarries, long the financial lifeblood of the community, have been replaced by a multitude of enterprises focusing on the technologies of the future. Amherst, unlike many of its counterparts, has found ways to move forward while integrating and making usable its physical and cultural past. Main Street coexists with suburban residential and commercial developments. Chain restaurants and the locally owned eateries both thrive. Old buildings are adapted, restored, expanded, and reused to fit contemporary needs. Today, Amherst residents have the best of both worlds.

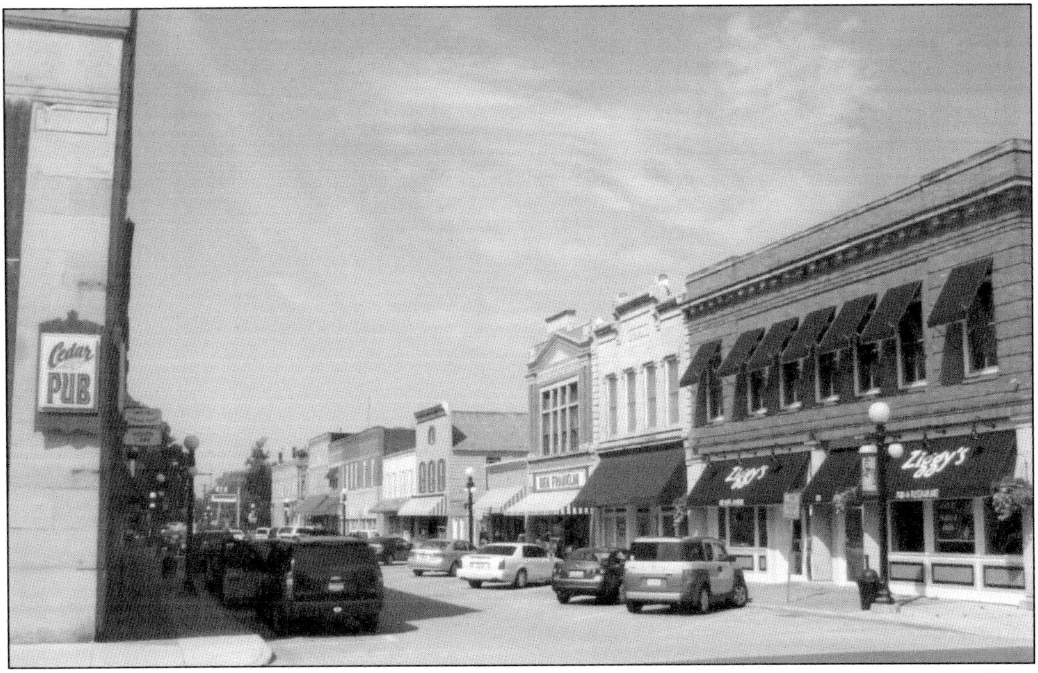

PARK AVENUE TODAY. Evidence of the activity of the Amherst Main Street program is nowhere more visible than on Park Avenue. The Main Street program, a project of the National Trust for Historic Preservation, was established in Amherst in 1999. A leading force for the revitalization of downtowns throughout the nation, the Main Street program emphasizes preservation of existing structures, encouraging their rehabilitation and reuse by businesses old and new.

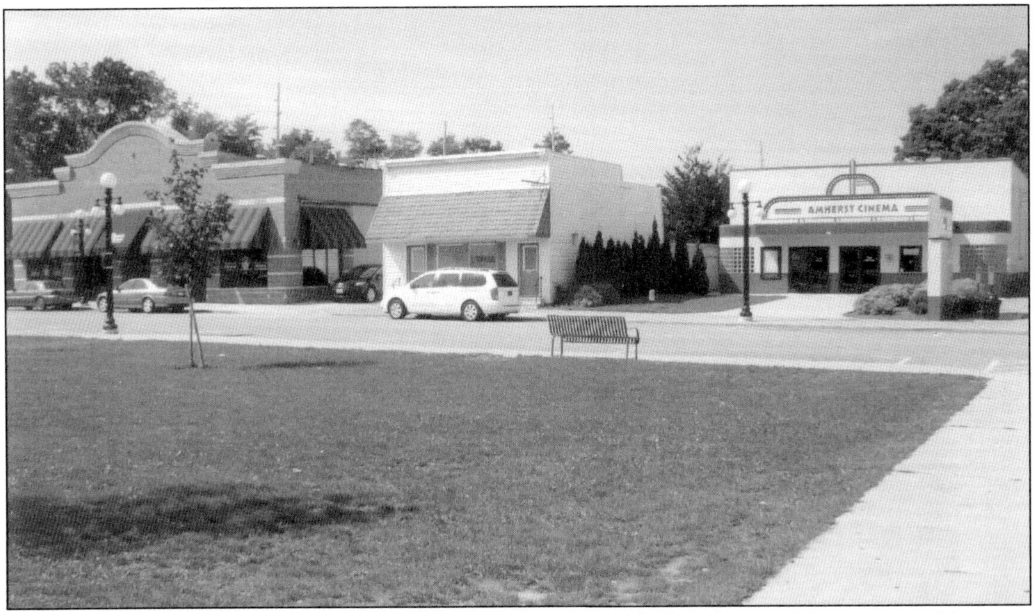

CHURCH STREET TODAY. This Church Street block is a blend of modern construction and historic fabric. It features the refaced Church Street Bar and Grill, the J. Taylor Salon housed in an early 1800s building, the city's original town hall moved from The Corners and a newly constructed Amherst Cinema, replacing the old Empire Cinema, across the street.

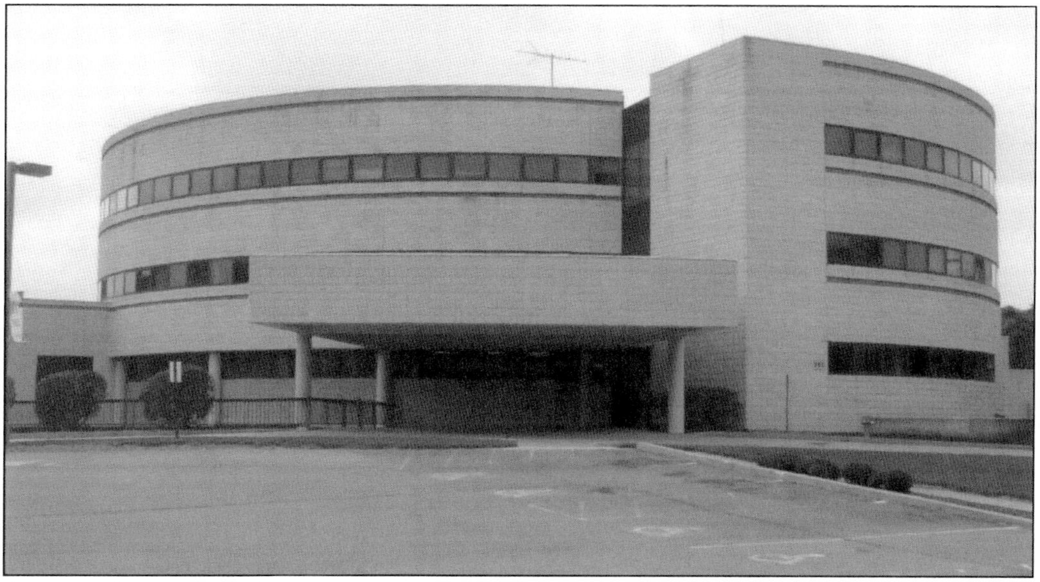

Amherst Hospital. Still an integral part of the community's life, Amherst Hospital has seen both new construction and adaptive reuse of its original building. In June 1978, the hospital dedicated a new 100-bed facility located adjacent to the original structure. Connected by an enclosed walkway, the old portion of the hospital now serves as offices and laboratory space.

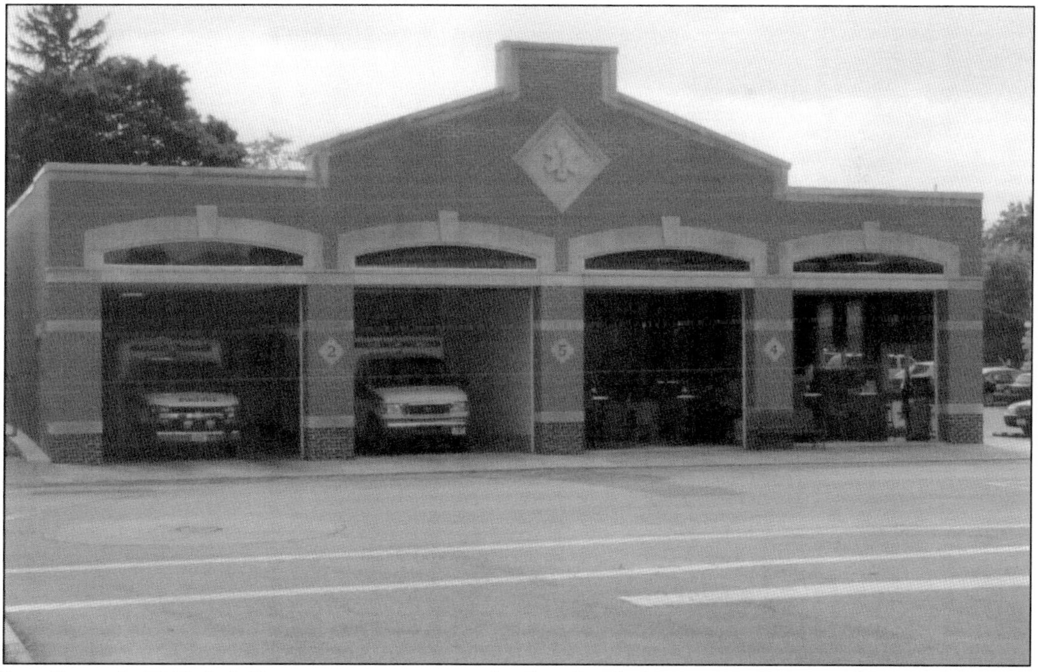

LifeCare. In 2009, LifeCare, an emergency medical and ambulance service, opened its operations in Amherst. In the best spirit of the community, the facility is housed in what had been an automobile repair shop on Park Avenue. It shares the space with a small coffee shop, Perk Avenue.

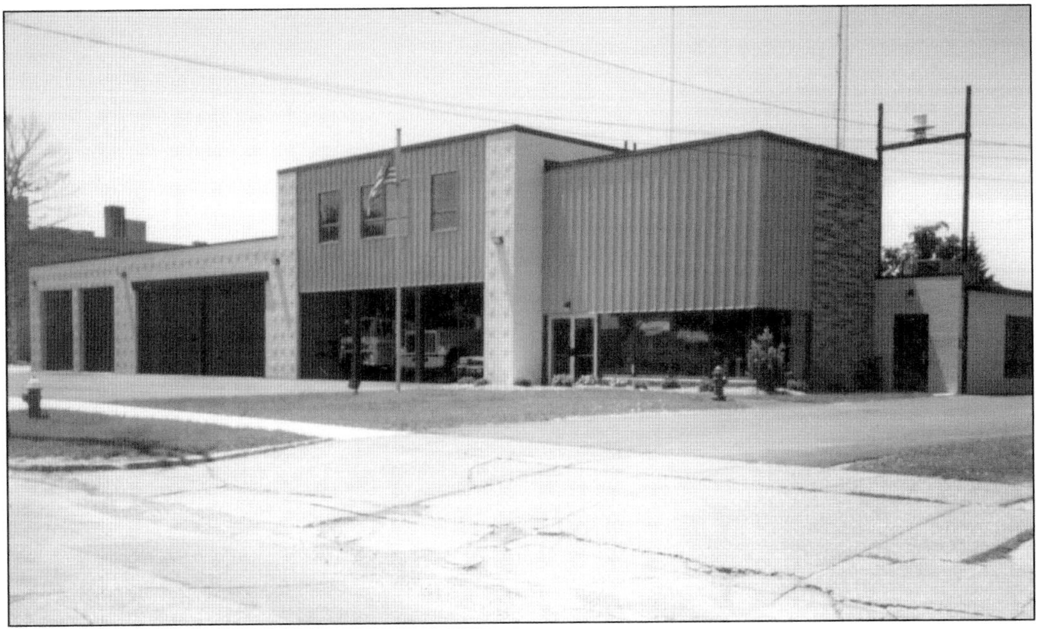

Amherst Safety Services. Once housed in the basement of city hall, the Amherst Police and Fire Departments later moved to larger and more modern facilities. The fire department (above) built a new structure in 1959, located at 414 Church Street. It completed an addition in 1996. The police department (below) moved into its new facility on North Lake Street in 1996. The Modernist structure houses both police headquarters and a jail.

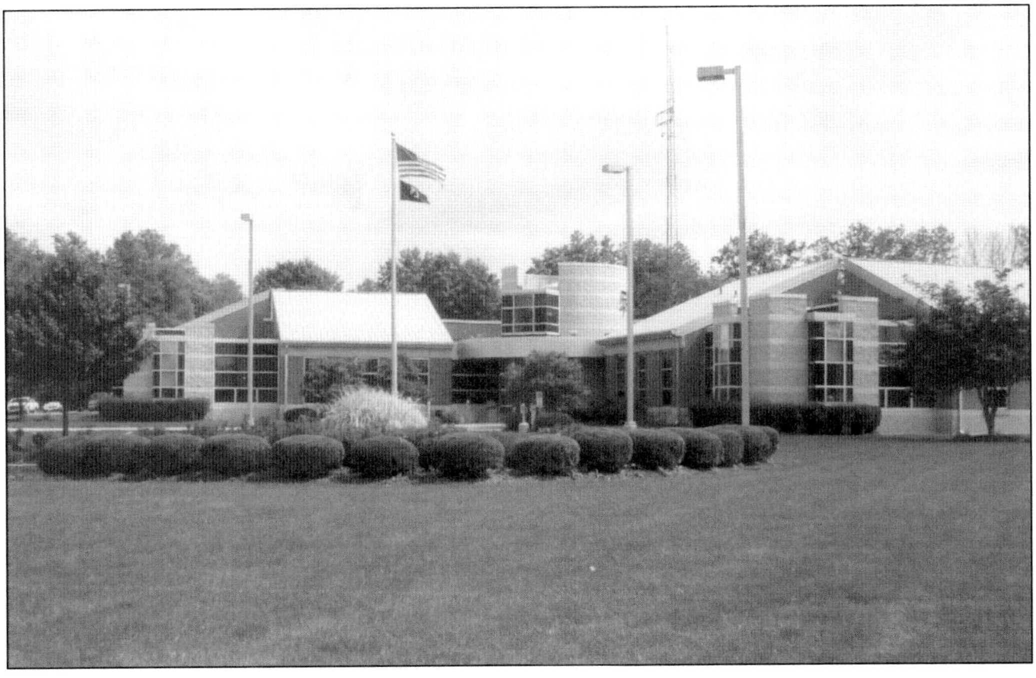

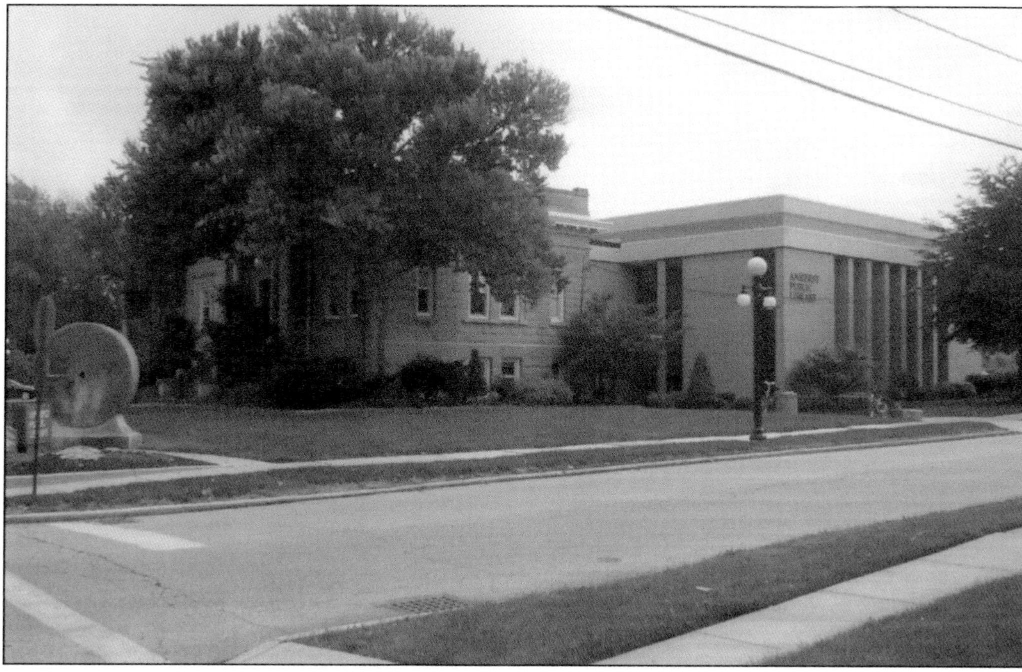

AMHERST PUBLIC LIBRARY. By the mid-1970s, the needs of a growing population required an expansion of its public library services. Unwilling to abandon their iconic historic structure, the library built an addition (above), designed by Clark and Post in 1976. The new structure allowed for an expanded collection and additional multimedia facilities. It is estimated that more than 14,000 visits are made to the library each month. Serving its clientele (below) from left to right are Janet Turner, the reference services manager, and Robin Wood, the library director.

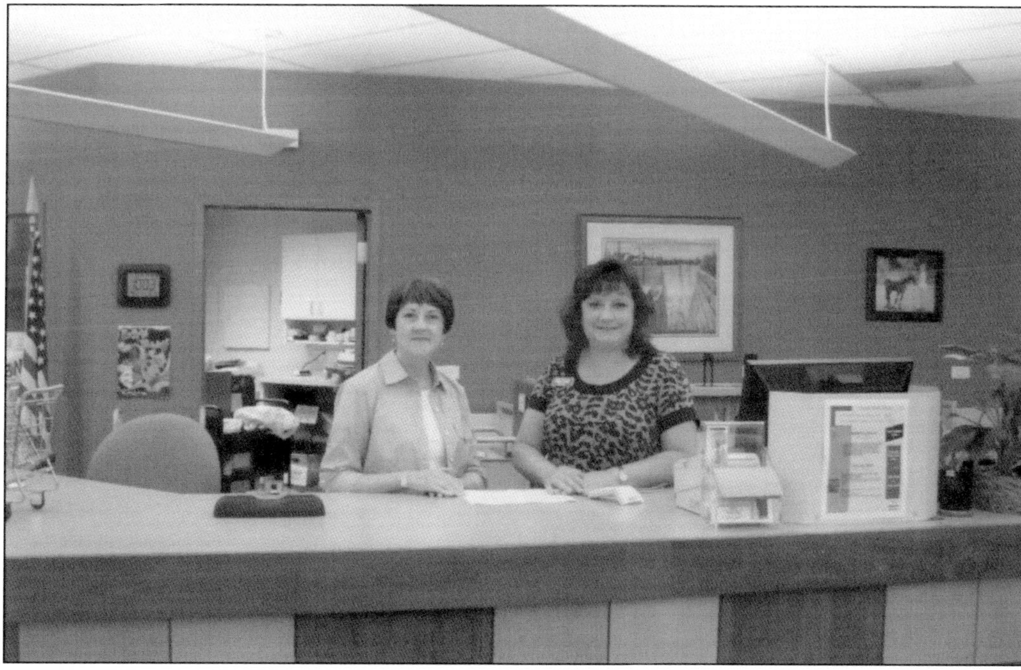

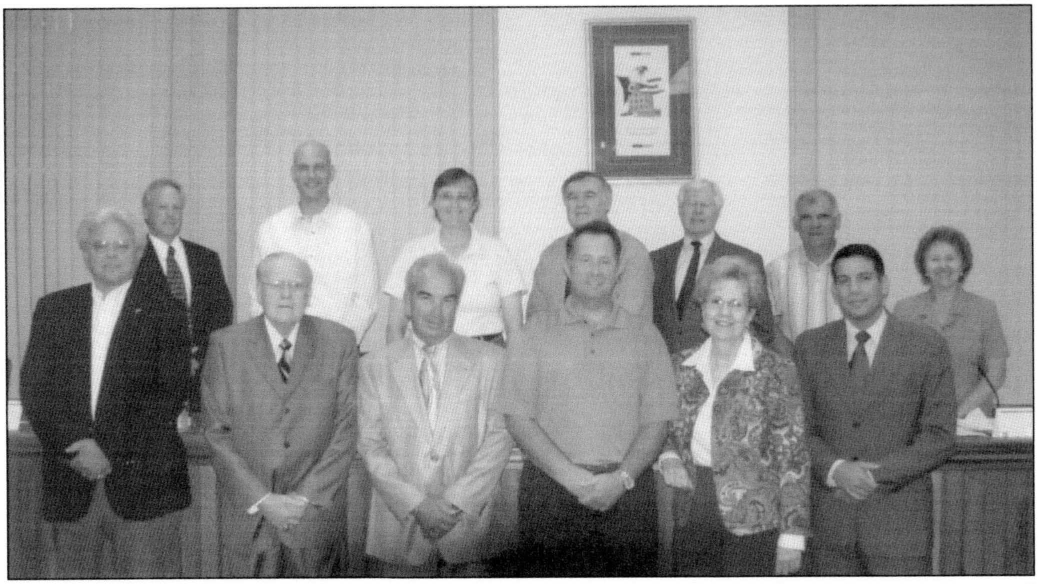

Elected Officials, 2009. Amherst city officials include a council, council president, an appointed council clerk, each serving a two-year term, and a mayor, who serves for four years. Pictured above from left to right are (first row) Dennis Clotz, safety/service director; David Taylor, mayor; John Dietrich, council president; David Kukucka, auditor; Kathleen Litkovitz, treasurer; and Anthony Pecora, law director; (second row) Glenn Loughrie, council at large Ward 2; Joseph Gambish, council at large Ward 3; Jennifer Wasilk, council at large Ward 4; Dennis Walters; P. William VanderWyden; Terry Traster; and Olda Sivinski, clerk of council. Equally important to the community is the Amherst City School Board, whose members serve a four-year term. Pictured below from left to right are (first row) Ron Yacobozzi; Valerie Neidert, president; John Funderburg, vice president; and (second row) Steve Sayers, superintendent; Nick DiMacchia; Rex Engle; and Shirley Antel, treasurer.

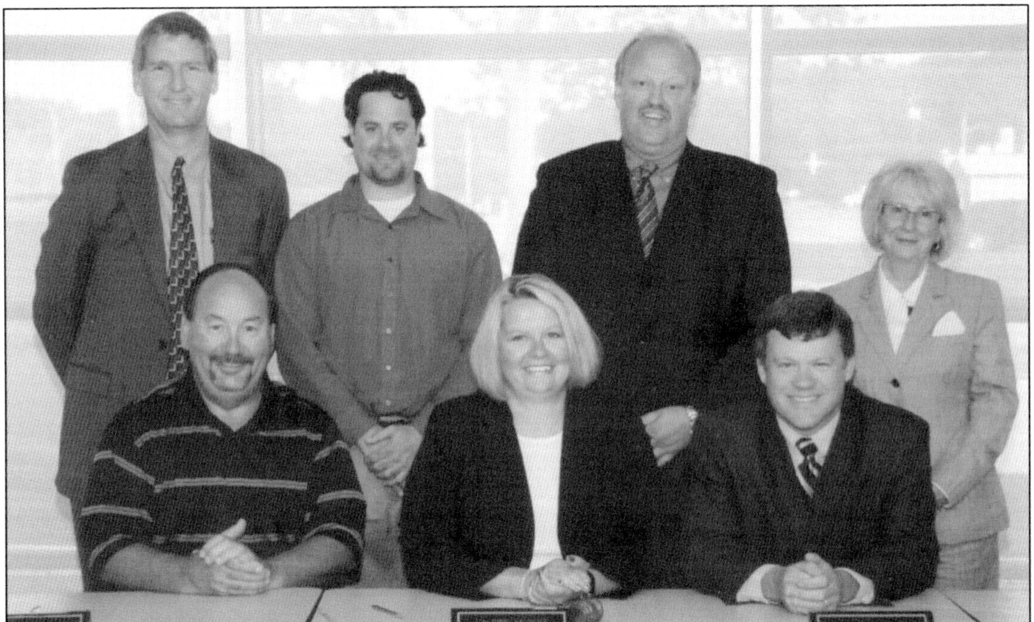

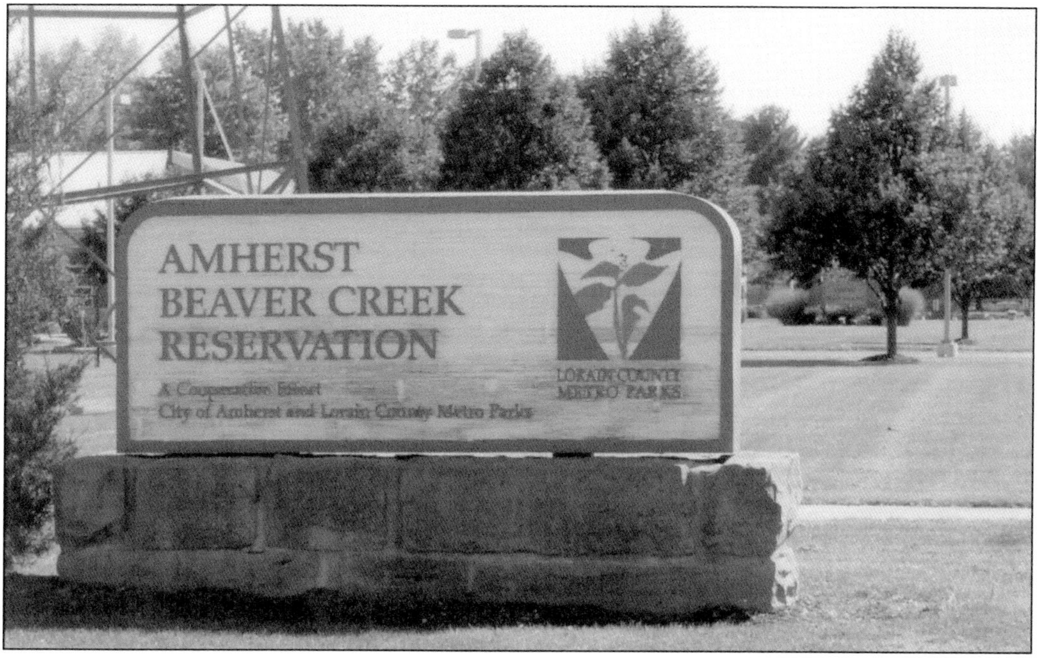

AMHERST BEAVER CREEK RESERVATION. Beaver Creek Reservation (above) opened to the public on July 1, 2001. It was unique in that it was the first joint effort between a metro park district and a city in the state of Ohio. It was the result of a cooperative venture between the city of Amherst and the Lorain County Metro Parks. The day-use area (below) features a visitor's center that is usable year-round, as well as park and picnic facilities. Visitors to the reservation can catch a glimpse of northern Ohio's flora and fauna in an uncontaminated setting.

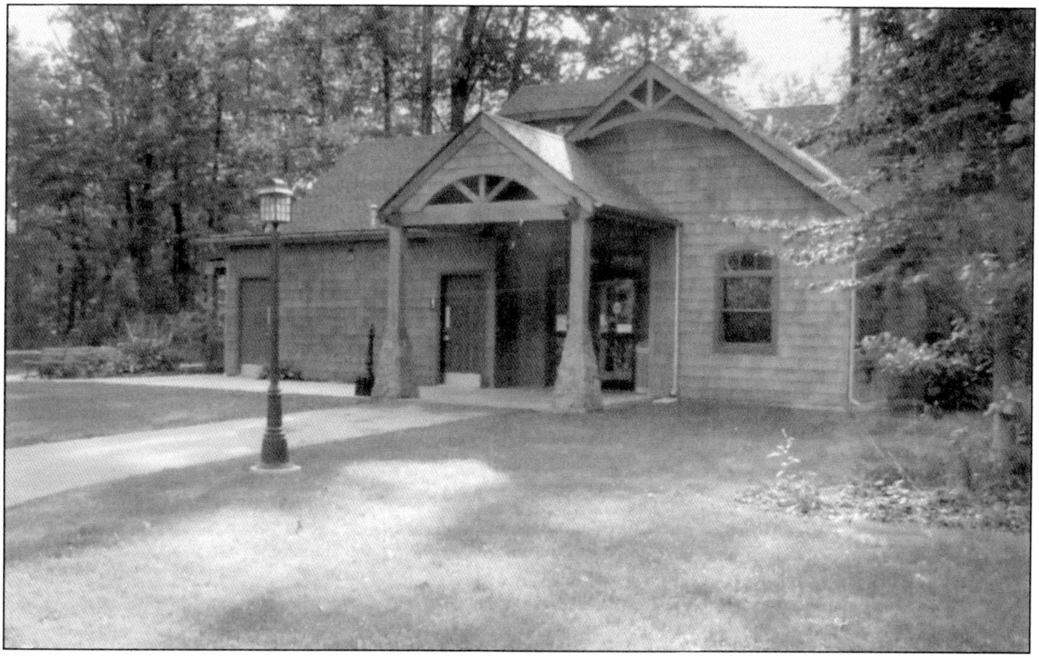

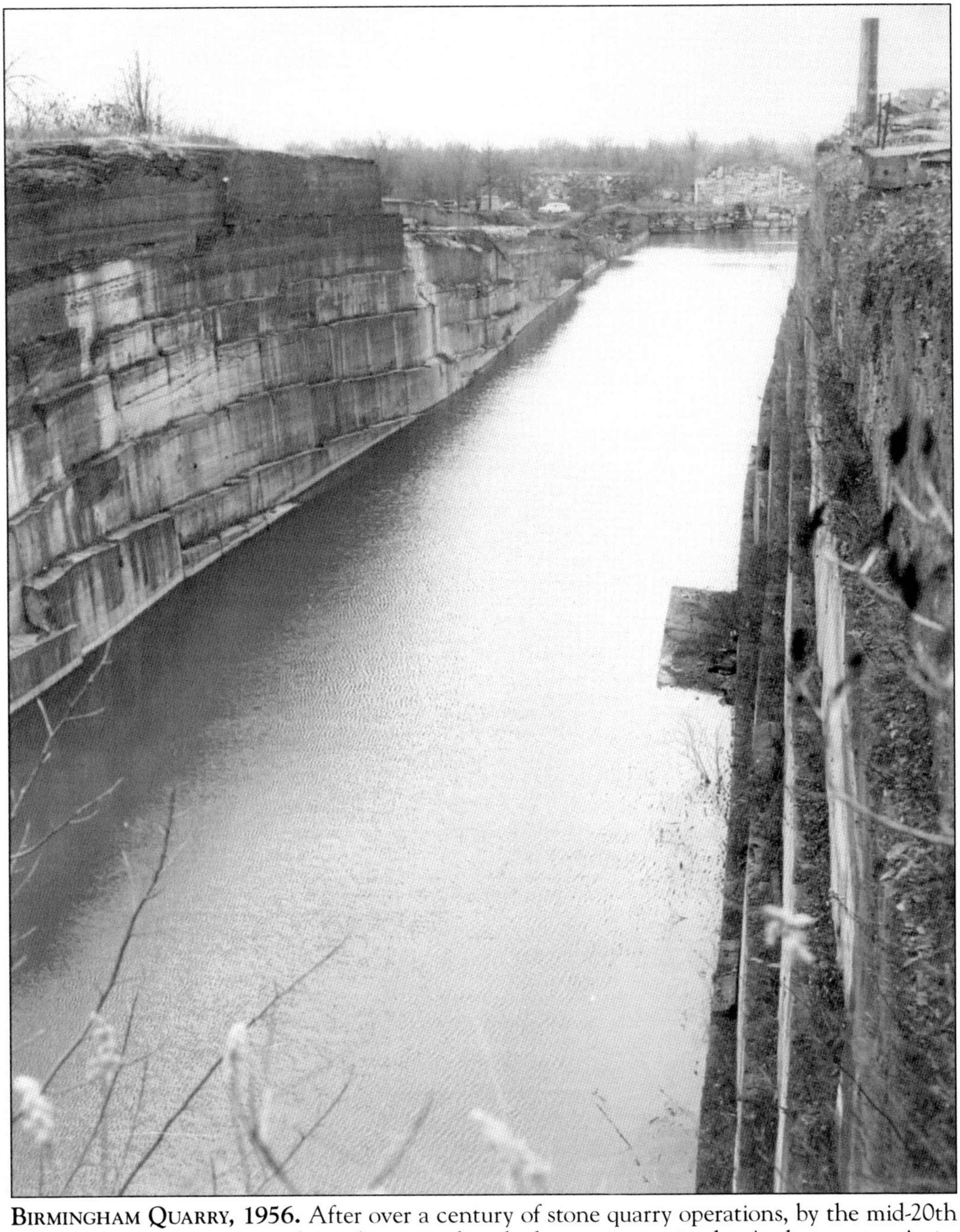

Birmingham Quarry, 1956. After over a century of stone quarry operations, by the mid-20th century, nature began to reclaim the sites of worked-out quarries in the Amherst area. At its peak, quarry production occupied several dozen small sites around the community. By the 1950s, however, a number of the locations had been worked out or abandoned for other reasons. While a market for Amherst sandstone remained, newer building technology and materials reduced its share of the market.

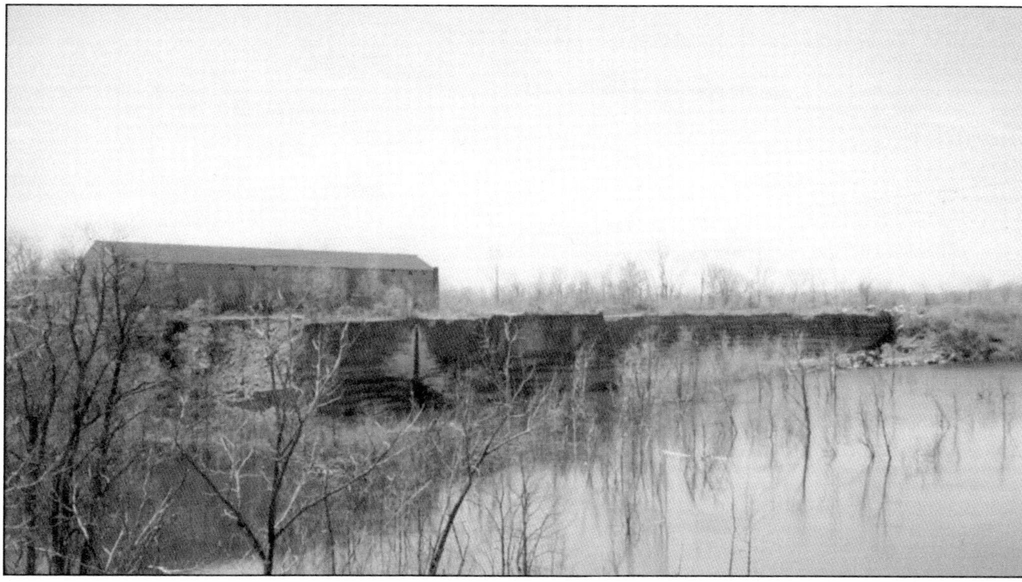

End of an Era. By 2000, Cleveland Quarries Company had entered a new stage of its existence. Now an affiliate of American Sandstone Industries, active quarrying had largely ceased (above) and nature continued to encroach upon the facilities. As the quarries filled with water, only the milling and finishing operations remained truly active. In 2007, Cleveland Quarries moved its remaining finishing operations out of the area (below). While a number of high-end developers initially expressed interest in the properties for residential and resort development, plans have not yet come to fruition.

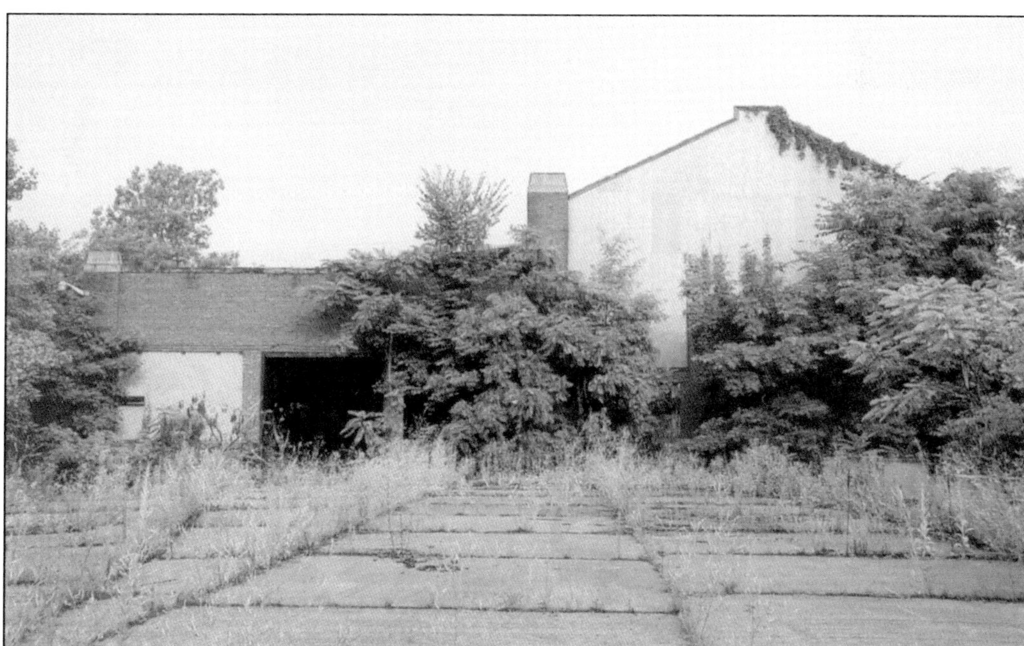

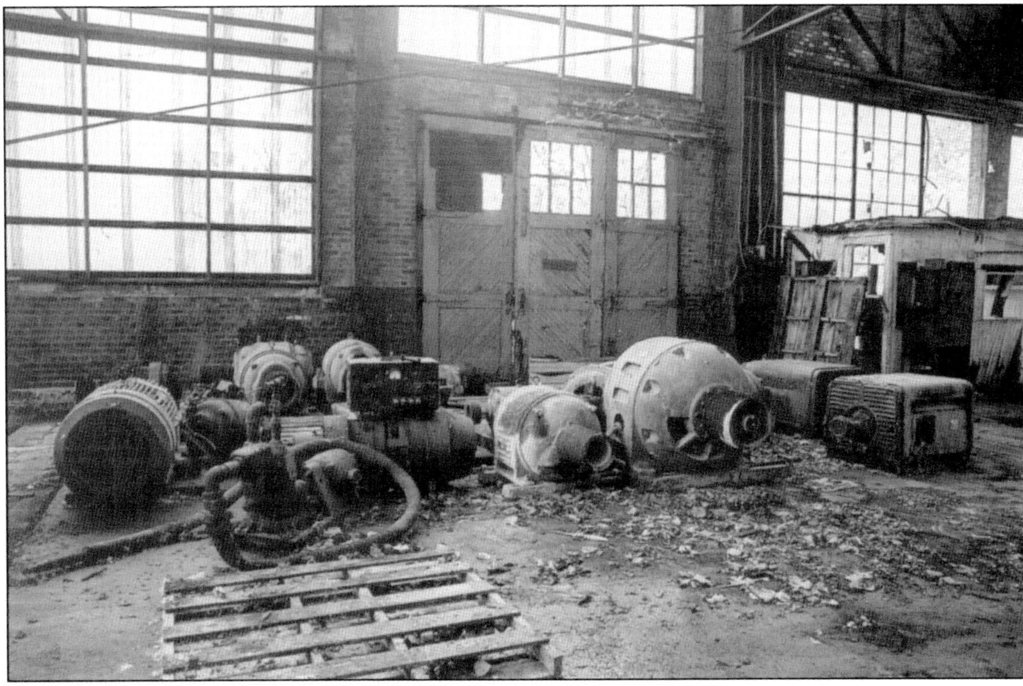

Cleveland Quarries. Since 2007, facilities of the Cleveland Quarries Company have continued to deteriorate. Left behind (above) are the remnants of abandoned machines, as well as the buildings themselves and stone scrap. However, the Cleveland Quarries logo (below) remains a symbol of the community and firmly ties Amherst, "the sandstone center of the world," to its past.

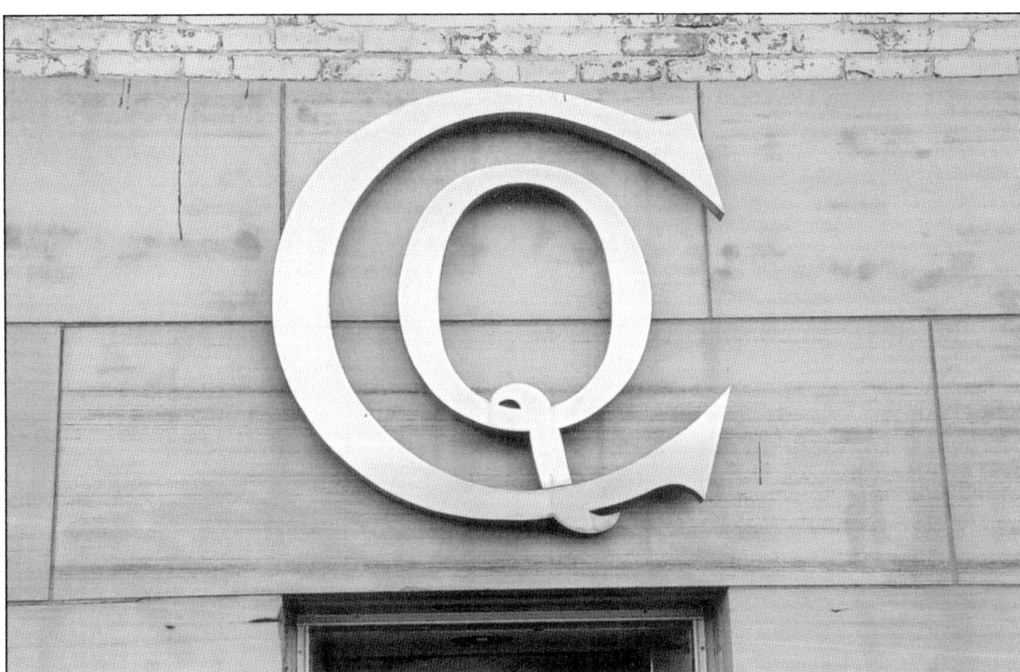

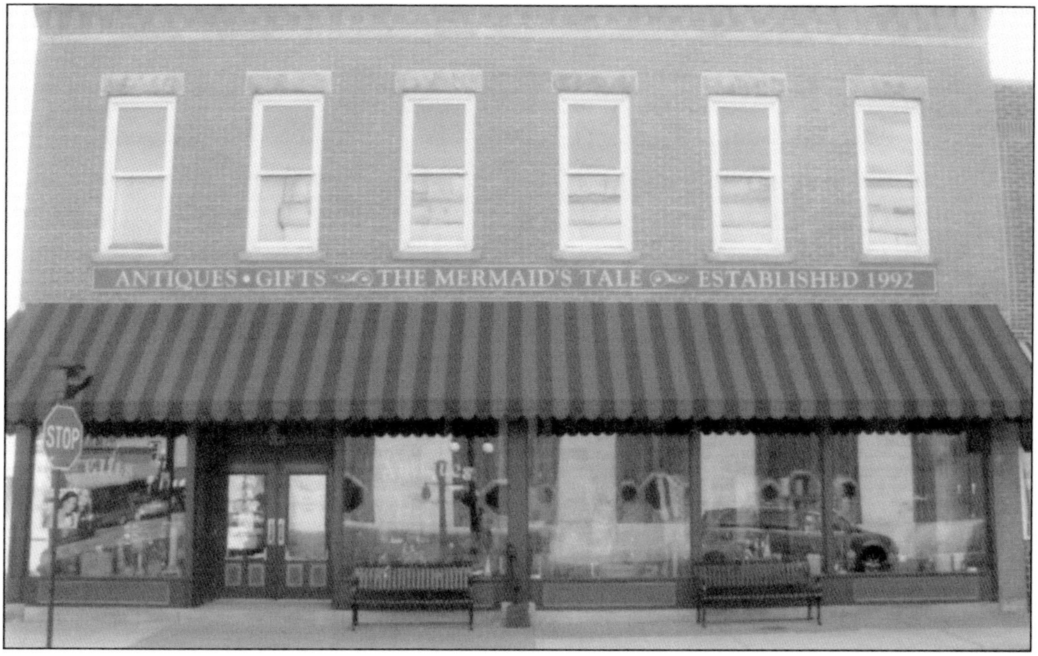

The Mermaid's Tale. Located at the corner of Church Street and Park Avenue, the commercial structure (above) that once housed Bodman and Company dry goods establishment (1900–1960) has long been associated with downtown commercial activity. Exchanging hands several times between 1960 and 1992, the facade underwent a number of superficial alterations. Under new ownership during the 1990s, the building was gradually restored to its original appearance. The new facility (below) takes its name from the unique inset in its restored tin ceiling.

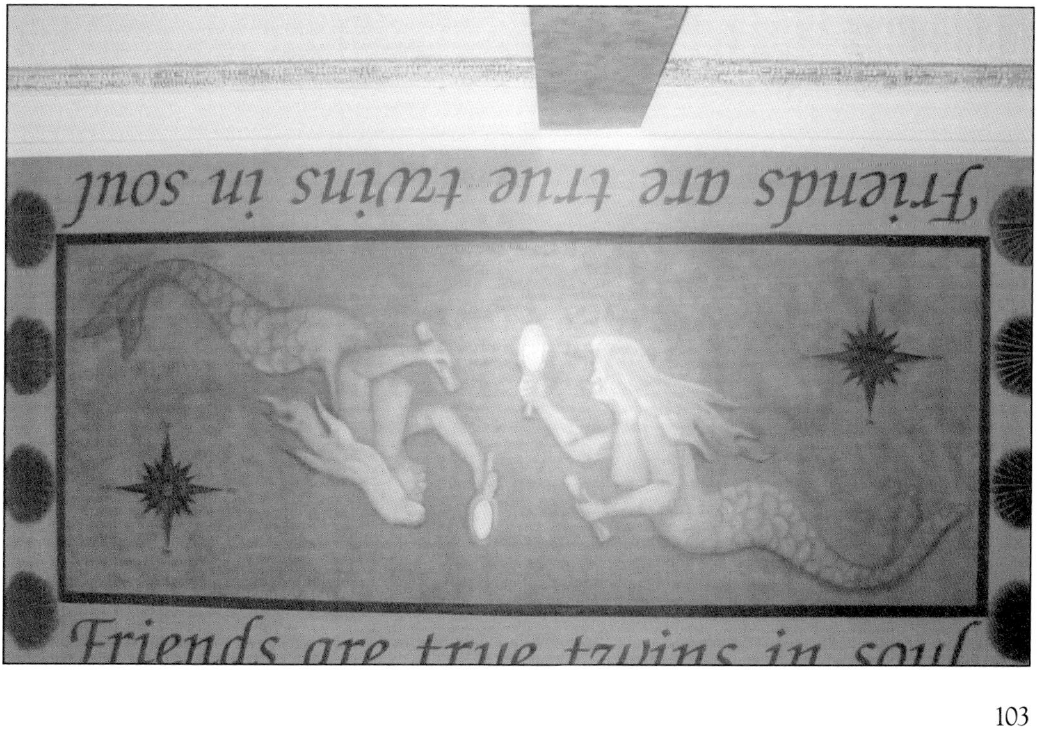

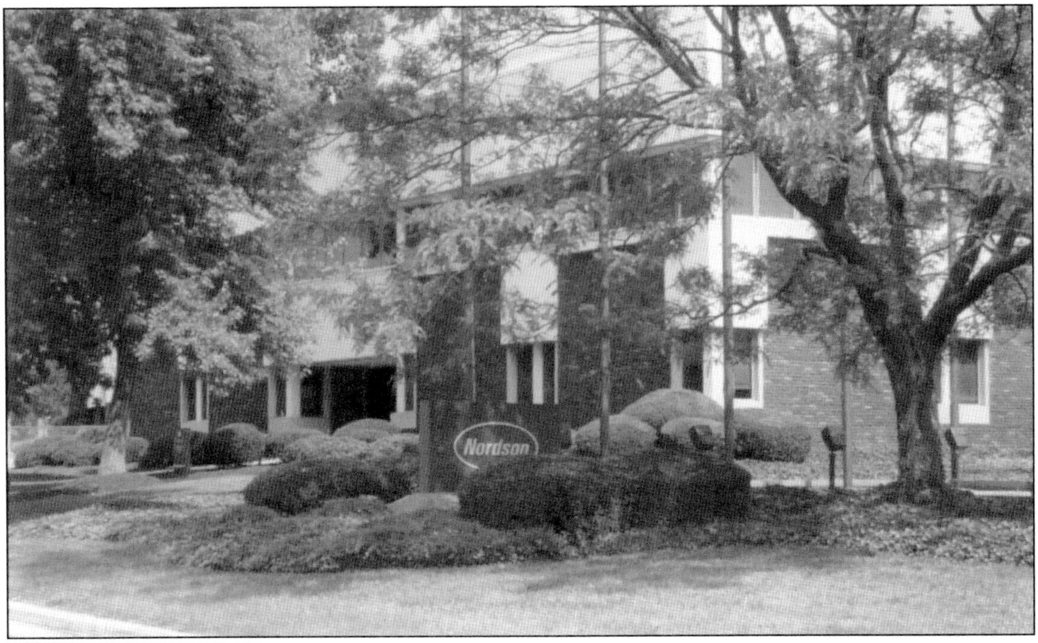

NORDSON CORPORATION. Nordson Corporation began its existence as American Specialties Company in 1919. When Uthe-Schibley (U.S.) Automatic Company went into receivership in 1929, and the court named Walter G. Nord as receiver. Nord's company survived the Great Depression and prospered during World War II. In 1954, it was reorganized into the Nordson Division of U.S. Automatic Company and in 1966 was wholly merged into Nordson Corporation (above). After Nord's (center) passing, his sons Evan (left) and Eric (right) gradually assumed control of the Nordson Corporation (below).

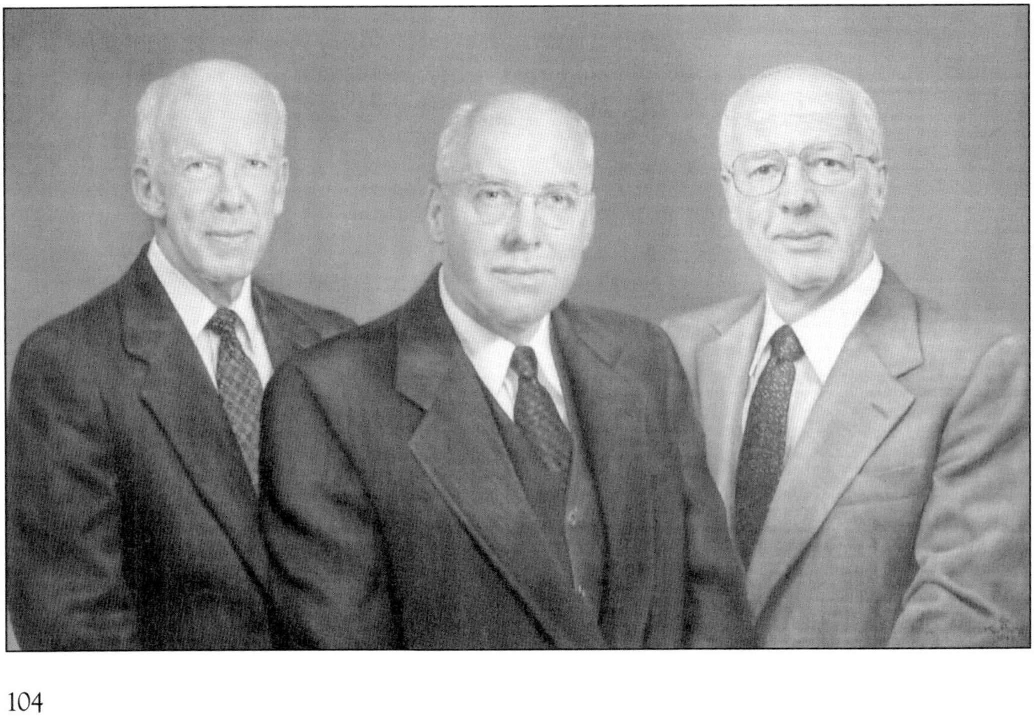

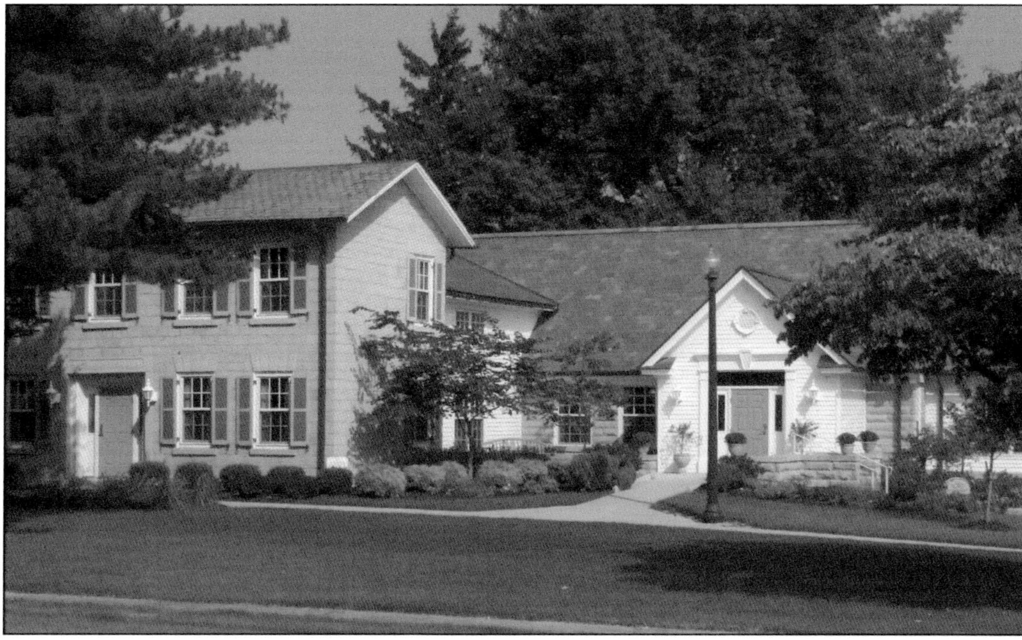

The Nord Family and Nordson Foundations. The Nordson Corporation Foundation traces its origins to 1952, when Walter G. Nord established the U.S. Automatic Foundation. In 1966, when the U.S. Automatic and Nordson Corporations merged, the foundation became the Nordson Corporation Foundation. This entity was reorganized in 1988 into the Nordson Corporation Foundation and the Nord Family Foundation, which today operate independently. The former continues the policy established in 1973 of contributing 5 percent of its pretax earnings for charitable purposes. The latter, under the direction of Nord family members, occupies a headquarters at the corner of Milan Avenue and North Lake Street. Among its projects is the former Amherst freight depot remodeled as the Nord depot in the 1970s.

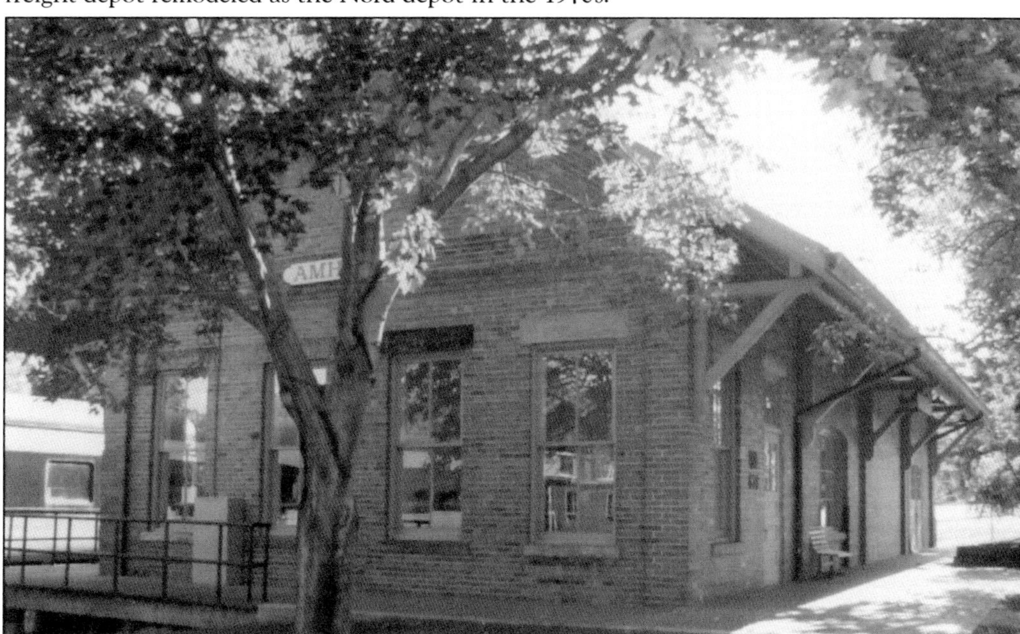

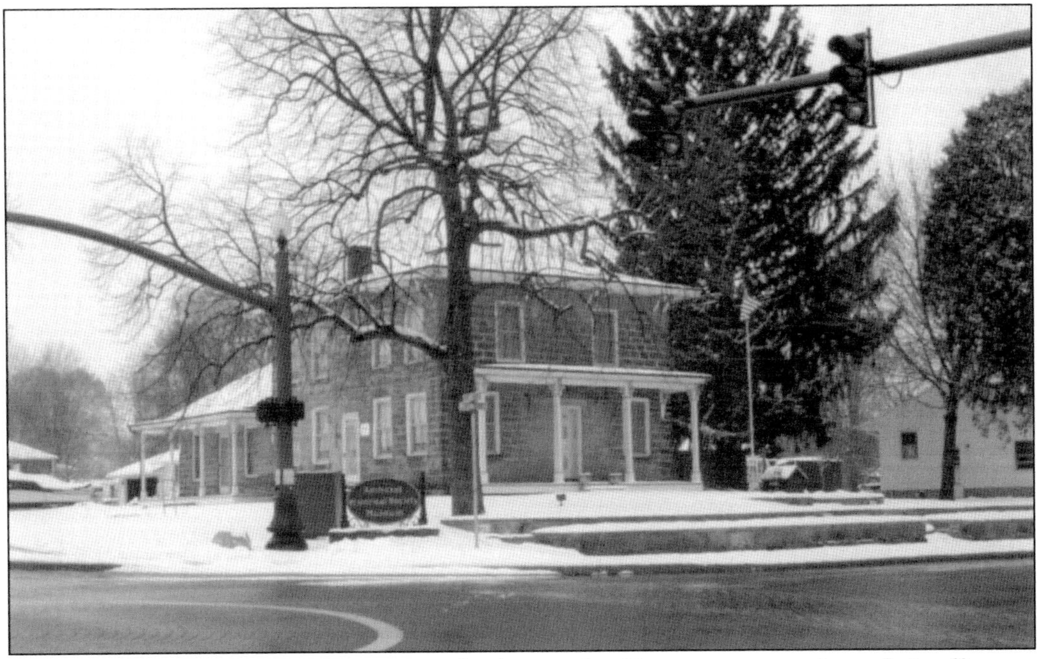

AMHERST BEAUTIFICATION. Community leaders in the 21st century continue their efforts to enhance the area's physical environment. In 2004 and 2005, three intersections, the Five Corners, Park Avenue and Church Street, and Milan Avenue and North Lake Street (seen here), were upgraded with simulated brick patterns embossed in the pavement.

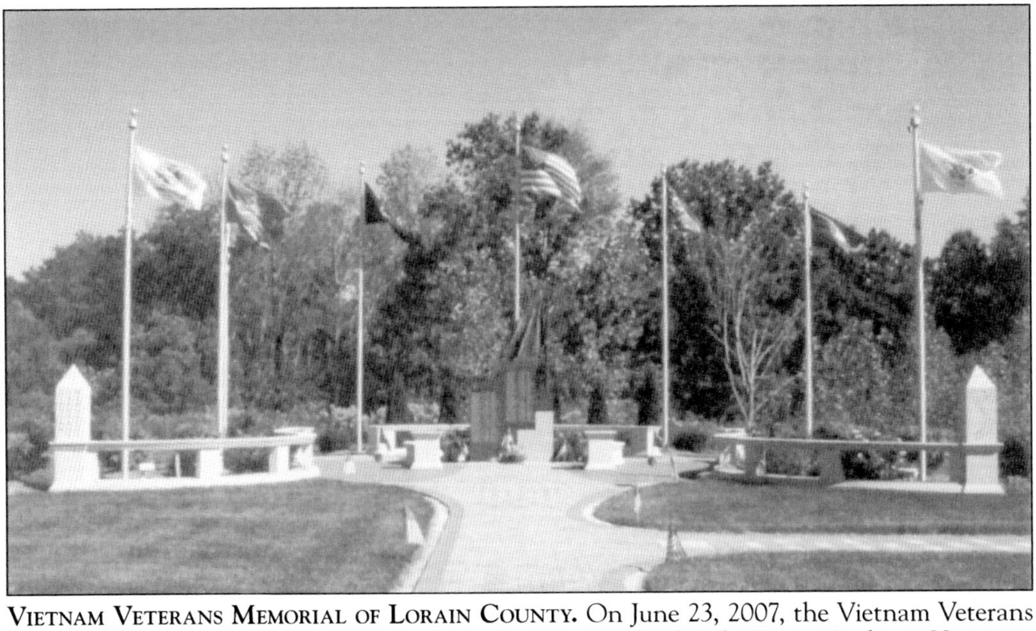

VIETNAM VETERANS MEMORIAL OF LORAIN COUNTY. On June 23, 2007, the Vietnam Veterans Memorial of Lorain County was dedicated at its location on North Lake Street, Amherst. Honoring the 98 individuals who died during the Vietnam War between 1965 and 1975, the memorial is made of Pennsylvania granite and engraved with the names of Lorain County's war dead. Construction and maintenance were funded by the sale of memorial paving stones.

Eight

Preserving the Past for the Future

Located at the corner of North Lake Street and Milan Avenue, the Amherst Sandstone Village was established to preserve and protect an integral facet of the community's history. Modeled on Henry Ford's Greenfield Village, the Amherst open-air museum features a collection of buildings original to the site, those moved from other locations, and a few created to fill specific niches. The project developed as the result of a partnership between the Amherst Historical Society, the citizenry of Amherst, and the foresight and generosity of the Nord Family Foundation and Nordson Corporation Foundation.

While the Grange and filling station were in situ, the Amherst Historical Society made arrangements to move or construct the remaining 14 structures. In the process, they saved many of the buildings from certain destruction thus preserving them for future generations. Most of the properties are doubly significant—they represent edifices typical to the region from the mid-19th century through the early 20th century and are constructed of Amherst sandstone, which is unique to the area.

Open year-round, the village has become an important gathering place and community symbol. It hosts events as diverse as Civil War re-enactments, weddings, and vintage baseball games, as well as programming more typical of a museum, such as school activities and site tours.

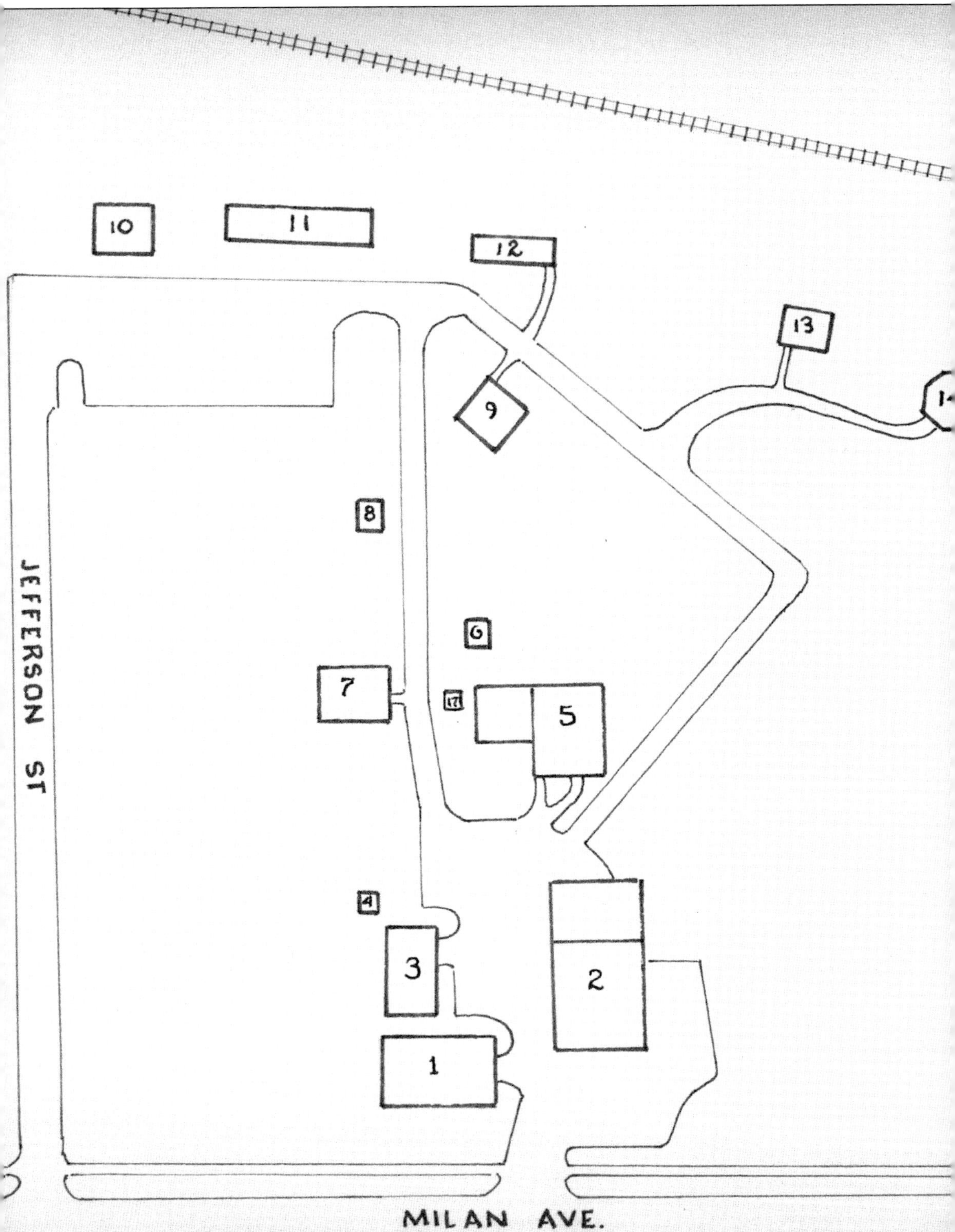
10
11
12
13
14
9
8
6
7
17
5
4
3
2
1
JEFFERSON ST
MILAN AVE.

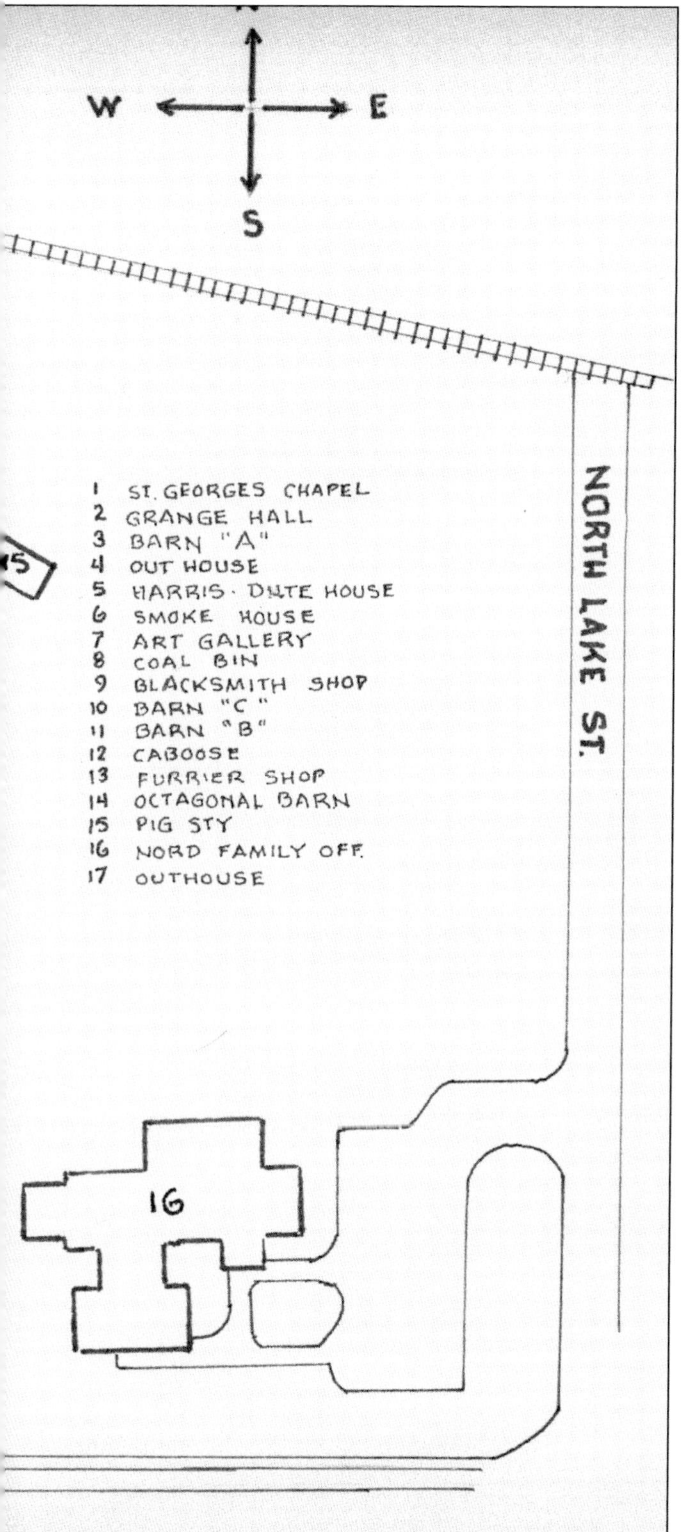

Map of the Amherst Sandstone Village. Located between North Lake and Jefferson Streets on Milan Avenue, the Amherst Sandstone Village boasts 16 structures in addition to the Nord Family Foundation offices. Much in the tradition of Henry Ford's Greenfield Village, the Amherst Historical Society deconstructed and rebuilt many of these structures on the new site. The only buildings on their original locations are the Grange Hall and the automobile garage. The historical society initiated operations in 1989 and continues to expand its programming and activities into the 21st century. In the village, the historical society celebrates the life and times of Amherst's earlier residents and preserves the history and heritage of all aspects of the community.

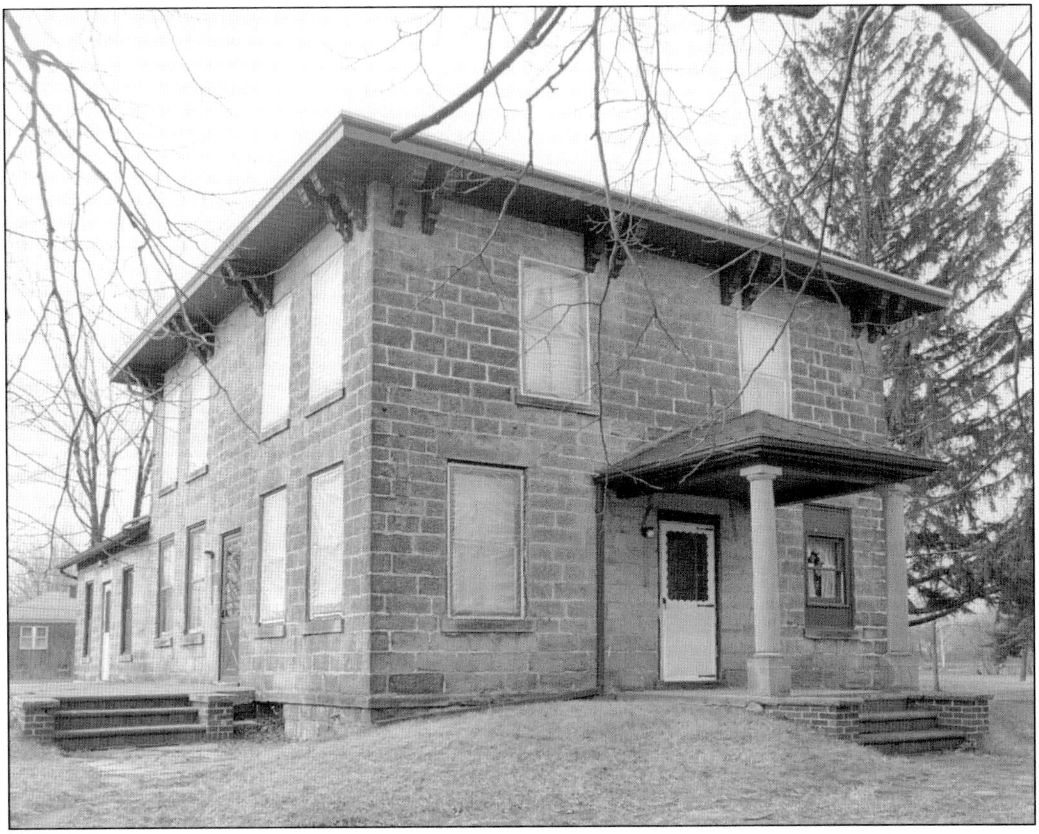

The Quigley House. The Quigley House was acquired by the Nord Family Foundation in 1988 and given to the Amherst Historical Society. It opened to the public in December 1989, launching its operations. The house (above) was built by Joseph Quigley out of sandstone from his own quarries about 1835. During the past two decades, the historical society transformed the interior (below) into museum exhibits interpreting various aspects of Amherst's past. This includes a representation of a quarry payroll clerk around 1920 at her period desk with her candlestick telephone and check writer machine.

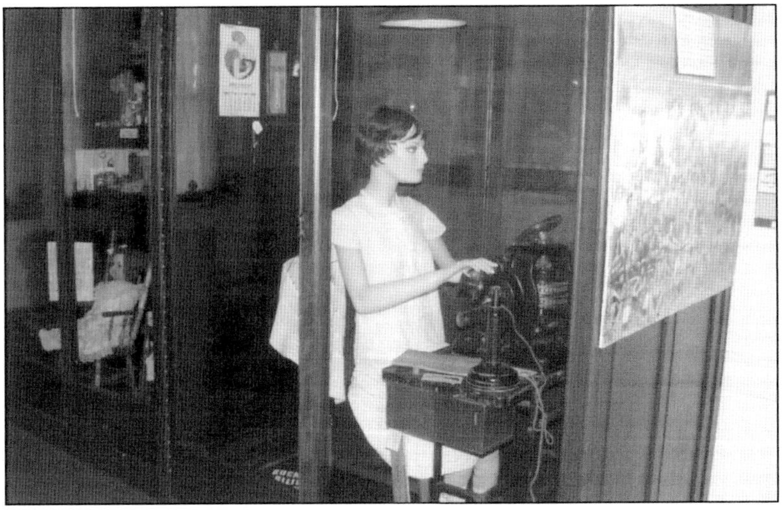

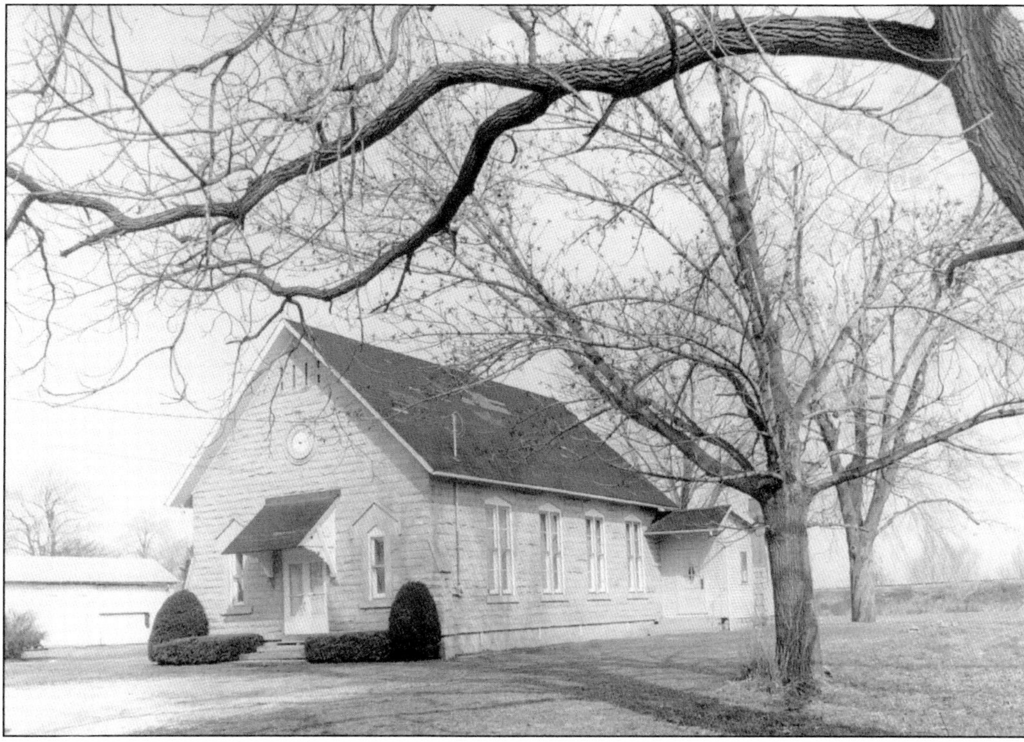

THE GRANGE HALL. The Hickory Tree Grange Hall, constructed in 1879 as a one-room schoolhouse, is one of two buildings original to the Amherst Sandstone Village site (above). Owned and maintained by the Nord Family Foundation since 1988 in conjunction with the Hickory Tree Grange, the building hosts one of the historical society's most successful programs, a one-room schoolhouse. Today it serves as a centerpiece of the village and hosts a number of community events, such as this set up for a mother-daughter tea party (below).

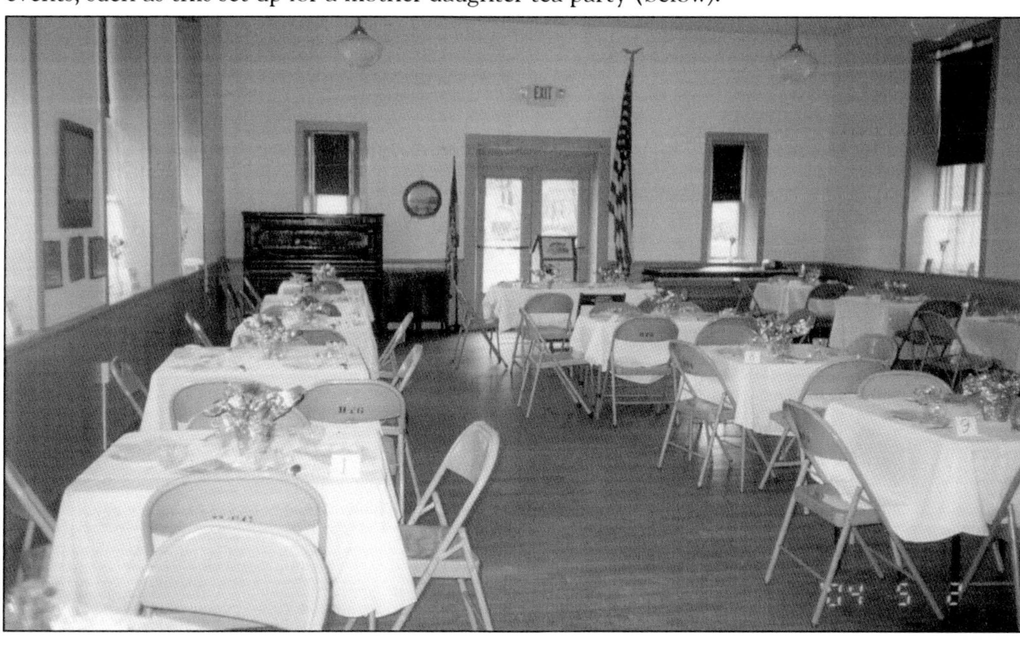

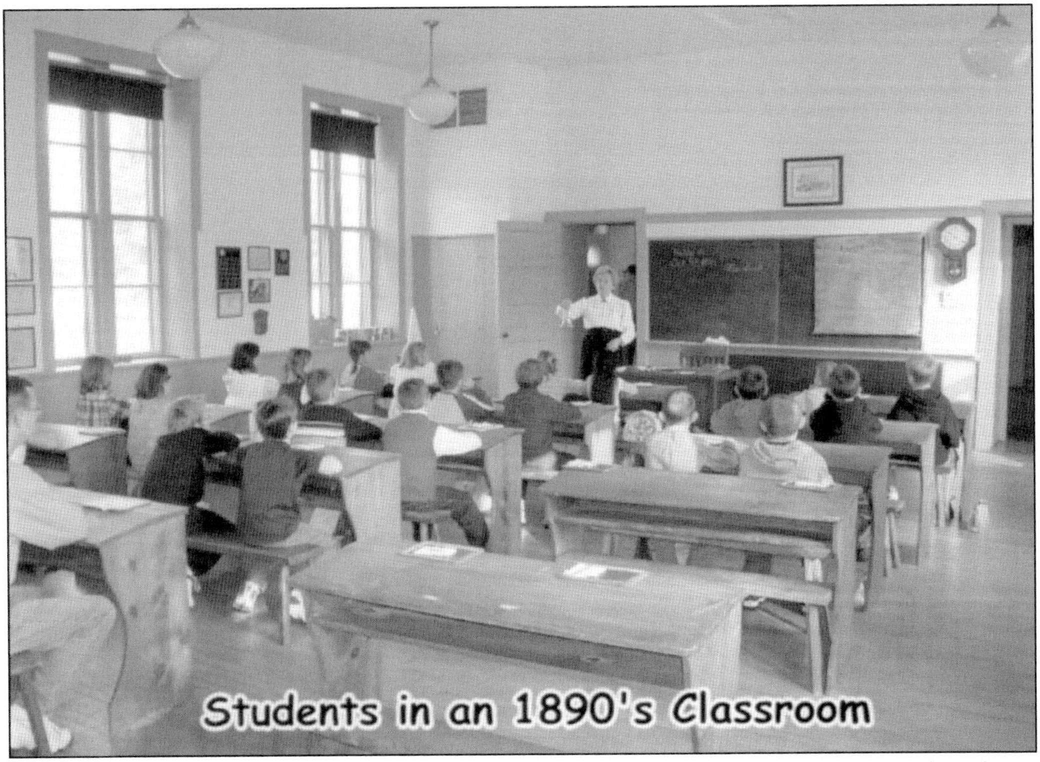

COMMUNITY OUTREACH. Finding ways to share information about the community's past has always been central to the mission of the Amherst Historical Society. Their award winning one-room schoolhouse program hosts third graders from the local schools and allows them to experience an old-fashioned curriculum (above). The village's St. George Chapel is an equally popular site for weddings (below). Its classical interior provides the perfect background for special occasions.

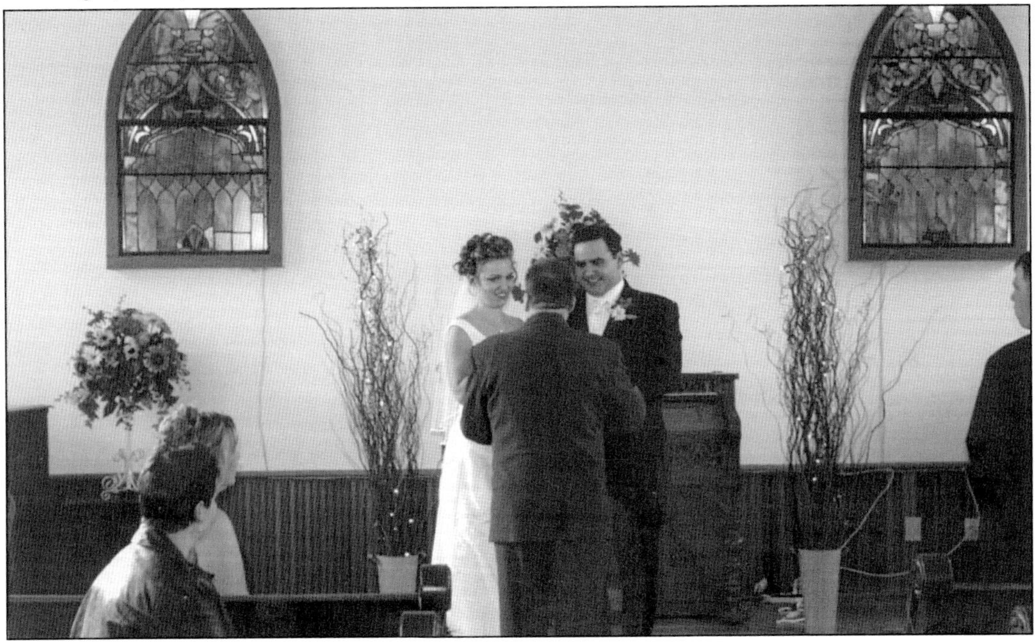

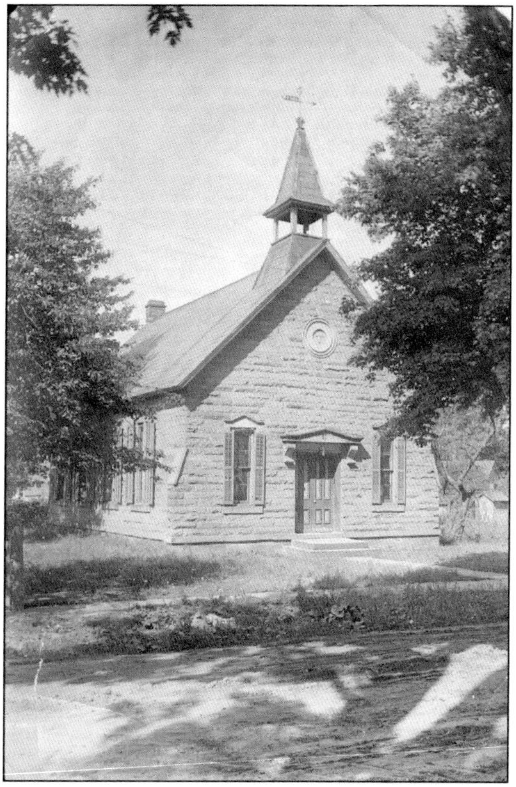

St. George Chapel. St. George Chapel, built in 1882 on Spring Street (right), was originally a schoolhouse and in 1913 became the home of an Episcopalian congregation. It later served as a two-family apartment building. By the 1980s, Amherst Hospital owned the property and opted to sell the building to the historical society in 1987 for $1, with the provision that it be moved from its original site. The historical society, in turn, opted to return the building to its function as a church (below), which is how it is used today.

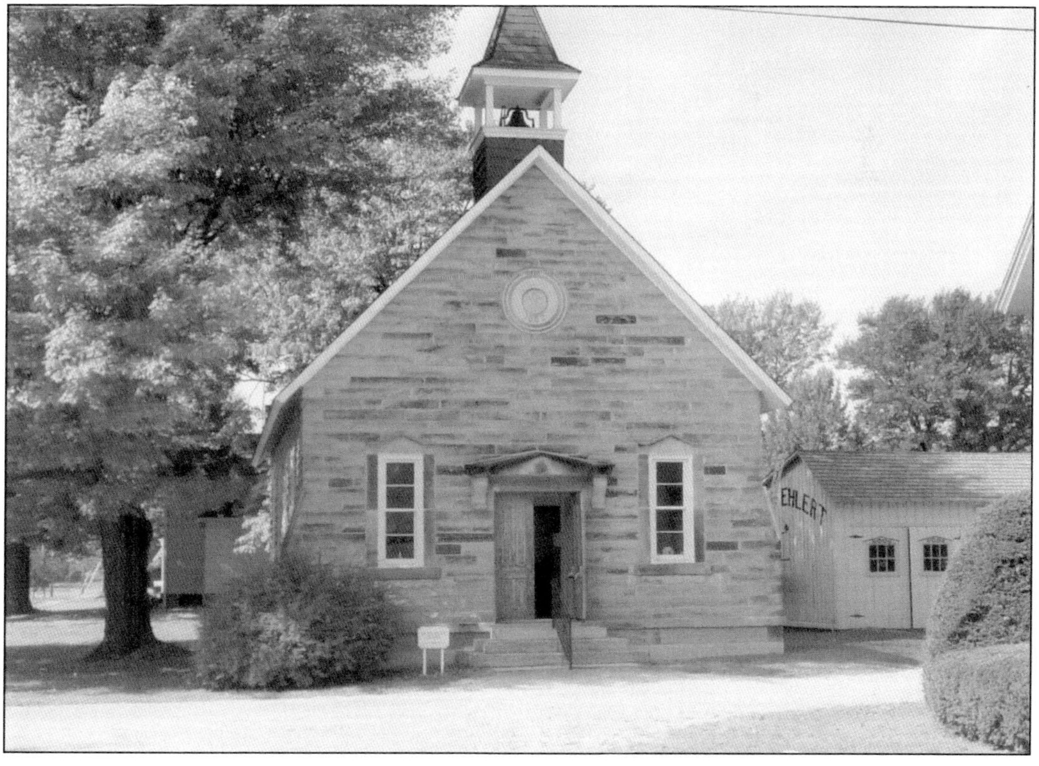

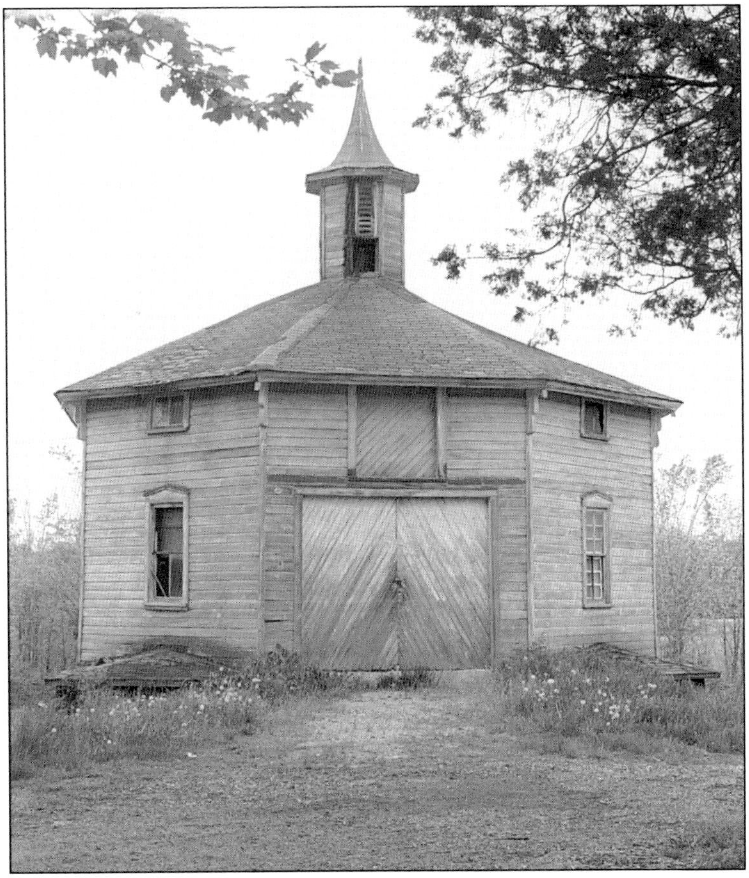

THE OCTAGONAL BARN. Originally constructed on Middle Ridge Road (left), the design of the Octagonal Barn, with its sandstone foundation, was an architectural form popularized in the mid-19th century. Having outlived its usefulness on the Pandy farm, this barn was sold to the Amherst Historical Society and moved to the village in 1991. Exercising historical sensitivity as it reconstructed the barn, the historical society re-created the site (below), placing it on the top of a mound. The structure now houses vintage farm tools, equipment, and a sleigh, which was donated by Evan Nord.

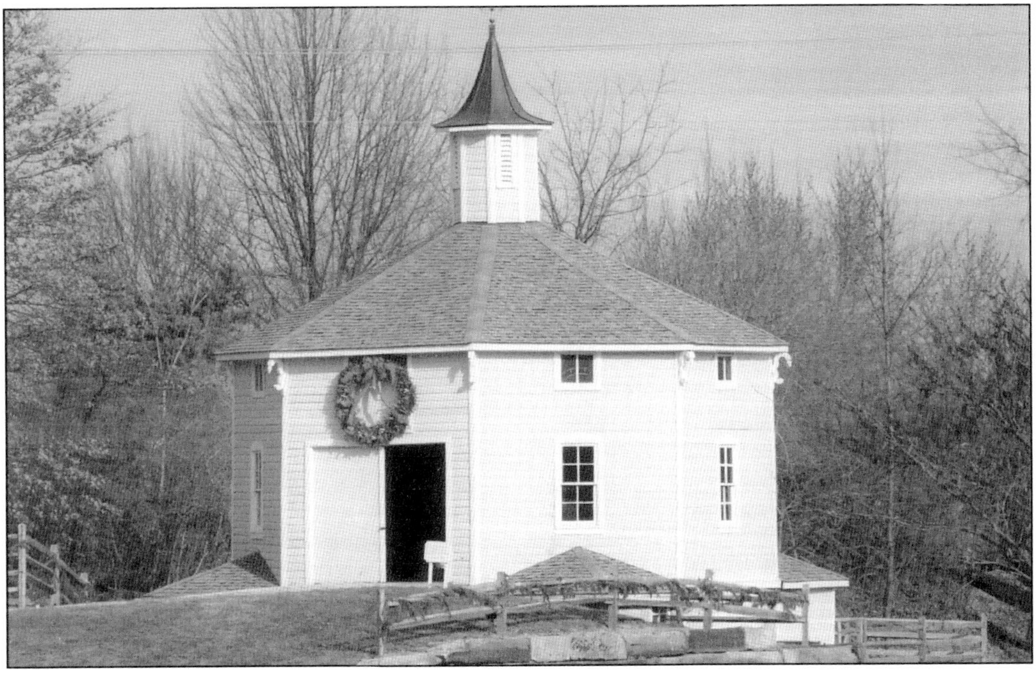

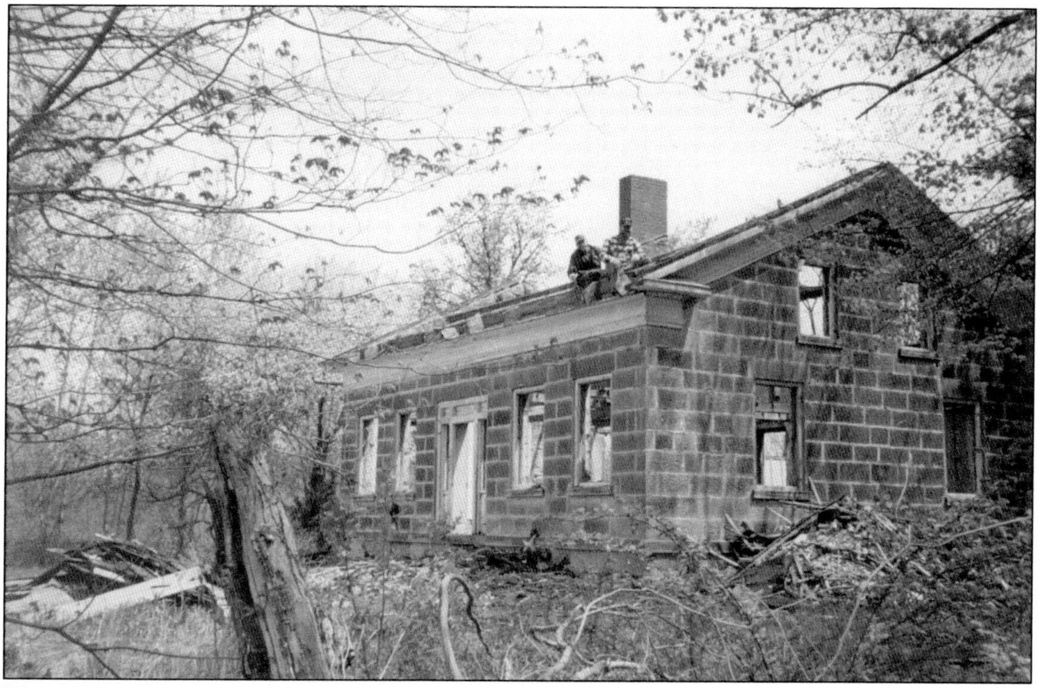

Harris-Dute House. The 1849 Greek Revival Harris-Dute House (above) was built by Lucinda and Calvin Harris. After Calvin's death, Lucinda sold the house to the Dutes in 1861. It was originally located on 105 acres at 8263 Oberlin Road in Amherst Township. Over time, the house was abandoned and left derelict. In 1974, Bill Starbuck and his wife purchased the property and in 1991 donated the house to the historical society. It was reconstructed at the village in 2001, where the historical society has furnished it with artifacts representing the 1840s through the 1880s.

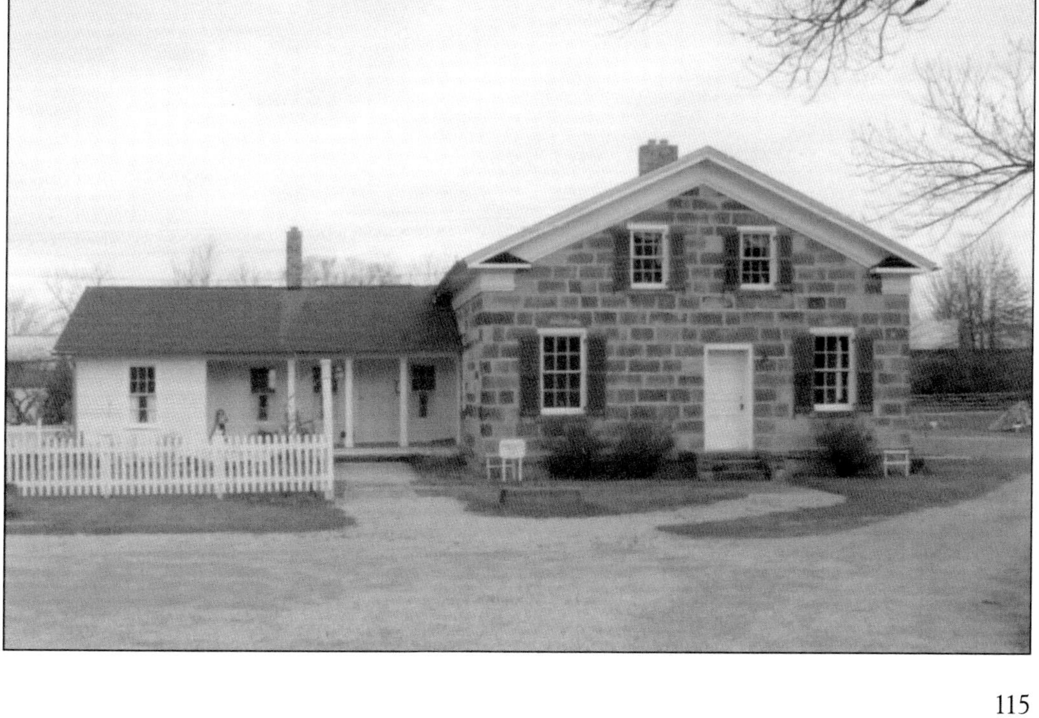

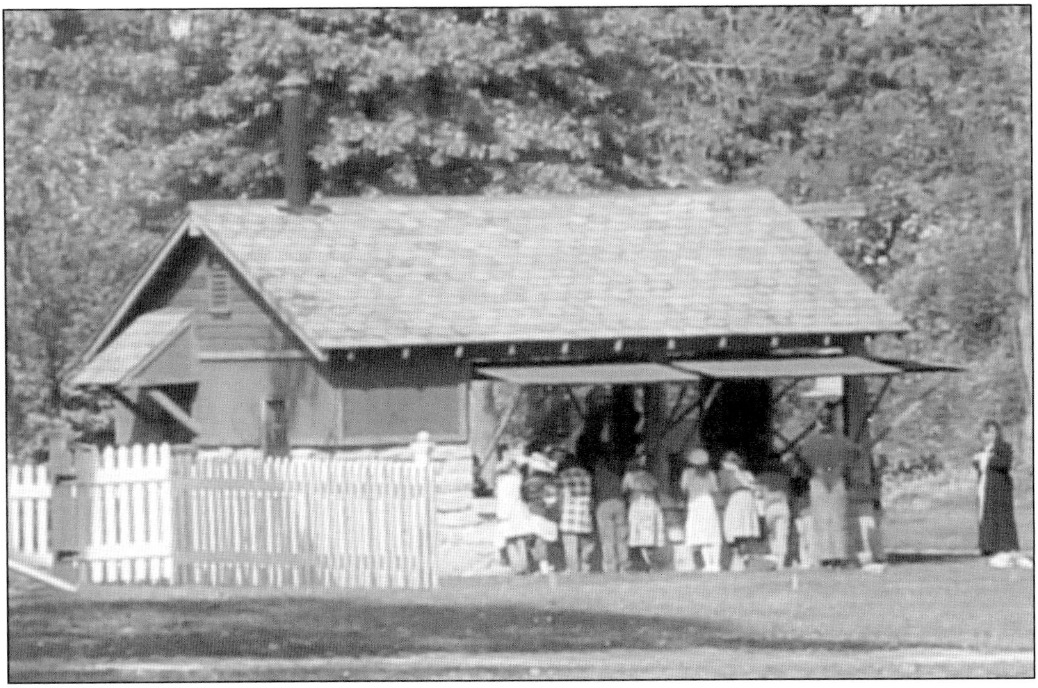

THE VILLAGE SMITHY. The Amherst Historical Society constructed a replica of a Vermont blacksmith shop out of pre–Civil War maple and Amherst sandstone for the village (above). It is an attraction that was popular with schoolchildren and adults alike, particularly when village blacksmith Bob Stilgenbauer gave demonstrations (below).

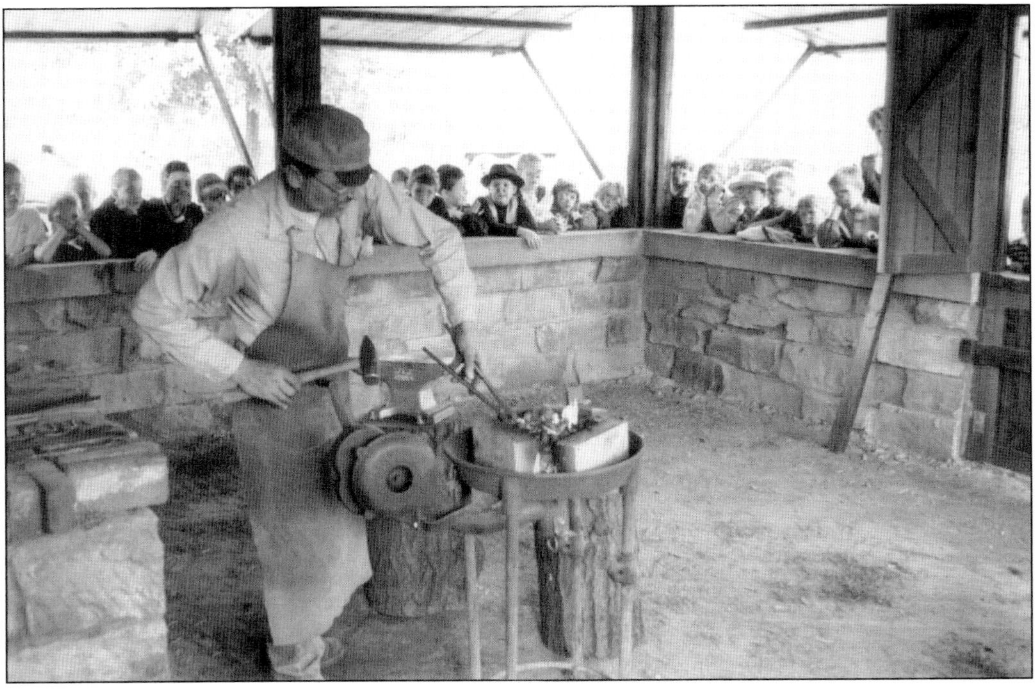

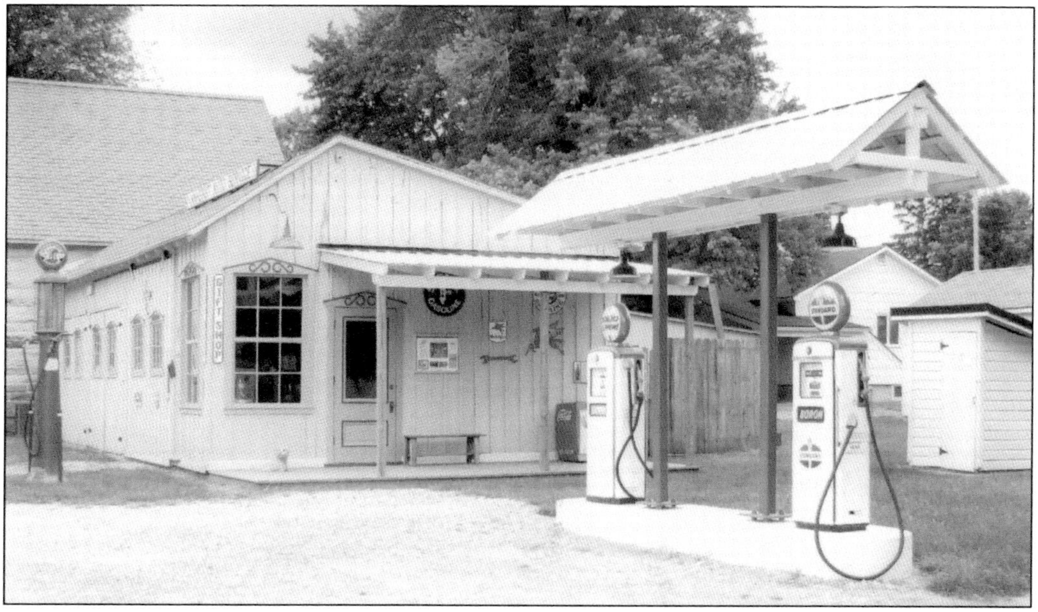

AMHERST AUTO GARAGE AND PRIVY. The Amherst Auto Garage is one of the two structures original to the village site. The two vintage early-1950s Standard Oil gasoline pumps are on loan to the historical society. The building itself houses a 1920 Ford Model T and a *c.* 1920 Chevrolet Stake truck, both of which were donated by Evan Nord. The privy next to the garage is emblematic of a time before indoor plumbing was widespread. This particular example is only a one seater; there is a three-seater version located behind the Harris-Dute House (below).

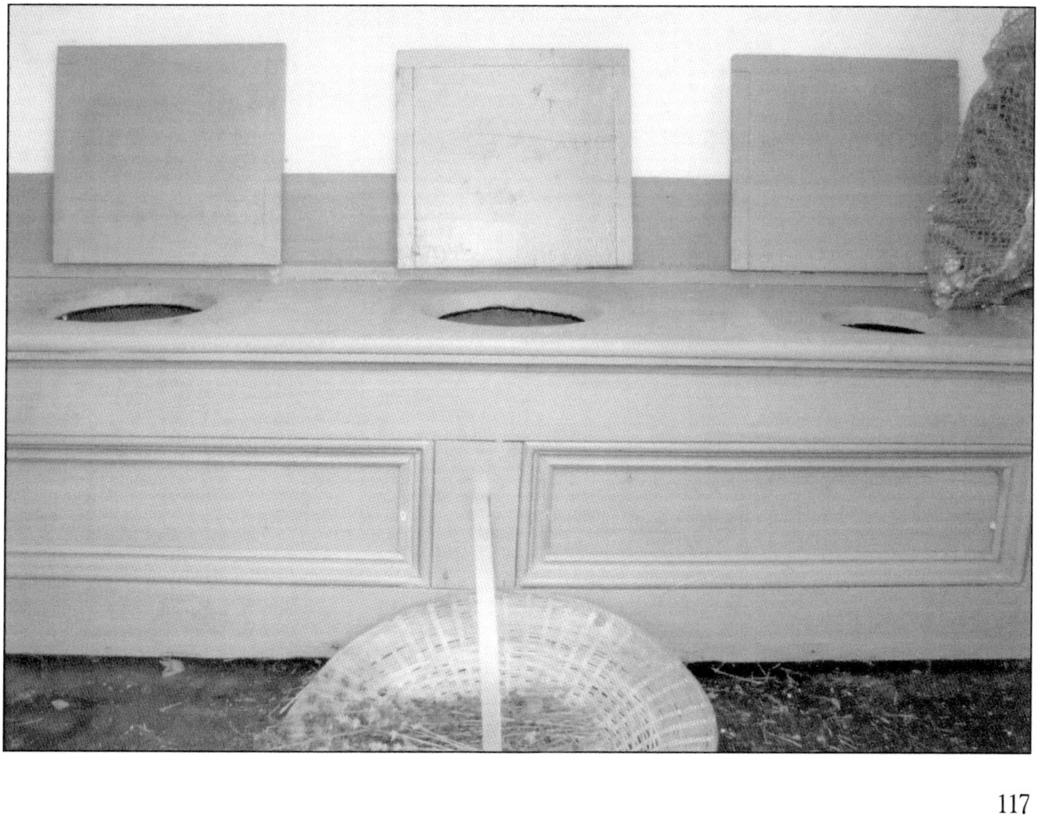

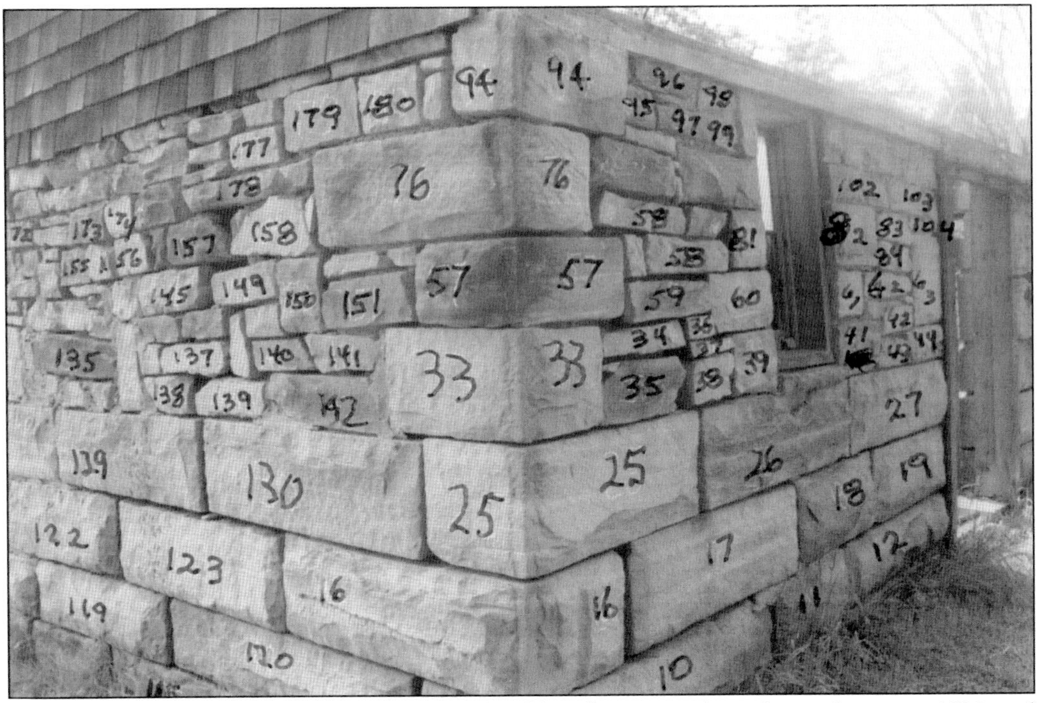

Pig Barn. The structure was originally built of locally quarried sandstone between 1890 and 1900. By the early 20th century, it was used to house pigs as part of a larger farm complex. It was originally located on State Route 58 between Amherst and Oberlin. It was purchased by the Amherst Historical Society, dismantled, and reconstructed on its village site in 2005. As it was deconstructed, its stones were numbered (above) and removed. The building illustrates an early-20th-century farm structure (below).

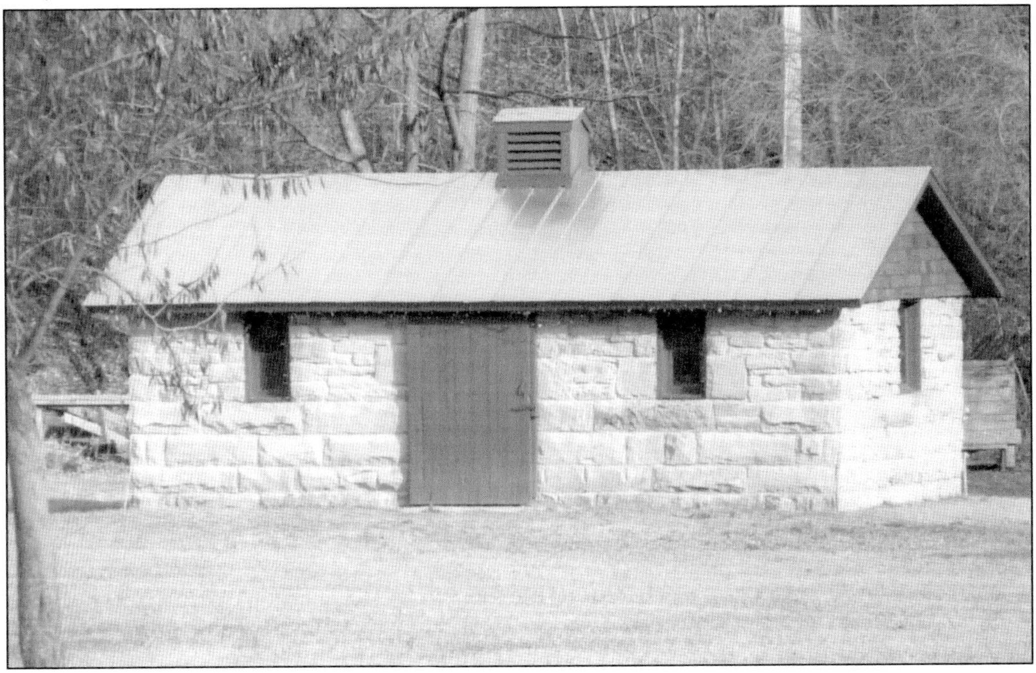

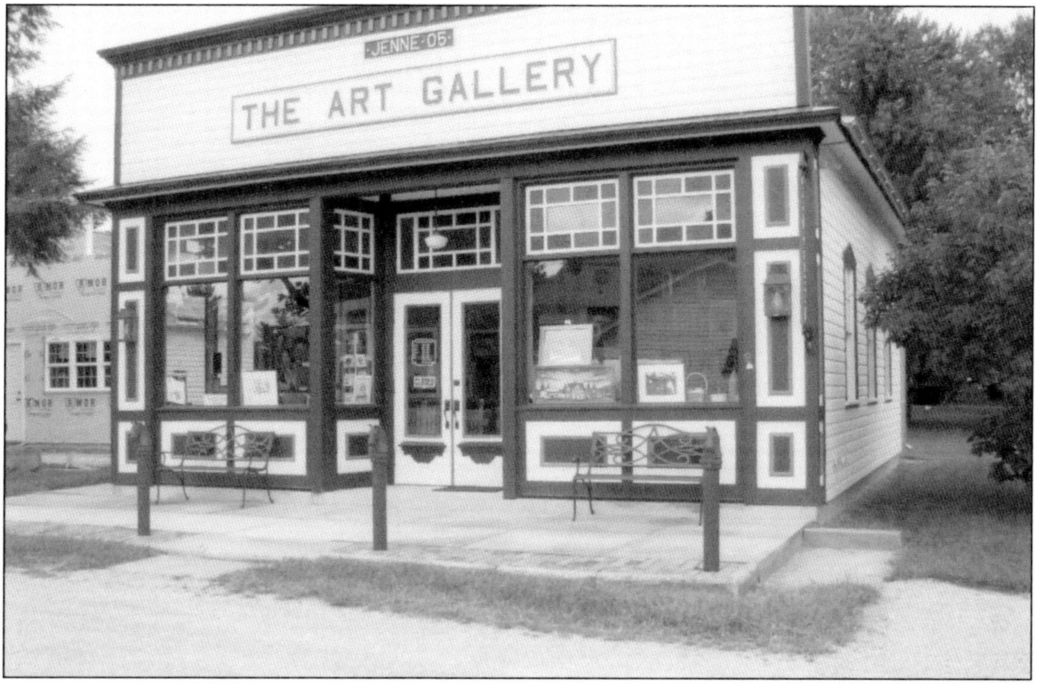

JENNE BUILDING. Representative of a late 19th- or early-20th-century commercial structure, the Jenne building was constructed by Marilyn Jenne in 2005 as an art gallery (above). Terry Traster designed the building and acted as contractor. Jenne and her nephew Neal Jenne (below), an artist in residence, oversaw the construction project and the gallery's grand opening. The building provides not only a space for artists to display and sell their work, but it is also a venue for art classes.

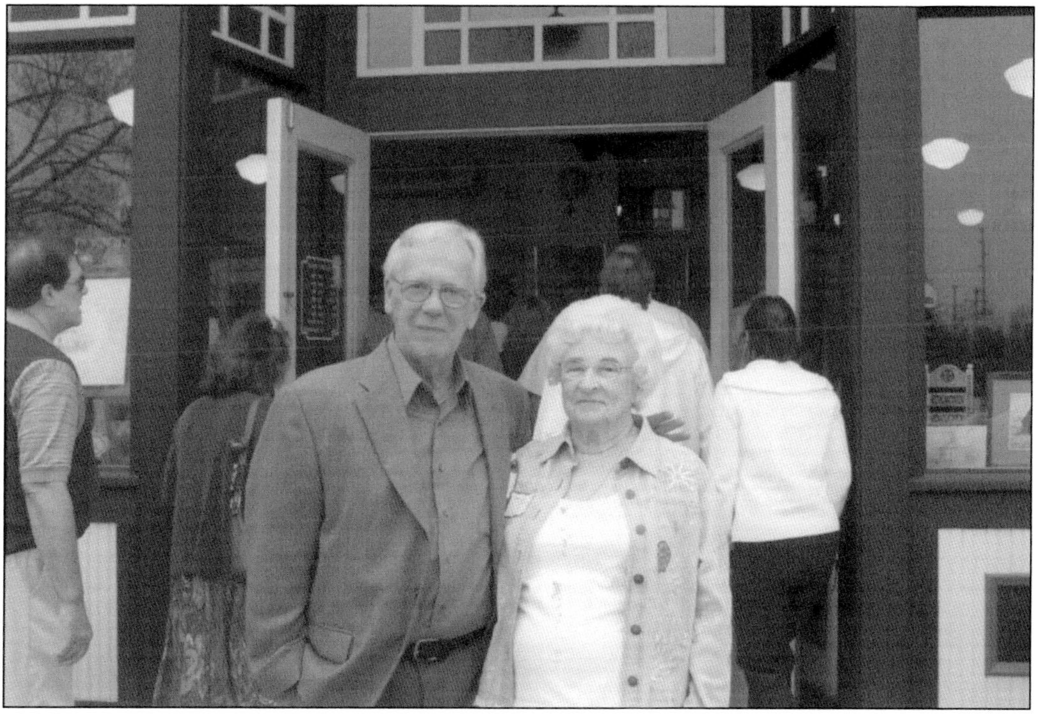

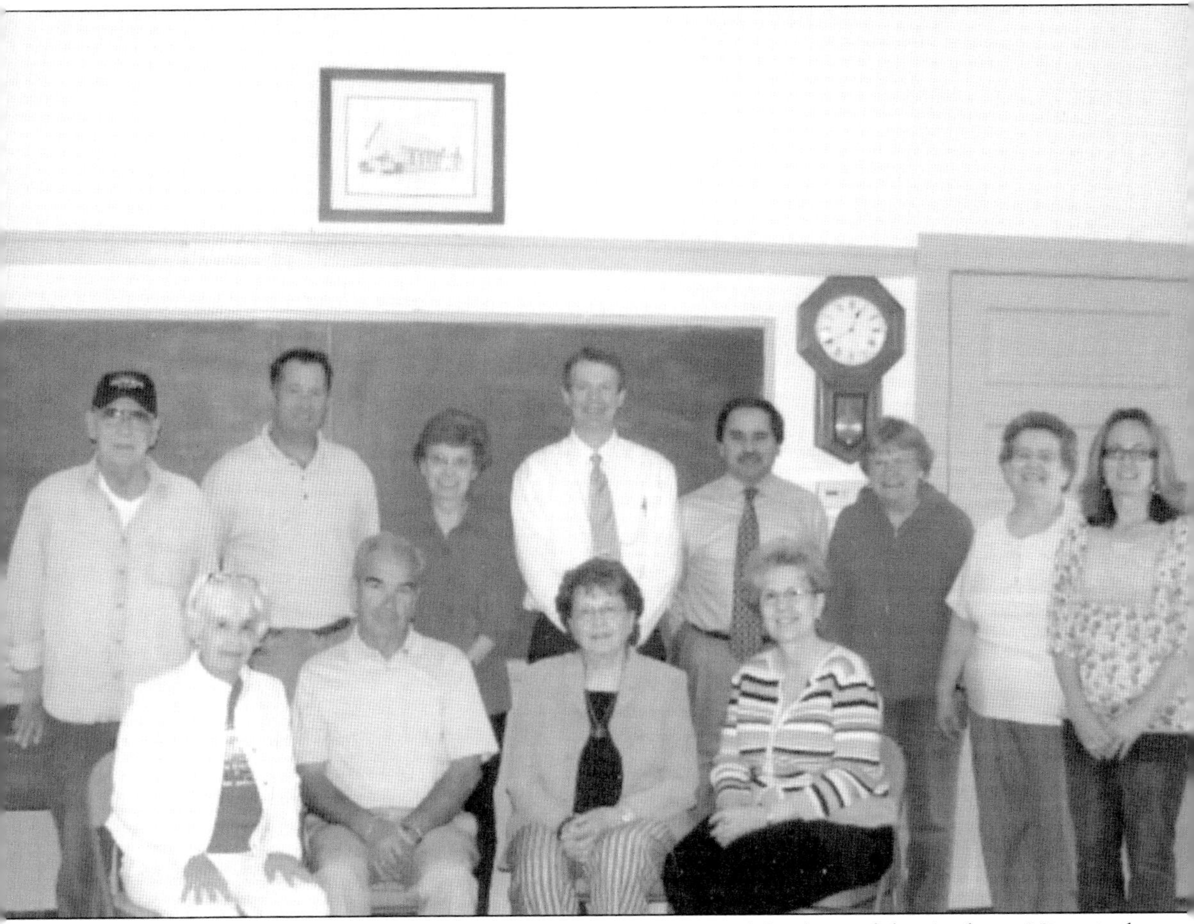

AMHERST HISTORICAL SOCIETY BOARD OF TRUSTEES, 2009. Members of the Amherst Historical Society Board of Trustees serve three-year terms. The 2009 board is seen here. From left to right are (first row) Judith Ryan (secretary), John Dietrich (president), Ruth Haff (treasurer), and Kathleen Litkovitz; (second row) Neal Jenne, David Kukucka, Martha Pallante, Eric Stocker, W. Zach Dolyk, Bernadine Wagner-Doan, Lilly Krebs, and Donita Abraham.

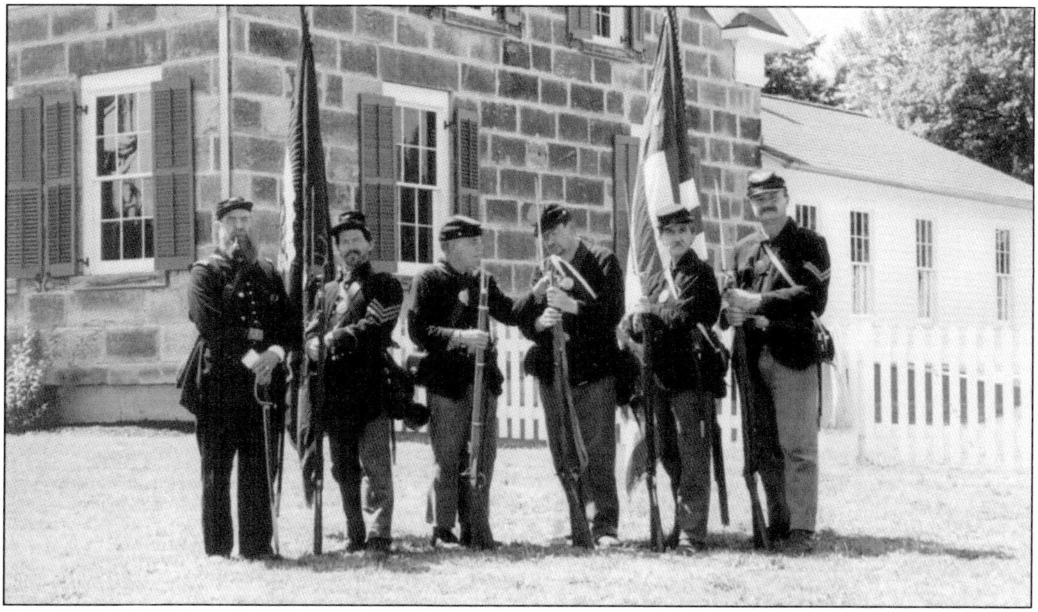

Re-enactments. With its period setting, the Amherst Sandstone Village has hosted a variety of re-enactors at the site. The American Civil War has long provided fodder for people seeking to re-create the nation's transformative struggle (above). A group of re-enactors representing the 69th Ohio Volunteer Infantry poses before the Harris-Dute House. Vintage baseball (below), which is played by mid-19th-century rules, is an increasingly popular activity at many historic sites. Amherst's team, the Sandstone Masons, is seen in front of the Harris-Dute House; their opponents include other Ohio teams, such as the Ohio Village Muffins from Columbus. Note the women in the photograph, who represent the "cranks" (the mid-19th-century term for fans) who often followed their favorite team.

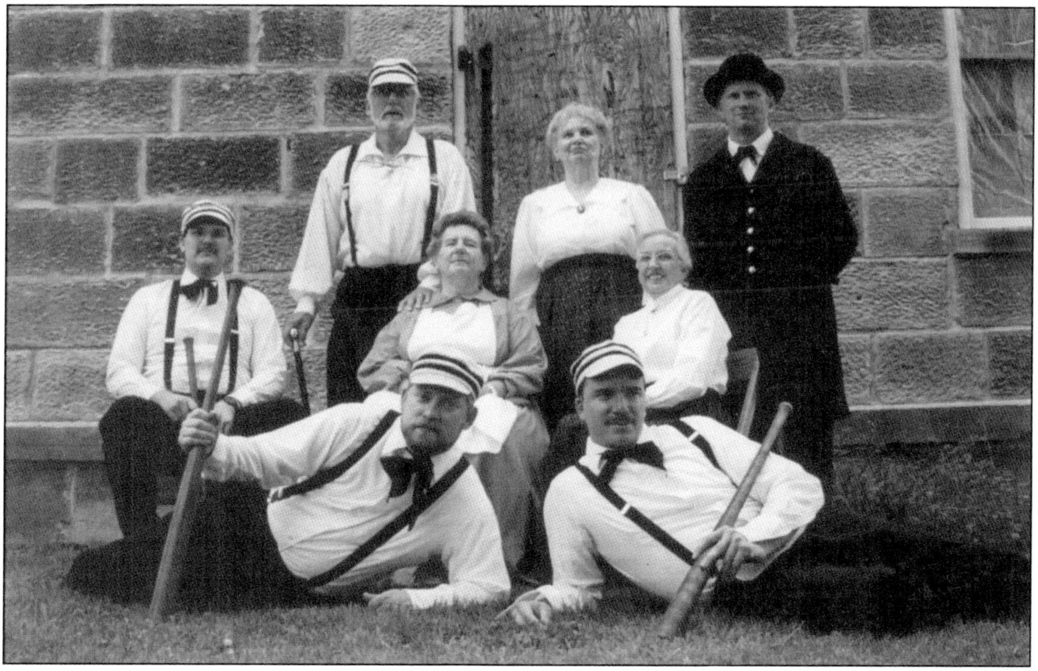

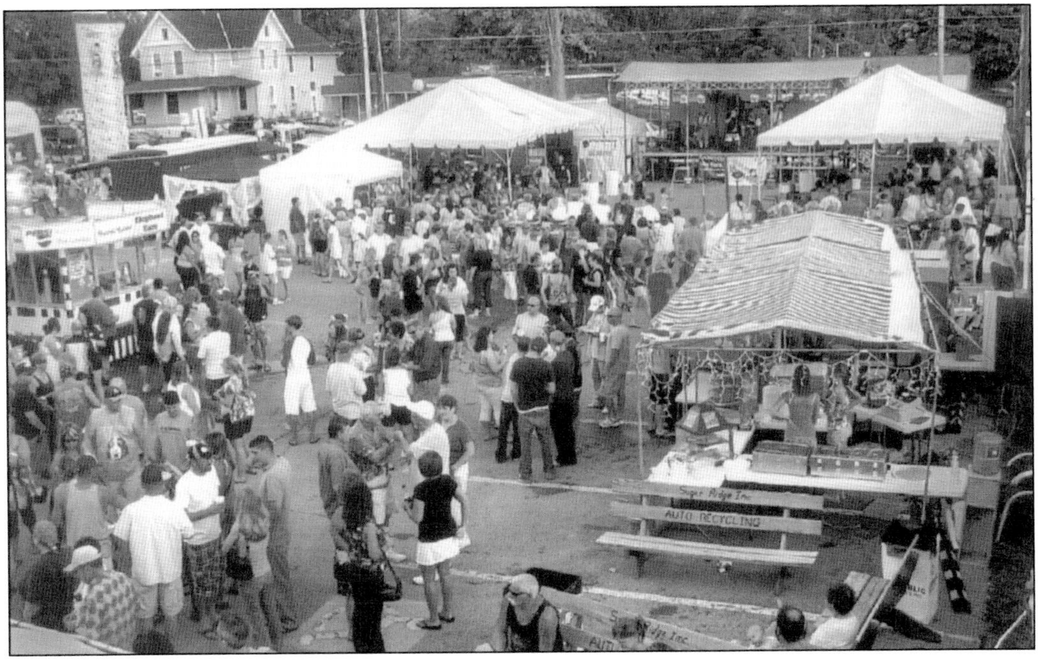

The Jamboree. One of the Amherst Historical Society's most popular annual events is the Jamboree, held every summer. The first Jamboree was held on July 14, 1974, for one day; it has now expanded to three days. It includes crafters, food vendors, and a variety of games. The 2009 Jamboree drew in large crowds (above) over the three days from July 11–13. The Amherst Historical Society (below) hosted the event from its booth in the midst of the celebration.

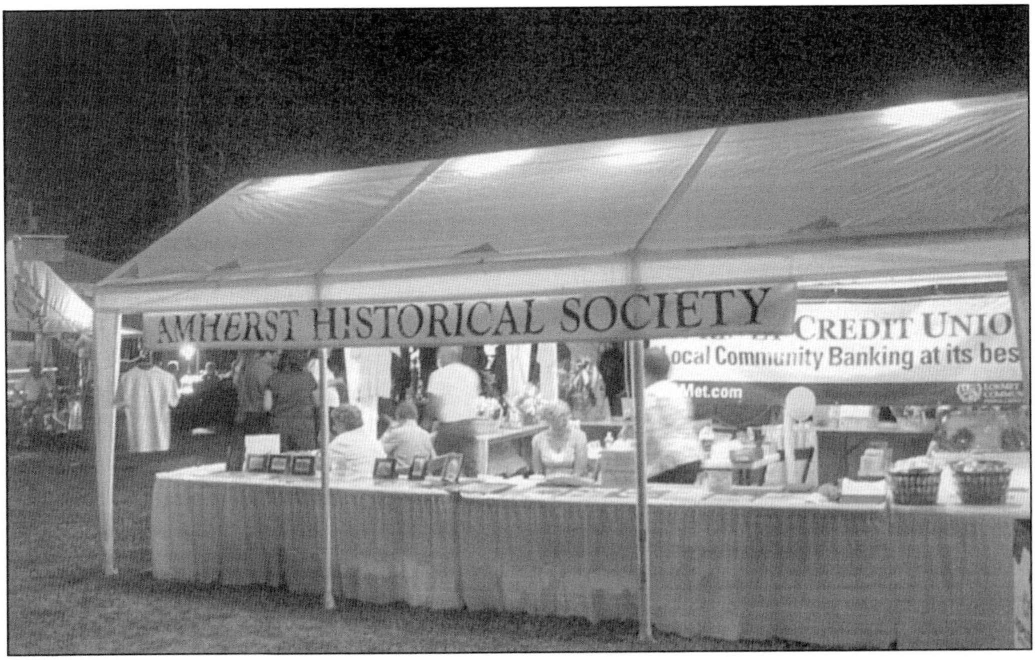

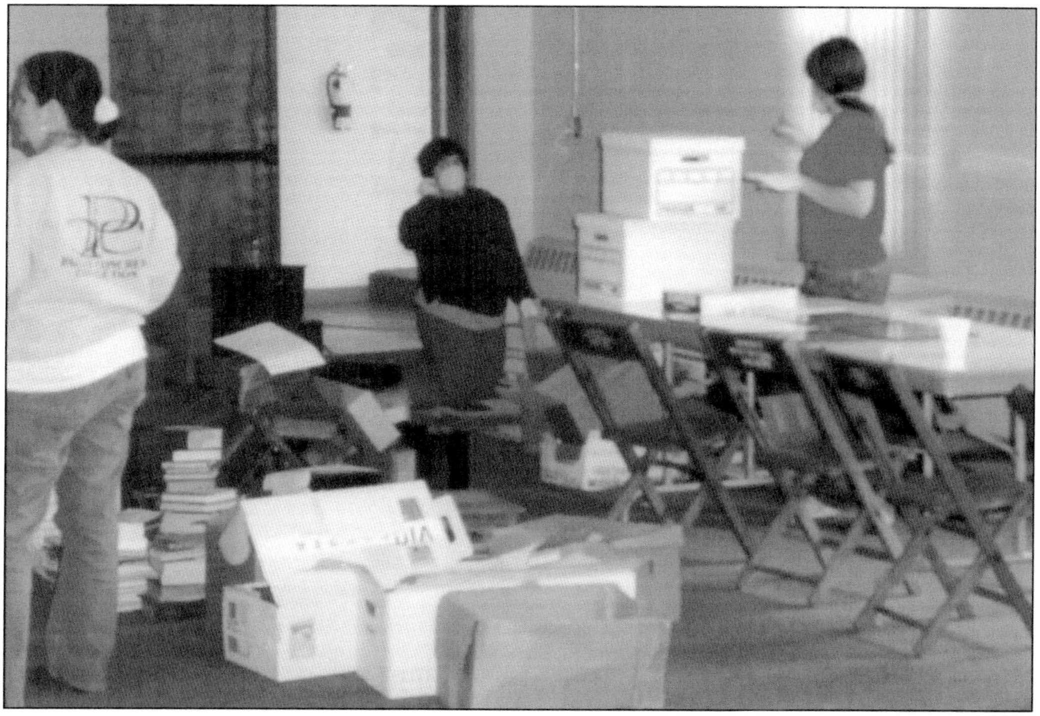

The Quarry Story. In the fall of 2005, the Amherst Historical Society became the proud recipient of what is now known as the Cleveland Quarries Collection. One of the finest examples of a corporate archive, it documents the history of Amherst's quarries from the 1870s through the beginning of the 21st century. With the aid of a group from Youngstown State University (above), the historical society began sorting and organizing the collection. Pictured from left to right are Dr. Martha I. Pallante, Ann Gillespie, and Sara Schaefer. Members of the historical society began the cataloguing of employee records (below) under the guidance of Dr. Marcelle Wilson. From left to right are James Mirey, Judy Ryan, Martha A. Pallante, Donna Rumpler, and Wilson.

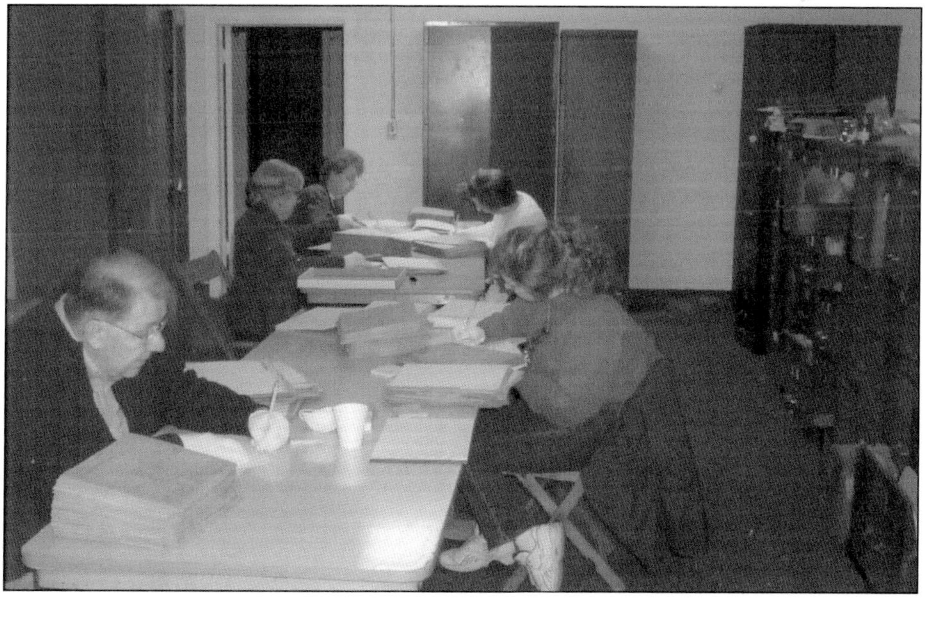

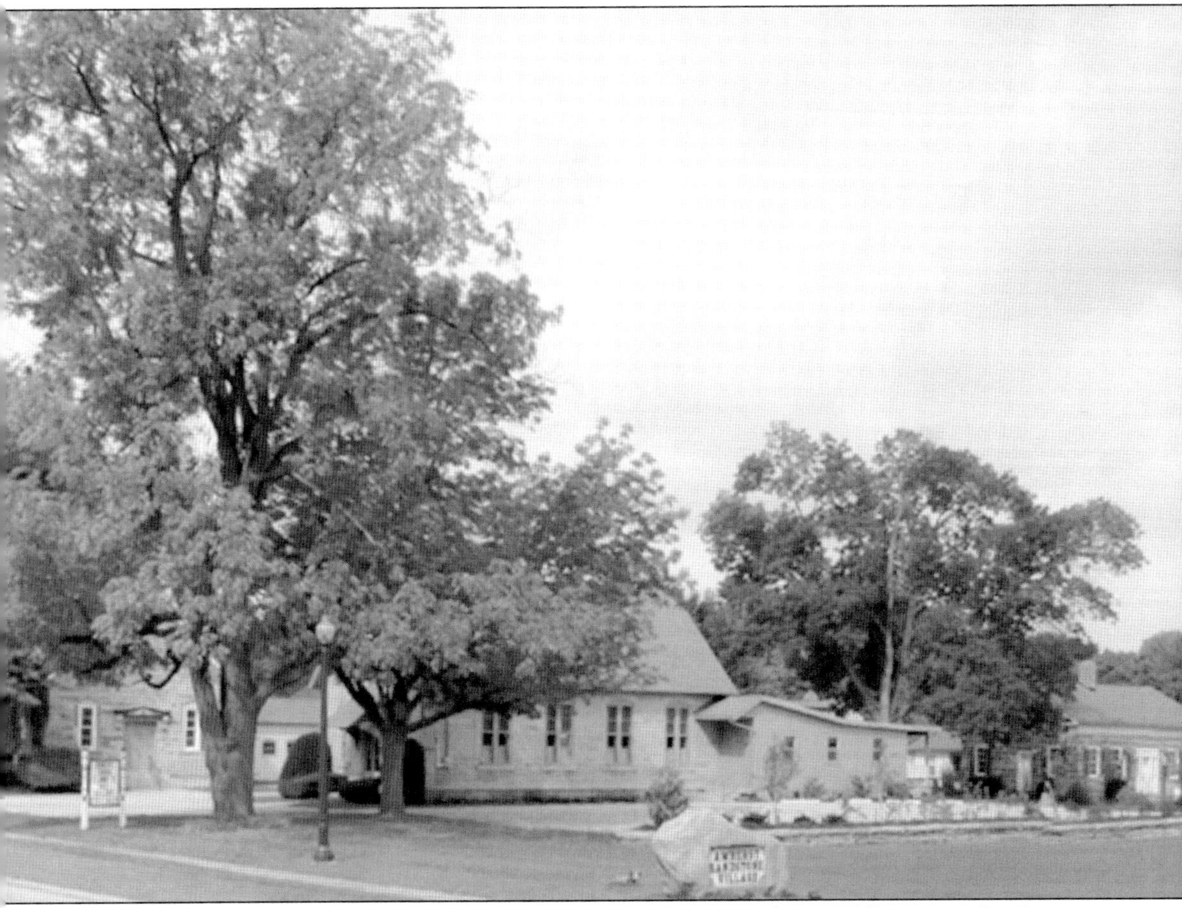

Amherst Sandstone Village Today. Today the Amherst Sandstone Village provides the citizens of Amherst with a glimpse of the past and a place to escape from the concerns of the modern world. The appeal of the property lies in its authentic historic structures and its interesting and

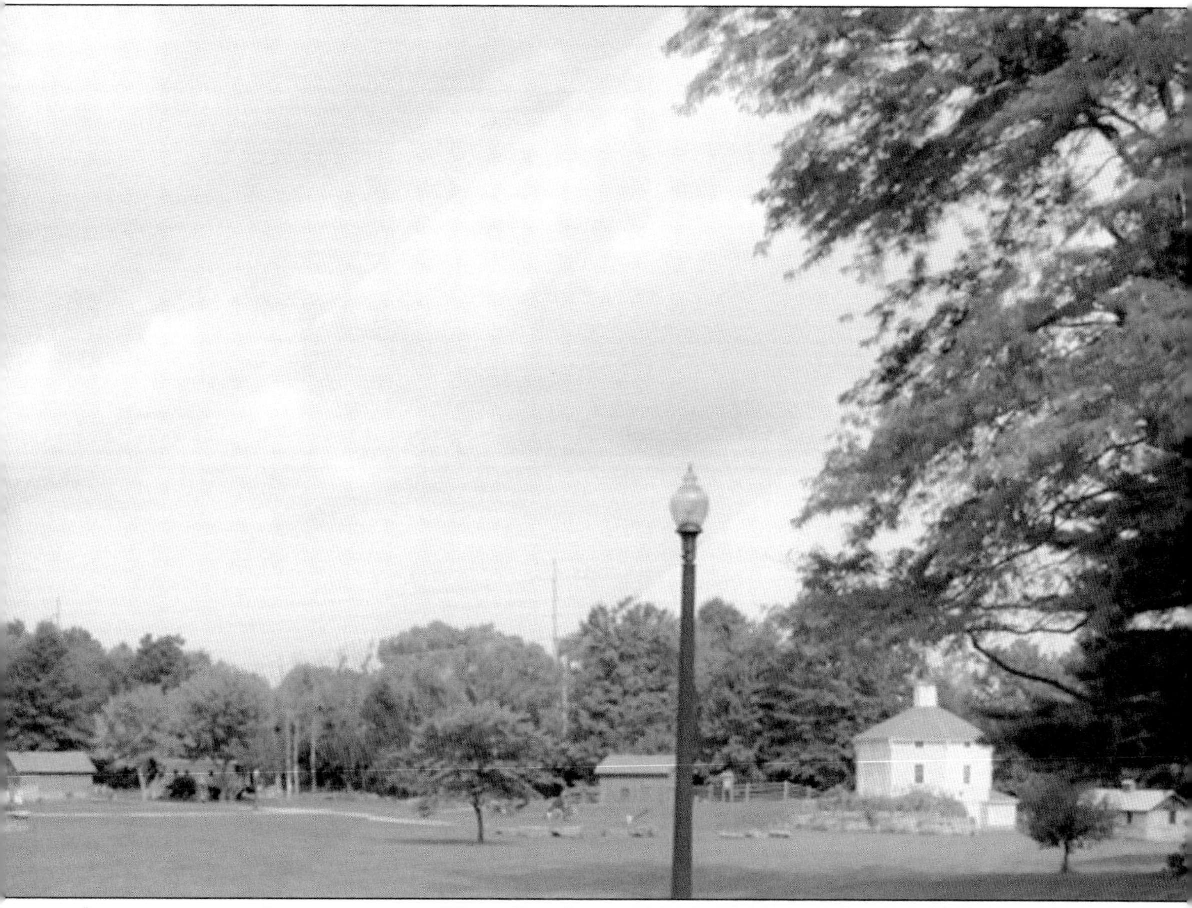

informative outreach programming. The village hosts 10,000–15,000 people annually. They come to participate in regular scheduled programming, school visits, and special events, as well as more casual tourists. A prime example of cultural heritage tourism, Amherst Sandstone Village provides a unique opportunity for residents and visitors alike.

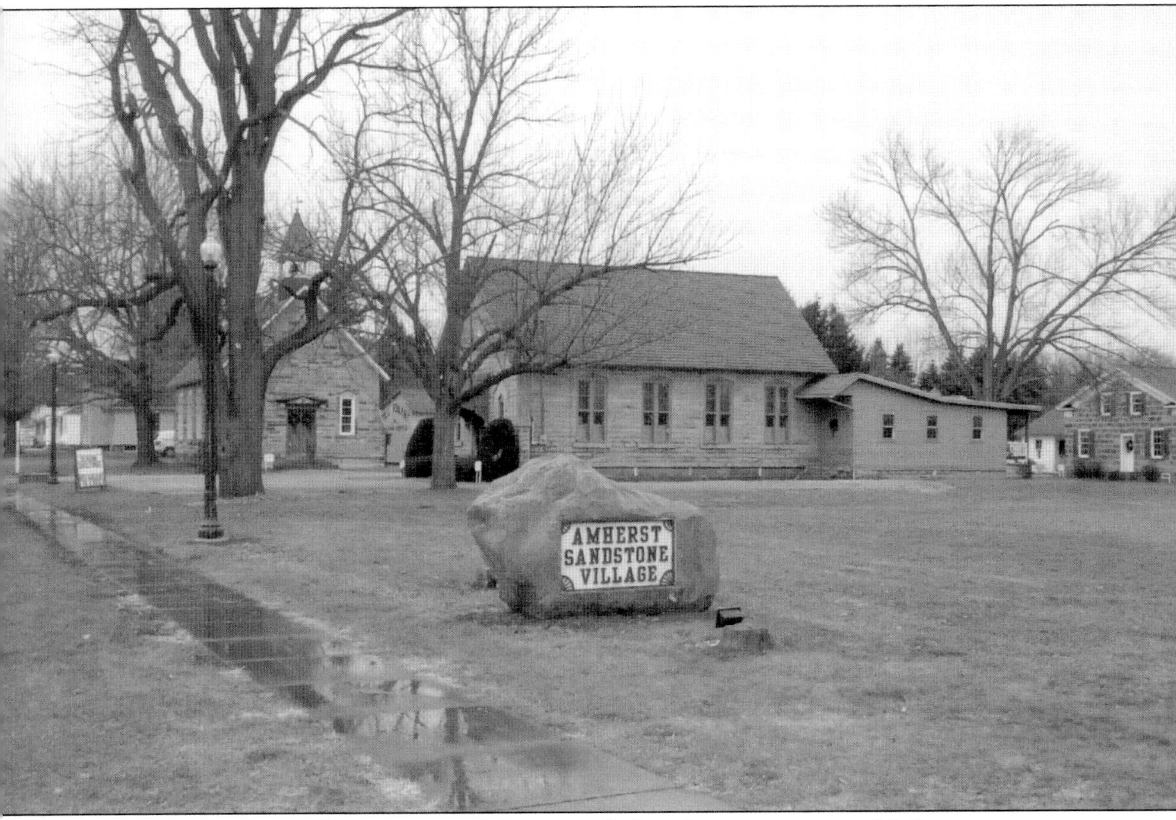

THE ROCK. The Amherst Historical Society is "where history comes to life."

Bibliography

Armstrong, Robert Grenville. *Amherst's Story*. Amherst, OH: Amherst Old Home Week Committee, 1914. Reprinted by the Amherst Historical Society, Evansville, IL: Unigraphic, Inc.

Hieb, James A. *Sandstone Center of the World*. South Amherst, OH: Quarrytown.net Publishing, 2007.

Middendorf, Lorna. *Amherst: Our Town*. Amherst, OH: Amherst Public Schools, 1960.

Paschen, Stephen H. *Quarry Town: The History of Amherst, Ohio, 1811–1900*. Self-published.

Pickrell, Martha M. *Investing in Community: The History and Legacy of the Nord Family of Ohio*. Oberlin, OH: Oberlin Historical and Improvement Organization, 2004.